Glad Tidings

Glad Tidings

A Friendship in Letters

The
Correspondence of
John Cheever and
John D. Weaver,
1945–1982

EDITED BY
John D. Weaver

HarperCollins*Publishers*

HarperCollins books may be purchased for educational, business, or sales promotional use. For information, please write: Special Markets Department, HarperCollins Publishers, Inc., 10 East 53rd Street, New York, NY 10022.

FIRST EDITION

Designed by Francesca Belanger

LIBRARY OF CONGRESS CATALOGING-IN-PUBLICATION DATA
Cheever, John.
  Glad tidings:a friendship in letters:the correspondence of John Cheever and John D. Weaver, 1945–1982/edited by John D. Weaver.—1st ed.
    p. cm.
  Includes bibliographical references and index.
  ISBN 0-06-016957-5 (cloth)
  1. Cheever, John—Correspondence. 2. Authors, American—20th
century—Correspondence. 3. Weaver, John Downing, 1912– —Correspondence. I.
Weaver, John Downing, 1912– . II. Title.
PS3505.H6428Z49 1993
813'.52—dc20
[B]   92-56218

93 94 95 96 97 CC/RRD 10 9 8 7 6 5 4 3 2 1

For Chica,
who made the lights
come back on

One has an impulse to bring glad tidings to someone. My sense of literature is a sense of giving, not a diminishment. I know almost no pleasure greater than having a piece of fiction draw together disparate incidents so that they relate to one another and confirm the feeling that life itself is a creative process, that one thing is put purposefully upon another, that what is lost in one encounter is replenished in the next, and that we possess some power to make sense of what takes place.

John Cheever, *Time,* March 27, 1964

CONTENTS

Introduction

We were both born in 1912, the year the Titanic sank and Democrats regained the White House, and in mid-December 1943 we were both wearing ill-fitting Government Issue with sergeant's stripes when we met in one of the more exotic battle stations of World War II. The old Paramount studio in Astoria, Queens, swarmed with writers, actors, directors, cameramen, cartoonists, film editors and sound technicians working on training and orientation films for the Army Signal Corps. Newly commissioned Hollywood producers who wanted to be mistaken for West Pointers worked cheek by jowl with West Pointers who wanted to become Hollywood producers after the war. They were distinguishable only because the Hollywood producers read Infantry Journal *and the West Pointers read* Variety.*

"I had a long talk with John Cheever, who I can see from here is going to be one of our good friends," I wrote Harriett on December 15, 1943, the day I reported for duty at the Signal Corps Motion Picture Center.*

Our paths might never have crossed if a hyperbolic screenwriter named Leonard Spigelgass had been less determined to wear the uniform of his country. As his friend Leo Rosten recalled at his memorial service in 1985, Lennie had been rejected by the military "for more reasons than any American since the war of 1812." His Los Angeles draft board capitulated when a two-star general called from Washington to ask whether Mr. Spigelgass's 4-F classification might be reconsidered if he agreed to absolve the Army and the Federal Government of financial responsibility for any injuries or ailments that might occur during his military service.

"The draft board chairman was absolutely flabbergasted; no general had ever before phoned him," Rosten continued; "the medical record of this Mr. Spigelgass was so awful that the enemy must be in Kansas City."

During a furlough in the spring of 1943, Mary Cheever, John's wife, reported in a letter to her father, John had been interviewed by "a Major Spigelgass, a Hollywood Special Service character who had told his publisher he wanted to see him. Between long-distance calls to Frank Capra and Louis B. Mayer, Spigelgass told John that he considered it unpatriotic for him to be in the infantry and that he would 'make with the General' immediately to get him into movie work . . . " Mary "thought it was very funny and didn't believe a word of it."

When John's transfer reached Fort Dix, the infantrymen in his barracks were awed by the speed and solicitude with which he was whisked from desk to desk, politely handed his travel orders, and driven off the post in a Jeep. He and his pregnant wife moved into a garden apartment at 329 West Twenty-second Street and he went to war each morning on the Eighth Avenue Subway.

"My division is still at Fort Dix and I imagine the schedule is largely fatigue details so I have no conscience about being out of the field," John wrote Mary's parents on June 14. Some weeks later Susan Liley Cheever was born. "Mary's been wonderful through the whole thing," John informed their friend Josephine Herbst, and went on to add, "my venerable division—the 'roughest, toughest, fightingest division in the world'—is still garrisoned in southern New Jersey going into their fourth year of pre-battle training."

His life in New York had "never been so well regulated, moderate, and quiet," John wrote on October 7. "Mary meets me at the door with a floury apron in the evenings. We eat dinner, play with Susan, read the paper, and go to bed. It's very pleasant, of course, but I sometimes wish it were more exciting, and that I could see more of the war. But the army is very big, moves very slowly, and the war may be very long."

★

Harriett Sherwood, a University of Kansas Phi Beta Kappa and beauty queen (Class of '34), and I had been married nearly six years when I signed up with the Army's Enlisted Reserve Corps in February 1943. I survived basic training at Camp Crowder, Missouri, and was working in the research department at Fort Capra (the Western Division of the Signal Corps Photographic Center in Hollywood, presided over by Colonel Frank Capra) when Major Spigelgass arranged to have me transferred to Astoria.

My new colleagues, still shaken from their own experiences in coming face to face with the city's wartime housing shortage, shook their heads and wished me well when I set out to find shelter Harriett and I could afford on our seventy-two-dollar monthly allowance. A friend directed me to the one-room basement apartment of a young army officer who was shipping out the following week. The monthly tab was forty dollars. I moved into 41 West Eleventh Street on New Year's Day 1944, and Harriett joined me two weeks later.

Our kitchen was a converted broom closet with a bar refrigerator and a two-burner hotplate. Every time we used both burners simultaneously we risked plunging the upstairs tenants into darkness. We kept a brown paper sack filled with fuses within reach. After dinner we stacked the dishes in the bathroom, the only source of running water.

"Harriett is one of the wonders of our day," John once wrote, and on his deathbed he recalled a chicken dinner she had served him nearly forty years earlier. He had been left with the impression that "she cooked the chicken on a curling iron."

For two years I crawled out of bed before dawn, slipped on my soldier suit, and rode off to war on the Sixth or Eighth Avenue subway. After standing reveille in a public street, I repaired to Borden's ice-cream parlor for bagels with lox and cream cheese and coffee with Sergeant Cheever and two other civilian-soldiers, Don Ettlinger (technical sergeant) and Leonard Field (private first-class). At noon we returned to Borden's for sandwiches or, if we happened to be in the mood for something more elegant (and could afford it), we headed for a midtown restaurant, Au Canarie d'Or. From time to time we were joined by one or more of a half-dozen other "Subway Commandos," but John, Lennie, Don, and

I were the four brought most closely together in a friendship that survived the next four decades.

John, a thirty-one-year-old New England prep-school dropout, had been a professional writer for thirteen years, ever since his account of his expulsion from Thayer Academy had been snapped up by Malcolm Cowley for the New Republic. *His stories had been appearing in* The New Yorker *since the mid-1930s and Random House had just brought out his first collection,* The Way Some People Live. *"A literary event," proclaimed the author of the jacket copy, who noted that "Cheever is in the army now, but when he comes back, the publishers expect that he will be a major figure in American post-war literature."*

Private First-Class Leonard Field, a stagestruck defector from Minneapolis, where his wealthy family had set up headquarters for its string of midwestern movie houses, had come to Manhattan hoping to get work as an actor or stage manager. Caught up in the draft, he was shipped to Astoria, where he and John shared the anxieties of approaching fatherhood. In that summer of 1943 Ruth Field and Mary Cheever gave birth to daughters, Kathy Field on July 17 and Susie Cheever two weeks later.

Don Ettlinger, a tall, eupeptic bachelor, who could have balanced the federal budget with the dental payments on his engaging smile, would have done well as a stock company leading man had he set out to become an actor instead of a writer. He had served with Major Spigelgass on the invasion of what turned out to be an undefended Aleutian island. As they stormed ashore, their cameras at the ready, their faces blackened for combat, Don had turned to his commanding officer and whispered, "Lennie, your mascara's running."

When Sergeant John McManus, *supervising editor of* Army–Navy Screen Magazine, *proposed that the Cheevers and the Weavers join him and his wife, Peggy (a Sarah Lawrence schoolmate of Mary Cheever), in sharing a $200-a-month town house on East Ninety-second Street, I was inclined to accept the offer, but Harriett put her foot down.*

"It would never work," she insisted.

Sergeant Cheever had similar misgivings, but, having finally wangled an overseas assignment, he left the decision to Mary, who was looking for an escape hatch from their cramped Chelsea flat. John expected to be in Europe filing feature articles for Yank, *the army magazine*, when his wife and daughter moved uptown. Four months later, however, after receiving "injections for everything except bubonic plague," he found himself living on "one of those bleak side streets leading east from Central Park, where stained limestone-and-marble houses stand like a deposit left by the great fortunes of the last century." There were five floors, eight flush toilets, and a paneled library shared by the Cheevers, the McManuses, and a civilian couple who had taken the floor set aside for us.

"They behaved toward one another with the restraint of people who have been forced into an unwanted intimacy by some perilous journey," John wrote in one of the six Town House stories he sold to The New Yorker. To an old friend, he put it more simply: "We're all in one another's hair."

Finally, in the spring of 1945, Sergeant Cheever boarded a train bound for the South Pacific by way of Los Angeles. He arrived on Easter Sunday. "The motion-picture industry has left a noticeable stamp on the appearance of the women here," he wrote Mary on Hotel Biltmore stationery. "They all seem to have breasts, they wear fancy hats, strong colors, flowers and furs. On the other hand there is a lovely breath of the middle-west blowing into every rock and cranny of Los Angeles. There are the old who came from the west to die and the young who came here to make their fortunes."

John, at this early stage of our friendship, had the mistaken notion that Harriett and I had headed for Hollywood to feast at the film studios' table. Actually we sought it out because her doctor had advised her to move to a dry, temperate climate. I took a six-month leave of absence from the Kansas City Star in the fall of 1940, but after a few weeks of awakening each morning to a day that was ours to do with as we pleased, we decided to break with the nine-to-five world into which we had been born and brought up to regard as inescapable.

I resigned from The Star and, years before either of us had heard the term, Harriett and I were two consenting adults practicing role reversal. She took a job with an advertising agency and I worked a seven-day week at home, writing, cooking, and cleaning. In December 1941, after ten dry months, I had stories in three magazines (The Atlantic, American Mercury, Esquire) and Macmillan had bought my Virginia hill-country novel, Wind Before Rain, for publication the following April.

Harriett quit her job, and we were living on a rigid $25-a-week budget when our New York agent put us in touch with her Hollywood representative, who called one afternoon to say that although we would live longer, happier lives if I never set foot in a film studio, he felt bound by the nature of his calling to tell us of an opportunity to work for David O. Selznick, producer of Gone With the Wind. "He wants a bright young man to bounce ideas off of." The job paid $250 a week and we were both tempted until the agent mentioned that my hard-driving employer might call me at two o'clock in the morning and tell me to come right over. Harriett shook her head. "No one ever calls you at two o'clock in the morning to go anywhere," she said. We turned the job down and, as promised, lived a long, happy life together without ever spending a single day on a studio payroll.

After the war Harriett and I resettled in Los Angeles, leaving John and Mary, Don and Katrina, Lennie and Ruth (later, Lennie and his second wife, Virginia) in New York, where they continued to keep in touch with one another through phone calls, regimental luncheons, and dinner parties. Harriett and I usually managed to get back East every year or so for a reunion, and in the fall of 1960 John came West and fell under the spell of the little cement-block house in the Hollywood Hills we'd bought in 1948 and Harriett had remade in her own radiant image. She wove wall-to-wall wool carpeting for the living room, built a desk for my workroom, and laid the bricks for three patios.

"I can't think of a place more intimately associated with two people than Hillside Avenue," John wrote us in the summer of 1964 after we had sold the house and moved to a canyon near Beverly Hills. "I know that Harriet made the rugs but I've always felt that she spun the grass and roses and I cannot yet see her on another terrace with another view. You must realize that many of us, at the end of an uneasy day, conclude that we can eat crab-meat with the Weavers but if you wander around like nomads we will all be lost."

In his teens, writing of his expulsion from Thayer Academy, John had noted how strange it was "to be so very young and have no place to report at nine o'clock." Throughout his life he seemed to be groping for a place to report, seeking it in his marriage, his church, and the company of his friends. He had a special attachment to the first of Harriett's houses, but he fitted comfortably into all the others. They became his sanctuaries, consecrated places where he was walled off from the demons that lay in wait for him in the outer darkness.

"I think you and Harriet and I share some sense of what love amounts to," he wrote us in 1974. "I remember standing on the terrace of your old house, by the Cinzano ashtray. The door was open and I heard Harriet flush a toilet and open and close a drawer. The sensation of my aloneness was stupendous."

In the spring of 1980, when we moved again, John suggested "it would help your friends if you sent photographs of your new house when it is completed. As a very old man, nearing the end of my journey it is my pleasure, when darkness falls from the wings of night, to recall those domiciles where my oldest friends enjoy repose. This has produced some shocking discoveries such as whips, thumb-screws, needles and other erotic facilities that I do not chose to mention. The wave motif of your last swimming pool has meant beauty and reason to me for many years now and I would like to know what replaces this."

A year later John wrote to tell us of a dream in which he had spotted Harriett and me at some sort of crowded gathering in Central Park and "was hurt to see that you had come east without calling and when I said as much you said that you had come east to go trout fishing with Frank Stanton and that you were pressed for time. You both looked very well and I thought you'd like to know."

"If we'd gone east to get in some trout-fishing with Frank Stanton," I replied, "we would certainly have called and made our way to the Cheever kitchen with the pick of our catch, but a dream is about the only way we could manage a trip east just now. As a result of the radiation therapy, the bones in Harriett's hip have deteriorated to such *an extent that she moves about on a cane with some difficulty and, at times, with considerable pain.''*

We had lived with cancer since the summer of 1969, when a dermatologist snipped a bit of tissue from a small dark mole a few inches above the ankle of Harriett's left leg. The biopsy turned up a melanoma, which was promptly excised. Five years later a recurrence of the malignancy necessitated the removal of her lymph glands. The following year, after another nodule had been excised, she was subjected to radiation therapy.

"It is not possible, of course, to sympathize with anything so dark, frightening and painful as Harriet's illness must have been," John wrote, "but one can try as I've tried, for most of my life, to pray. My love to Harriet and I can hear the hills ring with her sawing. Twenty-five years ago I wrote: 'Which came first? Christ the Saviour or the smell of new wood?' "

During Christmas Week 1981, our mutual friend, Pamela Fiori, editor-in-chief of Travel & Leisure, called to say she'd seen a newspaper reference to some tests John was undergoing at a New York hospital. "I called John this morning," I wrote her the following day. "It's bone cancer, left leg and hip. He said he'd had a kidney stone removed last July for what appeared to be a localized malignancy. Then he recently went to a doctor for what was at first thought to be a pulled tendon. 'John,' he said of this new development, 'it is in no way illuminating.' Then he laughed and described the waiting around for radiation therapy as 'a kind of laundromat. We sit there in our hospital gowns, not like people who have no washing machines, but like people whose machines haven't been repaired yet.' "

"We know what you mean about that surgical-gown laundromat scene," I wrote him on December 30. "Harriett has been going through it for some weeks now, with a view to finding out whether she can become a candidate for hip-replacement surgery."

Her operation went well, but what was supposed to have been a two-week hospital stay turned into a three-month nightmare. Circulation in the leg was so bad that gangrene set in. A vascular surgeon, drafted to perform an arterial bypass, nicked her spleen and another surgeon was called in to remove it. She spent a dicey week in intensive care, where her breathing became so badly impaired that still another surgeon was brought in. Her vocal chords were paralyzed, he said, and she went back to the operating room for a tracheostomy.

She was released on March 6 and three months later, as I wrote Don Ettlinger, "we had our first dinner out with friends in 1982. We came home to catch an eleven o'clock news and were immediately struck by the report of John's death. It was no surprise, of course, but it was nonetheless a shock. I called Mary next morning and was pleased to hear that the end had come peacefully at home in bed surrounded by his children."

John was our only house guest who attended church services. "There has to be someone you thank for the party," he was fond of saying. I was thinking of him and the comfort he found in his Anglican faith when I wrote his older son, Ben, in the spring of 1985: "It is our favorite season and after the chilling ordeal of the last three winters, it is especially pleasant to see Harriett out in the patio, surrounded by azaleas and camellias blooming in the warm spring sun. When I see her smile and reach down to play with the lion-colored kitten that came to us from God knows where a couple of years ago, my skepticism fades for a moment and I share your father's well-mannered belief that we have to thank someone for such a lovely party."

Harriett's long ordeal ended gently. She was asleep in a suburban Los Angeles hospital room, where her heart was being monitored. Suddenly a dozen nurses descended on us. She had finally been granted her wish to go to sleep and not wake up. I dismissed the nurses and kissed her good-bye. In her last conscious moment, when I bathed her forehead and held a glass of water to her lips, there was no indication of pain or fear in her eyes, only an unspeakable weariness. It was the eve of Thanksgiving 1988.

I envy the memories Don and Lennie have of their postwar New York years with John and Mary, but Harriett and I ended up with something more durable, a cache of 234 letters, which I photocopied and sent to Ben in the fall of 1985 when he set to work on The Letters of John Cheever (Simon & Schuster, 1988). He passed the correspondence on to his sister, Susie, who had already brought out her memoir, Home Before Dark *(Houghton Mifflin, 1984)*.

"I've been reading and savoring my father's letters to you both," Susie *wrote us. "In some ways his letters are his best writing—and yours is an extraordinary collection, certainly the best I've seen."*

The correspondence began in the spring of 1945, when John was on temporary duty in Hollywood at Fort Capra, and it ended with a note typed less than two months before his death when he had just been awarded the National Medal for Literature. The ceremony was held at Carnegie Hall. John, gaunt and hairless, supported by Mary, hobbled onstage with a cane, but his voice was firm when he declared that *"a page of good prose seems to me the most serious dialogue that well-informed and intelligent men and women carry on today in their endeavor to make sure that the fires of this planet burn peaceably."*

Digby Diehl, *covering the Carnegie Hall ceremony for the* Los Angeles Herald Examiner, *began his report by recalling an evening with John at our house in the Hollywood hills: "I was delighted by his wry, quick wit and his social ease. As he and the Weavers reminisced about literary adventures together, Cheever exhibited none of the stern Yankee Calvinist behavior, nor the shyness, that I had heard other people describe. He had feisty opinions about life and literature, all expressed with elegant turns of phrase that made his conversation sheer verbal music. And he had a penetrating gaze, a fire behind the eyes that burned and gleamed and riveted the listener."*

This is the John Cheever who comes bounding out of his light-hearted reports on the minutiae of his daily life as husband, father, writer, and, in the closing years, public figure.

"I get a lot of letters from ladies telling me not to be so sad *and* bitter," *he once wrote. "If they only knew, as you and Harriet do, what a sunny person I am."*[1]

We three were so close for such a long time that in conversation and in our playful, affectionate exchange of letters, we communicated in the kind of marital shorthand Harriett and I developed in our half-century

---

1. With the exception of one brief period late in life, John persisted in spelling Harriett with one "t."

together. The words "Fish Lady," for example, brought back the afternoon shortly before Thanksgiving Day 1960 when John and I stopped at the fresh fish stall in the Farmers Market to pick up some cracked crab Harriett had ordered for dinner. A shrunken, gap-toothed, Hogarthian crone, wrapped in a gray hand-knit shawl, turned to John and cackled something about having to spend Thanksgiving Day alone with her cat and a cold slab of leftover flounder.

"That character with the bit of flounder is still around," John wrote the following year. "I went into the local bookstore today and he [the owner] said: Hello, stranger, where have you been? but before I could say anything she was in there asking if he had any valentines."

The Fish Lady continued to crop up in our letters and small talk as a reminder of our advancing years and their accompanying discomforts. As the Christmas–New Year holiday drew to a close in 1981, John was dealing with bone cancer and Harriett was facing hip replacement surgery. John, Harriett, and I had become one with the Fish Lady, I noted, and assured him that "if I run into her during the next few days, I'll damn well let her know how we're spending our holidays on our respective coasts."

"Wrinkled Crotch," another of our code phrases, originated at our Hillside Avenue home the day John was to be taken to 20th Century Fox to meet film producer Jerry Wald. Out of this meeting in the fall of 1960 came John's assignment to write the screen treatment of a D. H. Lawrence novel, the fee for which provided the money he needed for a down payment on the house in Ossining where he was to spend the last twenty-one years of his life.

"My God, John," Harriett exclaimed, when he sauntered into our kitchen shortly before noon, wearing a navy blue Brooks Brothers suit, "your crotch!"

John cupped both hands over his genitalia. "What's wrong with it?" he asked.

"Give me your pants," Harriett said, and as he slipped them off, he asked me if he might have a martini.

A few minutes later his Hollywood agent, Henry Lewis, arrived to find John seated in the kitchen in his blue coat and white boxer shorts, sipping a martini, while Harriett stood over an ironing board pressing his pants. A bit shaken, Henry was quick to accept the martini I offered him. When he'd finished it (John had refilled his own glass to keep Henry company), Harriett and I walked to the carport to see them off. It was like watching our child being taken away to summer camp for the first time. When they came back in the late afternoon, we were waiting in the carport. John rolled down the window on his side of the front seat, leaned out and shouted to Harriett, "You should have seen Jerry's crotch. It was a disgrace!"

Over the years, the untidiness of John's crotch became a metaphor for the untidiness of his life. "It has gotten to be a serious problem," he wrote in a Christmas 1976 note, "now that I am spending my twilight years journeying from campus to campus, from podium to podium where some people seem to find my wrinkles more compelling than my countenance. How they stare; and when I drape my hands over my crotch this is generally misunderstood. . . . Very recently a lady reporter described my face as being linned by some force greater than time. The same seems to go for my crotch . . . I've just displayed my wrinkles at Syracuse, Bennington, Washington, Scarsdale and Cornell and I'll take them out to Utah after the holidays when I may continue to California for a touch of Harriet's healing iron."

Ben Cheever had a "queasy" feeling when he opened the box in which I'd packed two Vello-bound volumes of his father's letters, but, he wrote us, as he began reading them in bed that night, his outbursts of laughter distracted his wife, film critic Janet Maslin, who was "trying to read something else. She wants to know what's so funny, so I read it to her, and then she laughs too, in spite of herself, and then she goes back to her book, and I go back to the letters, and pretty soon, she wants to know what I'm snickering about this time. And so I read her the letter, and pretty soon she's snickering too."

While Ben was making his way through a stash of letters that encompassed his entire life up to the time of his father's death, Harriett was in a hospital recuperating from her first heart attack and I was seated by her bed, romping through Mark Amory's selection of Evelyn Waugh's letters, many of which I read aloud to her because they reminded me of John's letters to us.

"*His familiar gift of acute observation elegantly and precisely described is allied to a love of exaggeration that frequently takes off into fantasy,*" Amory pointed out,[2] and in commending the book to Ben I called his attention to the editor's "*harsh view that the feelings of children must be largely ignored; they must learn to live with the behaviour of their parents.*"

"*I'm part of the carping, complaining generation,*" Ben confided, "*and know that most of my more serious shortcomings can be blamed on my parents. They didn't feed me enough. They fed me too much. They touched me too much. They didn't touch me enough. My father was even successful, another enormous sin in a parent. So I should be relieved, I suppose, that he's gone. But, somehow, I'm not relieved. There was just too much good in that man. There were too many smiles. There was too much warmth. It seems impossible not to miss him, and to miss him hard.*"

I miss him too, as I reminded Ben on May 20, 1987: "*Your father, as always, is much in our thoughts this spring. We will lift a glass in the general direction of Cedar Lane on the 27th. His 75th birthday coincides with our 50th wedding anniversary on the 28th. We've made no plans for the occasion, and in the spirit of the Fish Lady who wove her way in and out of our friendship, we will probably end up with a tuna fish casserole.*"

Hardly a week and rarely a day will ever pass that I don't have something I'd like to pass along to John (and now to Harriett as well). I have no mail-drop for Harriett, but, until I defected to North Carolina in 1990 to start a new life in a new place with my new wife, Chica, I used to pass Firehouse 99, on a mountaintop overlooking the San Fernando Valley, almost every day, always with a tightening in my chest at the sight of the bronze tablet memorializing Harriett's work in

2. "I may exaggerate, but I do not lie," John often reminded us. "The telling of lies is a sort of sleight-of-hand that displays our deepest feelings about life," he told an interviewer for the *Paris Review*, and he once tossed into play a line he attributed to Malraux: "I do not lie. My lies become truth." He claimed to have written "the first sky-jacking five years before it ever happened. It's in *The Wapshot Scandal*."

making life safer for everyone who will ever live in the Santa Monica Mountains.

As for John, I now write Ben the letters I would have written his father and Ben's replies have taken on his father's light-hearted, self-deprecatory tone: "We went to an elegant Manhattan birthday party for a one-year old yesterday, where every moment was recorded on video by a famous Japanese woman movie maker, and the staff and parents wore T-shirts with the little celebrant's name on them. Phil Donahue wasn't there, but Tom Brokaw was. I comported myself very well, and felt that I'd made exactly the right sort of impression, until the cake came out. This excited a large bumble bee with black stripes on his tail and he flew about the crowded terrace, and then into my mouth and stung me on the right tonsil. I then swallowed him. A number of people were watching. I tried to be brave, but I couldn't think of anything witty to say. I just sat there swallowing and looking ill."

The letter reminded me of one John had written us twenty-five years earlier when he had been left alone in the Cedar Lane house with Ben and his baby brother Fred, whose pet name was Picci: "I cannot work much because people keep interrupting me. 'I don't want to disturb you,' Mary says, 'but I think there must be a fire in the attic.' Yesterday noon Ben knocked gently on my door and when I asked him angrily what he wanted he said he'd got his prick stuck in a zipper. I gave the zipper a yank and he let out such a howl that I nearly fainted. The dog began to bark and Picci ran around in circles, wringing his hands and saying, 'No Mummy here, no Mummy here.' Mummy was in the super-market. I called our doctor but he was out sailing and then I came at Ben with the rose shears, planning to cut off his trousers. He pointed out that even without his trousers his prick would still be caught in the zipper. Then I called the hospital but before I got through to the resident Ben had liberated himself. It's all part of the rich bulk of human experience, I suppose, but I don't seem able to work it into the novel."

In the spring of 1990, when Ben's wife was in France covering the Cannes Film Festival for the New York Times, he reported that both of their children had taken ill the moment Janet's plane left the ground and he was "dosing them heavily with Tylenol and toys."

"I rest more easily these cool spring nights knowing that Janet is back home," I replied two weeks later. "I worry about the ability of an all-male Cheever household to cope with an unexpected and unprecedented crisis. Fred saw that quite clearly the day your father came at you with the rose shears and he got at once to the heart of the problem, 'No mummy here! No mummy here!' "

"An unhappy marriage is a full-time occupation," John noted in his journal, and when his daughter brought up the subject in her News-week interview, he said: "It's been extraordinary. That two people of our violent temperament have been able to live together for nearly 40 years as we have seems to me a splendid example of the richness and diversity of human nature . . . and in this 40 years there's scarcely been a week in which we haven't planned to get a divorce."

In one of those weeks, when a breakup seemed imminent, he wrote in his journal: "I don't want a divorce; I want things to be exactly as they were, there having been much more good than bad in the relationship. I don't want to part with my children and I suspect that I don't want to part with the comforts of home, a place where I can count on warm meals and company. I am afraid of living in hotel rooms and eating in cafeterias and this seems to reflect on my courage. I am much too attached to cut flowers, to holding a seashell to my son's ear to see the intent look on his face, to the smell of peonies (oh how brief) in the stairwell. But is it wrong for a man to make a house a place where he can return in the evening? Is it wrong to avoid the venereal ghosts in cheap hotel rooms and the odd-sticks who share your table at the Automat? I don't want to make a life with my bachelor friends or be a dog in the households of the married people I know, bringing a bottle of wine for dinner or a present for the child . . ."

John was drawn to strength, Mary to need, their daughter wrote in her memoir. "An injured animal, a waif, a person in trouble—all elicit overwhelming concern for her." In the 1970s when John was staggering through the streets of Boston and passing out on park benches, it was Mary who managed to get him to the clinic that brought about his triumph over his addiction.

"How could I leave him when he was killing himself?" she explained.

Mary Updike, who first met John Cheever in 1964 when she and her husband spent ten days with him in the Soviet Union, got to know Mary Cheever afterward. "They looked as if they belonged together," she told Scott Donaldson, John's biographer. "He handsome, she pretty (very), both youthful, energetic, charming, funny, the same size. She had an amazing voice, I remember. One guessed they had a complicated marriage from the fiction but not from anything C. said about her."

Speaking as the wife of a brilliant writer, some twenty years younger than Cheever who also wrote about complicated marriages, Mary Updike once asked Bill Maxwell, who edited the New Yorker *stories of both men: "What is Mary Cheever like?" and he replied: "Vulnerable." Maxwell said it with "such gravity and respect that I knew it was an honorable condition. Mary Cheever became a kind of role model for me, I realized later, in the way she allowed herself to be written about. I've always liked and understood the wife in a Cheever story who rushes out to water the garden just before a downpour."[3]*

"You're a wonderful girl honey; a fine one and a brave one and a pretty one." Private Cheever wrote from boot camp, when Mary was carrying Susan, and in his old age, when Mary was upset by a bad review of her book, The Need for Chocolate & Other Poems *(Stein & Day, 1980), he gave her a piece of gold jewelry and eight lines of verse scrawled on a sheet of his Cedar Lane stationery:*

> The need for chocolat is much finer
> Than the need for gold,
> And I have hoped to find you
> Some of both,
> While we have sought the ghost of love
> Together—and better yet,
> Found something more enduring
> Than either gold or chocolat

3. "The sky got black," John wrote in "The Ocean" (*The New Yorker,* August 1, 1964). "As soon as dinner was over, Cora dressed herself in a raincoat and a green shower cap and went out to water the lawn."

"M comes into view," John wrote in his journal. "Her shoulders are bare, her dress is cut low. She carries an armful of lilies, trailing this way and that their truly mournful perfume. She seems content and so am I and when she takes my arm and we continue to walk under the trees in the last light, under the beeches that spray like shrapnel, arm in arm, after so many years and with so much sexual ardor I think that we are like two, sheltered by the atmosphere of some campus; that we are like a couple engraved on a playing card."

"Every writer should keep a journal," John said after dinner one night during his 1960 visit. "I happen to come from a long line of diarists," he added and proceeded to weave a Cheeverian account of seafaring progenitors who, at start of each day, would ease out of bed, *"pump ship,"* fling open a window, check wind, tide, and weather, and then commit their reflections to a daily journal, secure in the knowledge that what they jotted down would never appear in print. When they died, their oldest child burned the journal.[4]

"Would you like to see my journal?" he asked and ducked out to the guest room, returning with a letter-size notebook of cheap lined paper. I opened it at random and, as I was leafing through it, he remarked: *"Malcolm Cowley has the curious notion he's going to outlive me and edit my journals, so every now and then I slip in a notation, 'Fuck you, Malcolm Cowley.'"*

Harriett broke out laughing. *"But, John, you've given him the perfect title:* Fuck You, Malcolm Cowley: The Intimate Journals of John Cheever.*"*

I read John's description of a walk we'd taken along the beach at Malibu. (*"The tide is out, the rocks are bare and there is a whole family catching bait crabs under the direction of an old patriarch with a game leg in hip boots. Swastikas are painted on a wall; also, pray for surf to*

4. "It did occur to me one rainy afternoon that the journal might be publishable in the magazine," John wrote his *New Yorker* editor in 1955, "and then I seemed to be wool-gathering and forgot the whole thing. Why don't we talk it over?"

wash away the fags.") I was about to pass the notebook to Harriett when I spotted his portrait of us ("she is a sweet, pretty woman without a line on her face and he is a most gentle, affectionate and excellent man"). Harriett spent a couple of minutes with the journal, pausing to read one passage, and then handed it to John with a polite smile, but no comment. She had turned to an entry that revealed his bisexuality:

I spend the night with C and what do I make of this. I seem unashamed and yet I feel or apprehend the weight of social strictures, the threat of punishment. But I have acted only on my own instincts, tried, discretely, to relieve my drunken loneliness, my troublesome hunger for sexual tenderness. Perhaps sin has to do with incident and I have had this sort of intercourse only three times in my adult life. I know my troubled nature and have tried to contain it along creative lines. It is not my choice that I am alone here and exposed to temptation but I sincerely hope that this will not happen again. I trust that what I did was not wrong. I trust that I have harmed no one I love. The worst may be that I have put myself into a position where I may be forced to lie.

Twenty-odd years later, when Susan was doing some last-minute editing of Home Before Dark, *she called to verify the identity of C as Calvin Kentfield, the merchant seaman whose* New Yorker *stories had been published in a 1957 collection,* The Angel and the Sailor *(McGraw-Hill). John had brought Calvin to dinner one night during his 1960 stay, I told her, and I had taken them both to lunch a day or so later. After lunch, they had headed for a Finnish bath and I had gone back to work on an article I was writing about the Sunset Strip for* Holiday.

"They were lovers," Susie said, and explained that in her book she intended to confront her father's sexual orientation in order to defuse it. "I don't ever want to go in a grocery store and see a tabloid headline: JOHN CHEEVER A FAG."

Harriett and I heartily concurred in her decision, but not until after publication of Home Before Dark, *when we were reading some reviews Lennie Field had sent us, did she casually remark that she had known about John's affair with Calvin Kentfield ever since that evening he showed us his journal.*

"It was not a matter of great consequence to her in the 60s or to me in the 80s, except to arouse the fear in both of us, as it had in Susie, that journalistic violence might be done the memory of a gifted man we both loved," I wrote Ben Cheever, and sent a copy of the letter to Susie, who replied: "I was struck by the information that Harriett had turned to the passage about C. K. in the journals—do you think he may have wanted her to? It would certainly have meant a great deal to my father to feel that his behavior was forgiven if not approved by someone he admired as much as Harriett."

It was not in Harriett's nature to make moral judgments on those she loved and she would have considered any granting of absolution to John Cheever a meddlesome redundancy. He had already suffered enough from a self-imposed penance, and out of his confessions came the insights that, in the words of William Styron, cause us "to pause and realize, in wonder, that we have been told secrets about ourselves that we have never known."

EDITORIAL NOTE

When I deposited the text of John's letters in the memory bank of my Macintosh, I left his spelling and punctuation intact. I duplicated the text and edited it; then I printed both versions. The corrected text didn't ring true. In John's lexicon "it's" and "its" were interchangeable (even in the same sentence) and the room set aside for "dinning" rhymed with silver "linning." He never caught on to the difference between "principal" and "principle," and he sent his love to "Harriet," not "Harriett." His orthography, in some instances, struck me as an improvement. The shrillness of "shriek" seemed louder as "schriek," and why not "bagles" and "grisley bears" and Mother Seton's "cannonization"?

Typographical errors, however, were a different matter. I saw no merit in leaving two words jammed together simply because a finger had slipped. That sort of thing bespoke clumsiness rather than creativity. John also had a tendency to transpose letters, especially vowels. I have corrected these inadvertent misspellings.

He rarely dated a letter, other than to give the day of the week or of a particular month. Fortunately, Harriett kept not only his letters, but also the envelopes, so I have been able to make use of the postmark, a perpetual calendar and internal evidence to establish with reasonable certainty the year in which most of his letters were written. I have indicated such years in brackets.

In the last weeks of Harriett's life I spent many a sleepless night with my computer, typing John's letters in a room filled with love and laughter. Since then, I have reread his stories and novels, along with everything by and about him that I could run down, including hundreds of other letters and much of his journal, published and unpublished.

Some of what I read was painful and some of it disagreeable, but all of it reflected, in the words of John Updike, "a constant tussle between the bubbling joie de vivre of the healthy sensitive man and the deep melancholy peculiar to American Protestant males." He was, as has often been remarked, incapable of writing a dull page. Even on those rare occasions in our correspondence when melancholy prevailed over joie de vivre, his sadness was expressed in a choice and placement of words only he could have assembled.

"Malcolm says that I am mean and prideful," John wrote Muriel Cowley in 1959. "I know myself to be drunken and lazy, nervous and long-winded, runty and improvident but God preserve me from ever being balky with such an old friend as you."

With old friends, as so many have discovered, he could not only be balky ("stubborn; obstinate") he could also be mean in the sense of the seventh of the Random House Dictionary's definitions ("nasty; malicious"). About the same time he reminded the Cowleys of a friendship that dated back to his teens, he wrote his novelist friend Josephine Herbst: "Malcolm has never trod on a toe that was connected to a powerful foot."

"I don't think I would have started this book if I had known where it was going to end," Susan Cheever wrote in the preface of

Home Before Dark, *"but having written it I know my father better than I ever did while he was alive."*

I have the same feeling about my friend and I admire the honesty with which Susan and Benjamin, in The Letters of John Cheever, dealt with their father's drinking and debauchery. It is impossible for me to imagine the pain their mother must have suffered from so many relentless assaults on her privacy. I was pleased when she wrote to say that reading the first draft of Glad Tidings gave her *"some delightful giggles over Cheeverisms such as I had almost forgotten."*

Unfortunately, Mary never accompanied John on his trips to California, but in 1973, when she was visiting Susie in San Francisco, she flew down to Los Angeles to spend a day with Harriett and me. It was a joy to show her around a city she approached with the curiosity of a bright and tireless child. She wanted to see everything and we damned near did. Mary, as Alwyn Lee noted in his 1964 Time cover story, is *"clever"* and, as the English would say, *" 'brainy' in a way John has never been."*

I started to dedicate this book to John Moses Cheever and Andrew Hale Cheever, whose father, Benjamin Hale Cheever, has taken over a correspondence I thought had ended on June 18, 1982, but, with the kindness and generosity that have marked his life since childhood (in 1967 he was the only guest at his sister's wedding reception who wanted to share the wine with Bowery derelicts huddled outside the tented grounds of St. Mark's), he pointed out that the book belonged to Chica, who not only brought me back to life when I thought it was done with, but also installed me in this new home in a new place—Durham, North Carolina—where I can enjoy the Eastern foliage with which I grew up and, John always maintained, should never have left.

The 1940s

꧁꧂

*He was born in Quincy, Massachusetts, May 27, 1912, to Frederick L.
and Mary Liley Cheever, who, he had reason to believe, didn't want
him and denied him the love he spent his life looking for and writing
about. In the Great Depression, when his domineering mother took over
the family's support by opening a gift shop, the child's sympathies were
with his bankrupt father. Not until a half-century later, when a collection of his wife's poems was published and he saw her pride and pleasure
in having her name on a book instead of his, did he come to appreciate
his mother's feeling of intoxication at being able to write a check for a
new car without consulting anyone.*

*By 1940, ten years after selling an account of his expulsion from
Thayer Academy to the* New Republic, *he had written for* The New
Yorker, The Atlantic, Harper's Bazaar, *and* Collier's, *but, he told
a reporter for the Quincy* Patriot Ledger, *"I really haven't written
anything worth reading, yet." The war would undoubtedly have a great
effect on writers, he said. "Now they seem to be getting away from the
proletarian novel and there's an indication they may even go in for
fantasy."*

*He was working on a novel with a New England background, he
continued, and expressed the thought that "possibly it will be finished
in the spring." By the end of the decade, which embraced his marriage
(1941), his army service (1942–45), the publication of his first collection of short stories (1943), and the births of his daughter, Susan Liley
(1943), and his son Benjamin Hale (1948), he had written one of his*

most frequently reprinted short stories, "The Enormous Radio," a fantasy.

He was still working on the novel.

John was on his way to the Philippines, arriving a few weeks after the liberation of its capital. Two months later he was back in Los Angeles.

April 9 [1945]

Dear John and Harriet,

This is a hot time for writing letters because my general timidity about security makes it impossible for me to write about anything but my dreams and my reading. I've been reading George Eliot and dreaming about the farm in Erwinna where Mary and I used to spend our week-ends before the war.[1]

I never found the tar-pits in Los Angeles,[2] but I had a dish of Spam with raisin sauce at the Thrifty Drug Store . . .

As ever,

John

1. The farm belonged to novelist Josephine Herbst, a friend from John's early days at Yaddo.

2. I had once told John an anecdote about a Los Angeles book reviewer who rounded up a covey of village intellectuals to meet Sigrid Undset when she came to town on a lecture tour. He prepared a lavish smorgasbord for the Norwegian Nobel laureate, only to have her announce: "I loathe smorgasbord." When she found herself seated next to a distinguished educator named Von Kleinschmidt, she left the table. "I do not eat with Germans." An hour or so later she grunted: "Now I go home." Her host was delighted to accommodate her. Neither of them said a word as they headed east on Wilshire Boulevard. Suddenly the reviewer heard a shriek: "Stop the car!" He braked abruptly and a quite different Sigrid Undset pointed across the street, awed. "The La Brea *tarpits?*" When the reviewer nodded, she asked: "Is it permitted to go in?" He produced a flashlight from the glove compartment and spent one of the more delightful hours of his life listening to a scholarly discussion of this unique repository of Pleistocene flora and fauna. One Sunday afternoon in the fall of 1960 I took John for a walk around the

Handwritten note on the back of an envelope depicting the interior of Clifton's Pacific Seas Cafeteria, a downtown Los Angeles landmark combining a statue of Christ at Gethsemane with waterfalls, jungle murals, neon flowers, and thatched huts, including one on which rain fell at twenty-minute intervals.

This is for me what the tarpits were for Sigrid Undset.
John

Sunday
[postmarked 10 June 1945]

Dear John and Harriet,

It says here in the Los Angeles Times that Jupiter rules evening sky, Venus has morning: and an old lady on the bus yesterday told me that she was a very war-like person only that she had been born in the female form for the last seven reincarnations. I think continually of your affection for this place and sometimes I think you're right: But not often. Yesterday I strayed into a childrens birthday party at the Beverly Hills Hotel and saw thirty-five miserable tots being compelled to dance a Samba before they got their ice cream. Last Sunday I saw a bus-driver try to evict an elderly lady for non-payment of fare. He took her by the armpits and tried to pull her off the seat. They went down in the middle of the aisle. All the other passengers started hollering and yelling and one man—and he was not little, Godamit—said: "We are against people who push other people around . . ."

Military transportation has fixed it now so that I get to Astoria in time for the exercises on Monday and I'll look for you then.

Best wishes,
John

---

park surrounding the tarpits. "The explanatory notes posted by the archeologists are very dry," he noted in his journal. "They seem to regret the Pleistocene Age."

"*Cheevers & Fields down,*" Harriett wrote in her diary Saturday, June 23, 1945. "*Drinks then all to Nino & Nella's for dinner & to Don Ettlinger's for welcome-home party for Cheever—quite a party & not home till 3 but lot of fun.*"

"*Wonderful news (at last): we have an apartment,*" Mary Cheever wrote Josie Herbst the following month, and issued a final bulletin from the town house on Ninety-second Street: "*There has been constant disorder, hysteria, and vermin. But I won't try to write it because it would depress us both and anyway it's a saga which should be sung to the lyre. Our new address is 400 East 59th Street.*"

"*Here we are,*" Mary wrote in a follow-up letter to Josie, "*living like the wicked rich surrounded by swells and movie magnates and the reproachful stares of doormen and other dignitaries we can't afford to tip. Only Susie feels that this good fortune is perfectly her due and occupies her little suite, and ours as well, with ease and airs of a well-kept woman.*" John described her in "The Sutton Place Story," making imaginary martinis at play and thinking "*all the illustrations of cups, goblets, and glasses in her nursery books were filled with Old-Fashioneds.*"

"*To big separation lunch for Cheever, Don, Herbie[3] & McManus—home depressed,*" Harriett recorded Monday, December 3. We had reason to be depressed. I was still in uniform. I left for Fort Monmouth February 18, 1946: "*The big day! J up at 4:15 & off to separation center.*"

Five months later the marriage of our Astoria luncheon comrade, Ted Mills, to Joan Patterson elicited the first of John's letters from Treetops (family spelling), the summer home of Mary's father, Dr. Milton C. Winternitz, dean of Yale Medical School, and her stepmother, Polly Whitney Winternitz.

3. Herbie Baker, fresh from Yale, was the drummer boy of our outfit. One of his most vivid childhood memories was the night a skinny piano player kept him awake pounding out a new song for his mother, vaudeville star Belle Baker. The pianist was Irving Berlin, the song "Blue Skies."

Tree Tops Bristol,
New Hampshire.
July 15th [1946]

Dear John and Harriet,

I would have written about the wedding last night if I hadn't taken so much champagne but this morning will do. We may as well begin at the begining. It began in New York with Ed Sullivan's column which said that "NBC Television biggie Teddy Mills" was going to get married. It began up here with Mary trying on every hat in the attic. None of them fitted so Polly loaned her an emerald clip. I shaved with a fresh blade. We both took baths and Susie—who has the measles—had a relapse. We got so nervous and upset that we didn't leave here until after eleven. Andover was further down the road than we had thought and so we got to the church just as the happy couple were leaving. We were treated very roughly by a crowd of photographers that had gathered around the bridal car. Someone in the crowd told us they had been married by a Dr. Young-blood, but we didn't see this ourselves.

We got into our car (a 1928 Buick Roadster) and raced up a mountain road behind Teddy and Joan. This led us to a place called Horizon Farm which is not a farm by a long shot. It seems to be where the Pattersons spend their summers. It is on a mountain, but it is not on as high a mountain as the place where my wife's family spend their summers. We parked the car in a pasture and hid behind some bushes until some other cars had arrived. In the meantime Joan and Teddy had arranged them-selves underneath a white umbrella (which blew over) and Joan looked very pretty. She had on some pearls and a white dress that dragged behind her and Teddy had on some white pants and shoes to match. We got up our nerve and started across the lawn to congratulate them only to be intercepted by Mrs. Pat-terson (very nice) who said: "Not yet, not yet, the family of the groom hasn't arrived." We went back behind the bushes. Then a long line formed like the chow-line in Astoria when you got there late and we got into this line and shook hands with a lot of people and kissed all the women. In the meantime the photographers had reassembled and every time you tried to shake hands with anybody or kiss anybody they would give you a shove. The sun was hot and there was a fine view of the horizon, naturally, but not so good a view as there is at the place where my wife's family spends their summers.

Then they began to open champagne at a long table and I went over there to hear the noise the corks make when they pop. I kept saying: "Wasn't it the loveliest ceremony?" Mary was sitting on the edge of a well saying: "Wasn't it divine, wasn't it simply divine?" We ate chicken salad and a lot of toasts were drunk although I didn't make one myself. I had one all thought up, but I couldn't get a word in on the bias. Then they cut the cake and while they were doing this, Joan's younger brother put a big sign on the rear of the car that said: "Amateur Night." This made Teddy very angry and red and for a minute there you couldn't tell what was going to happen. Then Mary remarked that we hadn't been able to bring Susie because she had such a terrible case of the measles and everybody ran over to the other side of the lawn and the women I had kissed began to feel themselves all over to see if they had a rash. Then Mrs. Mills senior discovered that some hoydens were planning to throw rice instead of rose-petals, but before she could knock the rice out of my hand, the bridal couple came running out of the house and I hit Teddy with some rice which will make him fertile. Then they drove off and the caterer stopped opening champagne, so we got the Buick out of the pasture and followed the bridal car but they got away from us. We came back here and I pulled all the pickerel weed out of Polly's lily pond before I sobered up.

Love,

John

Tree Tops
Bristol, N.H.
Tuesday [1946]

Dear John and Harriet,

We have coons in the corn patch and they're eating all the corn. I think they're what you call possum in Virginia and maybe you can help me. I've been going up to the patch after dark with a rifle but it's been too dark to see anything. Then I tried traps and first the traps wouldn't spring and then I filed them down so that if I put them out before dark they catch sparrows. Yesterday Mr. Follansbee in the hardware store told me to hang little mirrors up over the traps. "This'll git their interest," he said. I've got plenty of mirrors and plenty of thread but I'm not going to do anything until I hear from you.

We got a letter from Don and Katrina last week who are drinking martinis and eating ducks. "By God and by Jesus," Don wrote, "this is Paris and it is marvelous . . ."[4]

When I was in New York I lost Lennie's address so I can't write him. . . .[5] Would you send me his address when you write me what to do about the coons. We'll be back in town on the second week in September, I think. Maybe sooner. It all depends on the coons.

Best,
John

JOHN CHEEVER
400 East Fifty-Nine Street
New York City

Bristol, N.H.
August 27 [1946]

Dear John and Harriet,

It was very kind of you to send me the note on the coon and the 'possum and Mary tells me that it contains some very

4. Don Ettlinger and Katrina Wallingford were on their honeymoon.
5. Lennie Field was visiting his brother in Beverly Hills.

useful information. I haven't had time to read it myself since I'm out every night from dusk until dawn, over hill and dale, swamp and mountain, tearing my clothes on briers and firing my rifle at humming-birds and skunks. I am a coon-hunter. I was blooded five nights ago. I won't go into the details of the kill except to tell you that Mary was wearing a gingham night-gown and curl-papers. Her job was to shake the flash light which kept going out. In the middle of the fracas I stepped into one of my own cunningly contrived traps and nearly lost a foot. My Father-in-law, a disagreeable man, tells me the catch is any-where from six weeks to two months old . . .

Since the kill I have been out every night with a man named Joe Plankey who runs the sawmill in Slabville and who has a dog named Ralphie. This has not been a successful combi-nation. We carry a lantern, just like you said, but no sack. Joe apologizes for his dog. I apologize for my coons. We walk a lot and I tell Joe about the islands. Last night Ralphie treed a bob-cat, right in the middle of my anecdote about the Manila whore house, and we were in the swamp until early in the morning, trying to get the dog back. We were both out there, standing in swamp and up to our knees, trying to bark like a hound bitch. I don't think Plankey will ever come back; but we're leaving on the sixth ourselves.

Best,
John

JOHN CHEEVER
400 East Fifty-Nine Street
New York City

January 2nd [1947]

Dear John:

. . . The weather here is cold and stormy and the city, under the first fall of snow, looks like an enormous ash-pit. We had a moderately good Christmas in New Haven and a very pleasant New Year's Eve with Don and Katrina who returned soon after you left. They got off the S.S. America one bright Sunday morning with paper hats and noise-makers from the Captain's dinner. They had spent their last weeks in Paris with Irving Wallace and his wife . . .[6]

I hope to finish my stories and get back to the novel on Monday, and perhaps I can write a fit inscription for your book; a double limerick or a sonnet.[7] And perhaps then I can write a fit letter.

My love to Harriet,
As ever,
John

"Up at 8 to find Mother dead in bed. . . ." Harriett's diary, January 14, 1947.

400 East Fifty-Nine Street
New York City

Saturday
[January 1947]

Dear John:

Lennie told me that Harriet's mother had died the day before we left for Vermont or I would have written you much sooner than this. I hope you're both allright—I remember the shock of my father's death—and give my love to Harriet . . .

We returned from Vermont last night where we had gone for a week's skiing. After the high, snow covered hills and the country cooking I find New York very depressing. The noise of

6. John had met Sergeant Wallace at Fort Capra.
7. John inscribed our copy of *The Way Some People Live:*

> There was a young writer named Weaver,
> Who thought urban life a deceiver.
> Said his wife, who was pretty:
> "City life's far from shitty."
> But Weaver didn't believe her.

THE 1940s
· ·
31

trolley cars kept us awake most of last night and after having listened to sleigh bells and church bells in the sub-zero cold the noise of the trolleys sounded very harsh. We had poor skiing and wonderful weather. I won't say any more because I don't want to seem to be trying to sell New England to you; but it's real nice . . .

In order to keep your memory green I've bought the Prairie Years.[8] Mary does not join me in sending her love because of something that happened a couple of weeks ago. We were walking down First Avenue when a rent, nearly a foot long, appeared in the stern of Mary's fur coat. "What shall I do?" Mary cried. "What," I said, "would Harriet have done?"

Love,

John

Sunday

[postmarked 9 February 1947]

Dear John,

I write you letters continually, but since I have to walk to Bloomingdales in order to get an air-mail stamp, and since I have to walk to 57th Street in order to get any kind of a stamp, and since (the vertigo is worse) this is very difficult for me the letters never get mailed. Lennie said he'd talked with you on the phone; that you were well and that Harriet was tired. I'm sure the Fields will join you in California soon. I'm sure that kind of mass-migration you led out of Kansas City will be repeated here in New York. This will be a brief report on the persistance of your memory, opening with a brief literary discussion. I've finished the Prairie Years and liked it. I read All the Kings Men and disliked it.

We went, one night last week, to a cocktail party at 425 West 57th Street. I give you the address because I know you'll appreciate the fact that we seldom go that far west. To cross Fifth

8. I was reading Carl Sandburg's *Lincoln*, Harriett's Christmas present.

Avenue is like crossing the Mississippi and the four hundred block might just as well be in North Dakota. The building appeared to be a remodeled tenement, the elevator was self-service and the gin was Dixie Belle. In the middle of the crowd we found first Howard Maier and then his wife and we spent the best part of an hour, talking about when the Weavers would return.[9] On the following day I was having my teeth cleaned in Chelsea when Friedman came in and asked about you—suspiciously, I thought.[10] I told him you were in Palm Springs. "Oh," the nurse said, "He has prospects there?" I asked her if she knew you and she said: "I'm terrible about names and faces. Its only the mouths I can remember. I'm terrible. I went out with a fellow from here four times and I couldn't ever remember his name until he opened his mouth."

We've had a good deal of snow here in the last few days and I drove up to Taconic State Park yesterday and went skiing. Susie has the vomiting-sickness and Mary comes home on Tuesdays and Fridays loaded down with Freshman themes . . . There are paper jonquils in Altmans window and they've turned off the blizzard machine at I. J. FOX so I guess we'll see you soon.

Best,

    John

February 24 [1947]

Dear John:

. . . We're very excited about your play here and I'm very envious to hear that you'll have the book done by spring.[11]

9. Howard Maier, author of *Undertow* (Doubleday, Doran, 1945) and his wife, Laurette (*The Stone in the Rain,* Doubleday & Co., 1946), were Village neighbors.

10. M. Joel Friedman, the Chelsea dentist we had shared with the Cheevers during the war.

11. Lennie Field and our Astoria colleague playwright Jimmy Gow (coauthor with Arnaud d'Usseau of *Tomorrow the World* and *Deep Are the Roots*) had arranged an off-Broadway production of our play, *Virginia Reel,*

Envious and glad. My book won't make the April first deadline and if you don't get them in by then they won't print them until 1950. I got back to work on the book about a month ago, was dealt some crushing financial blows three weeks later and now I'm back in the short story business. I want to write short stories like I want to fuck a chicken.

Mary journeys out to Bronxville twice a week and returns home with a lot of themes, written by young ladies named Pussy and Nooky. These names would give you no idea of the contents of these themes. She seems to like the job but it takes a lot of her time and the salary is something of a disappointment to me. Eddie Newhouse's wife, she plays the fiddle and she gets a minimum of a hundred a week but I guess its too late for Mary to take up a musical instrument.[12]

The days are much longer here, the winds are much milder, the skies in the late afternoon are cloudy and wonderful and in another month the hedge will be putting forth its tender green and the Weavers will be coming home.

John

"The Weavers returned hurriedly from California about a month ago because John's play is going to be produced by an experimental theatre group here," John wrote his old friends, Pete and Lib Collins, on April 2. *"Its a good group and all the producers and agents and other shits go to see the plays with an eye towards movie sales or commercial production in the fall so John and Harriet are very*

---

by the new Experimental Theatre of the American National Theatre and Academy. The book was *Another Such Victory*, a novel based on the 1932 Bonus March on Washington.

12. Novelist Eddie Newhouse, whose wife, Dorothy, taught violin at Juilliard, recalls a conversation in which John remarked to Mary, who was teaching English at Sarah Lawrence two days a week: "I could understand it if you were doing what Dorothy did, but why teach at an eighth-rate college?" "Now, John," Mary replied, "It's a fifth-rate college and you know it."

excited. John has also finished the first draft of his novel so the Weavers are in fine shape."

The play opened April 13 and the reviews, I wrote a friend, "skirted the laws against incitement to riot and lynching." One of the actresses who tried out for the leading role showed up at the Princess Theatre in an ankle-length sable coat. Nancy Davis didn't get the part. Later she moved to Los Angeles and married Ronald Reagan.

Handwritten note:

JOHN CHEEVER
400 East Fifty-Nine Street
New York City

Friday
[18 April 1947]

Dear John and Harriet,

I enjoyed it tremendously. I enjoyed the drinking scene more than anything I've seen on the stage for a good many years.

As ever,

John

JOHN CHEEVER
400 East Fifty-Nine Street
New York City

June 6 [1947]

Dear John and Harriet:

I'm writing you in case I don't see you before we leave for beautiful New England where so much that is fine in this country originated and where even the stone walls have a perfume of their own. We leave for New Haven (Venerable Yale college, aristocratic elms, Malley's department store, etc.) on Friday and thence on Saturday morning, to the only remaining shire of Bishop's Rock.

There are still a great many ugly sores about my face and parts and if I don't recover rapidly I may have to wear a veil to the train but we're bound to leave on Friday; bound to leave that is unless Mary comes down with the pox in the meantime . . .[13]

If I should get my papers from the Board of Health before Friday I'll give you a ring and if not, my best wishes for your vacation in the benighted south and when you get your car I hope you'll bring it north to where every black-smith translates Pindar and where they study Marx at the Grange.[14]

Best,

John

Thursday
Treetops
[postmarked 17 July 1947]

Dear John:

I have my troubles. Mrs. Fitch French, who does my wash, has a middle-aged and crippled cat she wants Susie to have. Susie wants the cat. I don't want Susie to have the cat so on Sunday I bought three rabbits; one for Susie and one each for Irene and Jackie, the cook's children. This cost four dollars. Then I brought the rabbits home. I put them in an old duck pen where I thought they would be comfortable. Irene went around behind the duck pen to take a piss. She sat down on a hornet's nest. The hornets waited until she got to her feet, which is typical of New Hampshire, and then attacked all of us with vigor. We weren't able to go near the duck pen again until after dark. I then moved the rabbits from an old duck pen to an old turkey pen where there were fewer hornets. The next evening when

13. "We have very little news excepting Chicken pox," John wrote Pete and Lib Collins this same day. "Sue was in quarantine for two weeks and then she was sick for two weeks. Then two weeks later I came down with the pox for a fair. I was and am sores from top to bottom and look like Hogarth's rake in Bedlam."

14. Harriett and I were planning to buy a car and drive down to Gooney Lodge, my family's summer home in Virginia's Shenandoah Valley, about seventy-five miles from Washington, D.C.

Susie went to the turkey pen to feed her bunny she found that he was dead. She screamed. She cried. She was inconsolable. I buried the rabbit at the head of the garden while the gardener stood beside me and told me I was wasting my time. I should throw the rabbit into the woods for the skunks, he said. He is a communist and is so steeled against bourgeois sentimentality that he hasn't even given his horse a name. I then went to the duck pen to investigate the cause of the bunny's death and found some poison there, left for the rats by "Guts" Winternitz, my father-in-law. This poison was manufactured by the Chemical Warfare Branch of the United States Army to be fed, presumably, to Russians.[15] All of the rabbits tasted the poison but only one of them died. Do you think this is a threat to our national security? Do you think there ought to be a shakeup in chemical warfare?

As ever,
John

Tree Tops
Bristol, N.H.
Sunday
[postmarked 24 August 1947]

Dear John,

We were both very glad to hear from you. Its been a very hot summer up here and even counting all the beauties of the village it must have been hot on stately 11th Street. We leave here on Wednesday, watch Mary's grandmother blow out the candles on her 90th birthday cake, have dinner with my mother and then return to 59th Street on Friday morning.[16] Its still hot

15. Dr. Winternitz had put together a book on the wartime uses of poison gas. In *Treetops*, Susan Cheever refers to her father's use of this incident in "The Summer Farmer" as example of the way he "took facts, his own fears, and a few characters, and wove them into a thoroughly transcendent story."

16. Mary's maternal grandmother was the wife of Thomas A. Watson, the mechanic who, on March 10, 1876, received history's first phone call, in

here and I like the country and I don't like to leave it, but my God, the people. I've finished the first draft of the novel, I think, but they tell me that eggs in the city are a dollar a dozen so I guess I'll have to write some more stories.

There aren't any down-stairs toilets here but if we had one it wouldn't be working. There are a lot of Mary's family here now and a good deal of venom is generated at the dinner table. After dinner everybody gets into the bushes and whispers. When I left the table last night Polly pulled me under a syringia and hissed: "They say he used to eat flies at Hamden Hall and now I believe it." From the other bushes around the lawn you could hear people asking one another: "Did you see her take that third helping of chicken? Did you see that look she gave him? When I asked him to pass the cabbage he pretended not to hear me. Etc." I went into my house and read The Return of the Native but the whispering raged in the bushes until after eleven. It was a beautiful night if you happened to look at it. Most of them have been. I love this country and I'm sorry you and Harriet haven't seen it. I've climbed a couple of mountains and I get up at six in the morning, not so much to work as to have my breakfast alone. The mornings are beautiful. Do you plan to return to the coast for the winter when you get your car? Won't you be coming to New York in the fall. I'll ask the Fields and I hope we see you in the city.

Best,

John

LOOK AWAY FROM THE BODY INTO TRUTH AND LOVE
[Typed across the top of the page]

December 16th [1947]

Dear John,

. . . I stuffed the pockets of my Norfolk jacket with manuscripts and went down to the Algonquin last week to have lunch

---

which Alexander Graham Bell is supposed to have said: "Come quickly, Mr. Watson, I need you."

with Ross, Dorothy Parker, The Duke of Windsor, et al.[17] In the middle of lunch a raggle-taggle bunch of hoodlums appeared in the dinning-room door. "Sardi's must be on fire," Ross said; and he was right. They had to close it for a week and naturally this has upset a lot of people, including me because Mary is giving me a membership in the Dramatists Guild for Christmas.

We've glimpsed the Fields, Ettlingers and the Maiers. The Maiers said you sent them a bible, which is nice, and I liked the tracts you sent me, particularly the part about standing at the window waiting for feelings, which is my predicament in a nut-shell. Have you got a good copy of Science and Health with a Key to The Scriptures? The Ettlingers came in town to do their Christmas shopping and see the shows just as if they'd come in from Minneapolis.

Best,

    John

My parents had taken over our West Eleventh Street burrow. John's concern for their welfare figured in a letter he wrote Mary's parents the following spring: "Some friends of our's, John Weaver and his wife, have just returned from California where they spent the winter. When they left for the west in the fall, John offered his apartment to his elderly parents who have spent most of their life on a farm in the Shenandoah Valley and who have always wanted to spend a winter in New York. John worried about them a lot, since they're old and rural and inexperienced, and he was pleased last week when he returned to find them in good shape. 'Oh we liked New York,' his mother told him. 'We thought New York was real nice and real cheap, all but the drinkin'. You can get a real nice lunch for a dollar and a half, but we found with

17. "My mother says he never owned a Norfolk jacket," Benjamin Cheever noted when he reprinted this letter. He also pointed out that his father "had to become a member of the Dramatists Guild in order to get paid for the production of the Town House stories."

the drinkin' and all it brings the check up, nearly to five dollars. We went up to the Plaza once for lunch and drinks there was a dollar a piece and we come away hungry.' "

Neither of my parents was "rural and inexperienced." Mother was born and reared in Washington, D.C. My father, the son of a county-seat merchant, was a lawyer and court reporter. He held a lifetime appointment to the corps of shorthand experts who recorded the daily proceedings of the House of Representatives for the Congressional Record. *Mother often transcribed his elegant Pitman shorthand notes. Both were superb editors. She would, however, have been less offended by John's solecism ("drinks was") than by his reference to her as "elderly." She was sixty-five that winter. In the fall of 1972 she was outraged when a* New York Times *article mentioned my age. She didn't want people to know she was old enough to have a sixty-year-old son. She was eighty-nine at the time.*

December 30th [1947]

Dear John,

I know that God's handiwork is manifest in the tarpits, but Jesus Christ you should have seen the blizzard. The village is still buried like an alp and I imagine that your parents can discourse with some bitterness on the arrangements they were induced to make for the winter. Everyone has a train story to tell. Gus Lobrano boarded the 5:19 for Chappaqua on Friday evening and reached Chappaqua at 7:10 the next morning.[18] The train was unheated, the commuters were unstable, and Gus still shakes. There was a riot over some coffee-cake from Cushman's one of the passengers was hoarding and a Yale man tried to throw the conductor out of the window. Ross boarded the Century on Friday evening (he's on his way to the tarpits) and vanished. I left New Haven Friday evening at about eight and got into Grand Central a little after three in the morning. People were sleeping all over the floor in the station. The drifts on Madison Avenue were shoulder-high but there was a little lane beaten in the snow

---

18. Gus Lobrano was *The New Yorker*'s fiction editor.

of the east sidewalk, winding from bar to bar. Every bar was overflowing and I've never seen such general drunkenness. People were wandering up and down the street, with their drinks, admiring the drifts and there were sleighs on 57th Street. The air was as still as the air in Brentwood. On Saturday night I went to Bleecks where hundreds of commuters were having a Saturnalia. The main streets have been cleared now but I think the village is still cut off and the two-cent press says there's going to be more snow this afternoon.

Base-pay at the Saturday Evening Post has gone up to eight hundred dollars. Teddy Mills has given up his country life (Joan had some trouble with her back teeth) and is trying to rent his house to Herbie Baker. We spent a week-end at the Ettlingers and were taken on Sunday afternoon to the opening of an antique shop owned by Buss or Buzz and Paulette. Max Anderson, Helen Hayes, Jinx, Tex, Buzz and Charlie were there but you couldn't get to know them very well since they, like the furniture, were roped off and only stayed with us long enough to be photographed.[19] Naturally this was very disappointing. Susie learned a new poem at school which goes like this: "The more you work the more you fight the more you fuck." Mary thinks always of Salvation. Love is reflected in love!

John

400 East 59th Street,
January 22nd [1948]

Dear John,

. . . I haven't seen any of the old gang except Lennie. Lennie said he was going out to the coast in February and

19. Don and Katrina had rented (and would later buy) Waldo Pierce's house in Rockland County. Herbie Baker, a comedy writer in civilian life, was about to remarry and, for a brief period, become their neighbor. Buzz (Burgess Meredith) was married to Paulette Goddard. Tex McCrary, a sportswriter, and his wife, Jinx Falkenberg, a model, were hosts of a popular radio talk show. Helen Hayes's husband, Charlie (MacArthur), was, like Maxwell Anderson, a neighboring playwright.

seemed to me rather tight-fisted with his news so I guess he's saving it up for you. The only news I can think of is that we were supposed to go to Vermont and didn't go. Herbie Baker is buried in snow. Irwin Shaw's play closed after eight perform-ances.[20] We've been to the theatre five times this year; that is to five different plays.

M. Joel Friedman has expanded tremendously and Mary had a rather unfortunate experience here. She needed to have some of her teeth recapped and Friedman recommended a Japa-nese. She went to the Japanese and he put into her mouth so many long, large, white teeth that it is difficult for her to close her mouth at all and she hisses when she laughs. Otherwise she is fine and sends her best.

As ever,
John

[postmarked 11 February 1948]

Dear John,

In order to check up on all the angles of the news before reporting to you, Mary and I got into a taxi ~~yesterday~~ *Sunday* evening and went west to Park Avenue, then down, down, down to 14th Street, then west again to Hudson, and then down, down to 96 Perry where Joan and Teddy were giving themselves a farewell party before leaving New York for Chi-cago where the rivers run backward. Teddy has a big job work-ing for McCormick in television and after Joan has had her baby she's going into the Chicago office of TIME. We arrived at the party too late to see Lily and Arthur Mayer and we left too early to see Tony and Nixon Griffis but we did talk with many ornaments of the radio, television, and news-weekly world and my head is still spinning.[21] Both Teddy and Joan seemed in a fine

20. *The Survivors,* written in collaboration with Peter Viertel.
21. The Mayers were the nude-bathing couple John drew on in writing "Roseheath," which had come out in *The New Yorker* the previous

humor and we came away without a bruise. After leaving the party we walked along 8th Street, happy to hear the maracas from Don Julio's and to see that every Russian blouse, every moonstone bracelet was in its place.

Then yesterday, still searching for truth, I went to a party at the Ritz. There, sitting on a piano was Howard Maier. He took out of his pocket a letter from you and read it aloud. Quite a large crowd gathered for this and agents from Howell Soskin and Lipincott took your address. Then a man named Louis Untermeyer came along and he took out of his pocket a letter from you—creased and spotted—and he read aloud from his letter.[22] Then I read aloud from a letter I chanced to have in my pocket and then we all sat down at the piano and sang a rousing chorus of "Another Such Victory. Viking. Two-seventy-five" in the face of a good deal of spiteful interference from a woman named Laura Hobson or Hopson.[23]

John

February 16th [1948]

Dear John,

. . . We're having here now what the doctors call the ebb of winter. A lot of people are killing themselves or having heart trouble and lung trouble and I'm the only man in the East Fifties who hasn't finished his novel. Mary and Sue are both well and we're trying to get Sue into a fashionable school called Brearly.

---

summer. Griffis was a wealthy young Astoria officer who now presided over Brentano's bookstores.

22. We had met in Kansas City in 1939 when he spent a month on a local campus as poet in residence and Harriett served as his secretary.

23. Laura Z. Hobson was the author of *Gentleman's Agreement,* a popular novel about a Gentile journalist (Gregory Peck in the film) who poses as a Jew to expose anti-Semitism. After praising the book in a Brooklyn lecture, Louis Untermeyer was cornered by a woman who said she had "learned a lot" from his talk. "What did you learn?" Louis asked, and she said, "Be nice to Jews. They might turn out to be Christians."

She goes up to take what they call her "tripos" tomorrow. She's already had her "vivas."[24] Mary's brother Bill is going to be in Los Angeles sometime this month and I told him to look you up. He wears a uniform, but he doesn't like to and if he rings your doorbell look for the medical insignia on his collar before you slam the door on his fingers. Irwin Shaw writes seventeen pages a day but he can't ski as well as I can. Neither can Jack Kahn who broke his left leg in two places a couple of Sundays ago.[25] Have you read the new biography of Fielding? I'm going to buy it.

John

"On May 4th which is Mary's birthday, she spent the afternoon pricing bathrobes at Bendel's, and in the evening went up to Harkness and had a seven and one-half pound son whose name is Benjamin Hale Cheever which I made up myself," John wrote Pete and Lib Collins.

Treetops
Bristol, N.H.
July 5th [1948]

Dear John and Harriet,

Mary will write to thank you for the bib whenever she gets out of the diaper can and in the meantime I want to tell you how much Ben and I appreciate your thoughtfulness, and how handsome and practical the bib is. He wears it whenever he's fed in the presence of company and he sometimes wears it at his private feedings. He is greedy and since the milk overflows from his mouth and drops down his back and his stomach a bib is what he needs. He needs a bib more than most babies and I guess you must have figured this out from watching me eat.

The weather, the country, the company, the drink and so

24. "Sue seems to feel that she satisfied them," John wrote her maternal grandparents; "but we're not so sure. 'They asked me,' she said, 'to draw with a pencil how a little boy could get home from his house to his school without crossing the street but it was very easy because all the little boy had to do was to jump over the hole in the street!' Somehow this doesn't sound like a winning answer."

25. John's friend and neighbor, who writes for *The New Yorker*.

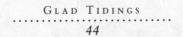

forth are all fine; so fine that I'm afraid I'll have to leave in the middle of July for New York, if I'm going to get any work done. I won't describe the beauties of New England to you again, and I'm sure there's a great deal to be said for Virginia, but it is, as everyone who has been here admits, country of unusual character. One of its principle characteristics is that a hangover here is painless. People come from all over the world to see its old churches and to drink its cheap booze (gin is $2.60 a quart) and how much is gin in Virginia.

Mary is well, Sue is bursting, and Ben looks a lot better than he did on 59th Street. We think, we hope that he's going to be a big boy and he can already do many wonderful things like lifting his head off the pillow and swatting a rattle. Mary will write you, and many thanks again.

John

John's letter was written at Treetops. Harriett and I were at Gooney Lodge.

August 2nd [1948]

Dear John,

It's been so long since I got your letter and so much has happened that I don't know where to begin. I may as well begin with the deer. Well first they ate the broccoli and the spinach and then they ate the carnations and the gladioli and I fired guns off at them and did everything that it said to do in the Boston Herald but when I left they were eating the lupin and the salpaglosis; but I'm getting ahead of myself. Then I got crocked one night and forgot to put the chickens in and I guess you have weasles in the Shenandoah Valley and will understand about this. Then Susie told my father-in-law, who is really Lionel Barrymore, that Treetops didn't belong to them at all and that it was only by my grace and charity that he was allowed to stay there. Then there was a stern letter from a collection agency and putting two and two together I took the plane for New York one evening and have been sitting at my desk opposite the Queensboro Bridge ever since. I've seen almost no one since no one knows that I'm here excepting the Ettlingers, the Fields, the Werners, the Collins, the Lindsays, the Kahns, the Lobranos, the Brickens and the Mayers. They don't seem to be doing much about it, but after all I've only been here three weeks.

It's very pleasant here, all alone, and by missing the blizzard and the heat wave I think you and Harriet have missed the best of New York. Also the Lion's Convention which was here last week. New Hampshire was allright, if you like that sort of thing and before I left I killed thirty-six roosters, intentionally, and had a discussion with the hired man about Kautsky. The hired man is going to vote for guess who. He hung the Daily Worker in the garden to frighten away the deer but that didn't do any good either. In my spare time I read the novels of Liley Saportas and shellac the floors around here, always wearing a fresh white shirt with a button-down collar and a Brooks' foulard, just in case the telephone should ring. Mary's going to give me a signal when the deer have finished and when Lionel Barrymore's cholers have passed away and I'll return then; but perhaps I'll see you here before that happens.[26]

Best,

John

26. The summer at Treetops ended happily, as John recorded in a bread-and-butter letter describing the train trip home (September 19): "The porter in Concord stowed our luggage conveniently on an empty berth and told us to relax in the drawing-room until it's rightful owners boarded the train in Lowell. Ben was put to bed and Mary and Sue and I established ourselves with the scotch, the chicken sandwiches and the backgammon board in drawing-room A and ate and drank and played backgammon and watched the scenery roll by. We tucked Sue in at Manchester and at Lowell Mary and I took the backgammon board and the scotch into my berth and played there until the other passengers objected to the rattle of dice and Mary's exclamations when she trapped two of my men on her board and forced all my checkers onto the one point. Then we went to bed and slept soundly until three when Benjamin woke and wanted to be tickled. Mary tickled him industriously for half an hour. Then Sue woke and the rest of the night was a sort of quiz program. New York was humid and overcast when we pulled in on Wednesday morning and so ended one of the best summers we've ever had. . . ."

John's handwritten note on a Metropolitan Museum of Art Christmas card, "The Virgin of the Annunciation," engraving by Martin Schongauer, German 1445(?)–1491(?)

[postmarked 15 December 1948]

Dear John and Harriet:

We would have written much sooner if it hadn't been for the pressure of head-colds and disorders here; and I'm snatching these few moments away from my house work while Mary is at school listening to Susie sing "Away in a Manger."[27] I've just rocked Ben to sleep and Electroluxed the Christmas tree. Lennie called us as soon as he heard the news of the bonanza and we were delighted to hear it.[28] It is the first time I think that anyone about whose success we've cared, has enjoyed this kind of a sale. I think of it as a blow against Spigelgass and Chauvinism.

It is snowing here and I think continually of your poor parents getting fire-wood in Washington Square. Also "The Harem" has closed. Mary bought this card at the museum and I don't know what it has to do with Christmas, but our best wishes anyhow.

John

400 East 59th,
January 18th [1949]

Dear John,

Mary didn't let Ben eat your letter but sometimes I wish she had let him eat it because she was made curious and I'm sorry to say, restive, by a remark that came towards the end of your letter where you are leaving this cocktail party and Harriet is

27. "On the Sunday before Christmas Sue is going to be an angel on the alter at Saint Thomases, wearing genuine high-church episcopal wings," John wrote the Winternitzes (November 25). "I hope they don't expect us to repay them with a stained glass window, but I know that they do."

28. Toward the close of a financially troubled year a Christmas story I'd sold to *McCall's* was bought by RKO and made into a film the studio called *Holiday Affair*.

fingering her new mink coat. What new mink coat? If she was fingering it does it mean that it is a finger-tip length mink coat. Or is it full length. Or is it a cape or a stole. Is it wild, is it ranch, is it backs or is it stomachs? Why does Harriet need a mink coat out in California if the climate is so good. What about this?

Here, of course, we are at the top of the brilliant season, and more often than not I can't remember how I got home. Last month one of Susie's baby-sitters gave a party to which we were invited. I wish you could have seen the collation. People kept coming up to me and whispering: "I guess you'll be able to write a story about this." They were wrong. Then right after that we went to a dinner at Sue's school that was given by the Parents and Teachers Association. I was put right between Mrs. W. T. Beauchamp who teaches carpentry and a Mrs. Maguire who said that she was a parent. What repartee. What chicken fat. It cost us two dollars and a half a piece and it was worth it. Then the next day I met Herbie Baker on 59th Street. Then after this was Christmas. Mary gave me an alarm clock and I gave her a sweater that didn't fit her. This put her into sort of a bad frame of mind for the news of Harriet's coat. She says that she hasn't had her shoes on since Christmas eve, but that's certainly not true.

I have a hangover and am putting an undue strain on my left eye so I will stop this. Please tell me about the mink coat— send me a snap-shot if you can.

Best,

John

[April 1949]

Dear John,

I went down to the village yesterday, I had to go down to the village on business, and I walked over to 11th Street to take a look at the hedge. The hedge nearest Sixth Avenue is clipped but your hedge is a riot of green, climbing well up beyond where the funks used to live.[29] Speaking of the funks, they wrote a letter to the New Yorker saying they were surprised to see a story of mine that lacked the accuracy of detail that is imposed on *their* work. But to get back to the hedge. It can be seen from both Fifth and Sixth Avenues and it sticks way out on the sidewalk. The hedge is fine but the house looks abandoned. I looked in the windows, the basement windows, but I couldn't see anybody moving. Are your parents still there? Do they get enough to eat? Are they all-right? Then I walked out to Fifth Avenue and up to Macmillan. I hung around there for a long time but nobody came out. The double bill at the Playhouse is Le Sang d'une Poete and Le Jour de Colere. Then I took a bus home.

Lennie is well and happy with his hands on a show and it looks like a reasonably good thing.[30] All the Fields are bright-eyed and happy and it would be wonderful if this turned out. I'm not too sanguine about Jerry Chodorov, but then I didn't think Saint Subber would ever get a show open. They tell me that the only thing wrong with George Kaufman last year was his metabolism and that this has been fixed up with some new kind of pill and I'm sure glad that he feels better and I sure hope he remembers to take those pills. Lennie and Jerry and everyone else connected with the show speak of Kaufman with that rich blend of respect and excitement that I enjoyed last year. Kaufman must have lost his friends and relatives at least five million dollars, but everyone still speaks of him as if he were in his prime. Maybe Jerry knows how to handle him.

I've been having some difficulties with the New Yorker so

29. Tom Funk and his wife, Edna Eicke, were *New Yorker* artists who lived on the floor above us at 41 West Eleventh Street.

30. *Pretty Penny* a musical revue with sketches by our Astoria colleague Jerry Chodorov and directed by George S. Kaufman, who had directed *Town House,* based on John's *New Yorker* stories about his wartime living arrangement with two other couples. It closed after twelve performances, making John richer by fifty-four dollars.

that while we've had a quiet winter we've also had an exciting one, but now that it's over I'm sure that I'll finish my play, my book, my poems, my operetta, and my essay on the Concept of Dread. In the evenings now Susie and I play parchesi.[31]

Best,
John

400 East 59th Street
June 19th [1949]

Dear John:

. . . Olga organized John and Harriet day at Ebbett's Field[32] and at the seventh everybody stood up and sang the last two verses of Another Such Victory. It was thrilling. I bought you a pennant (Navy Blue: fifty cents) but Susie got it away from me and packed it in her suit-case. She wants to carry it in the Fourth of July parade in Bristol. I may be able to get it back after the holiday. But the biggest news I have is that the A&P has stopped redeeming waste fats. This blow came without any warning. It was our last source of income. I don't know what's going to happen.

We're taking our waste fats up to New Hampshire tomorrow with the hope that the bottom won't have dropped out of the market up there and in order to escape the worst weather I remember in New York. There hasn't been any rain for three weeks (we like rain here) and there hasn't been any change of air. As soon as I've unloaded the fat and marched in the parade I'm coming back here to write on my nvl.

I haven't seen Lennie but I've talked with him on the phone and he seems contented. He says that Kaufman has been renewed, not only by his pills, but that his marriage has worked

31. "My long love affair with The New Yorker," John reflected in his journal, "seems like an unhappy marriage, repaired, now and then with a carnal exchange, a check."

32. When Jackie Robinson joined the Dodgers we started going to Ebbets Field with Olga and Jimmy Gow.

on him like monkey glands. Ha ha. He never had any trouble that way anyhow. Everybody talks as if he was directing the show with his prick. We're not going to see it in Pennsylvania but I'll see it in Boston on my way back and maybe we'll all see it in New York in the fall. Mary sends you both her love and Susie says you can't have the pennant.

John

The opening game of the subway series at Yankee Stadium turned out to be a pitchers' duel between Allie Reynolds, a Yankee of Cherokee ancestry, and Don Newcomb, a Dodger with African roots. Neither team had scored when Tommy Henrich came to bat in the bottom of the ninth inning. Newcomb threw him a curve. It ended up in the lower right-field stand.

> 400 East 59th Street,
> Wednesday
> [October 5, 1949]

Dear John:

I didn't want to write you until I heard the game today and until after I'd been to lunch at Sardi's and The Algonquin and investigated these old stamping grounds of yours. You couldn't help but hear the game, wherever you were, and I was in a bar across the street. The elevators in this building stopped running at one o'clock (that's when they play baseball in the east) and everyone in the street who wasn't listening to a portable radio was asking the score from people who were listening. This is the best of New York. Sardi's and the Algonquin are a good deal less. I went to Sardi's with Lennie so they let me in and I had the canneloni. Marty Gable was there too.[33] They have a new bar right in the middle of the dinning room now, but it isn't worth the trip east. Lennie said that you might come east for the Columbia picture. Stanley Kramer and Carl Foreman did . . .[34]

33. Martin Gabel, actor and producer, had coproduced the 1947 Irwin Shaw–Peter Viertel play.

We had a good summer. During the winter Wezul, the hired man's wife died and he buried her with his membership card in the Communist Party and his tendency to compare me to a plant upon which too much fertilizer has been lavished and in exchange for his civility I gave him driving lessons which he didn't want. I also borrowed an apple-press and made ten gallons of hard cider which, with the money we get in refunds from the gin and tonic bottles we bought in "good times" make us practically self-sufficient.

After New Hampshire the city looks like a bucket of shit but I'll get used to it I guess and why don't you come east for yuletide. Don't you miss the village, the snow, the maracas at Don Julio's, the firelight in the Jumble Shop Windows. Come, come, come, come.

Best,

John
[*handwritten postscript*]
My love to Harriet

John's handwritten note on a Metropolitan Museum of Art Christmas card, "Kneeling Angels":

[postmarked 12 December 1949]

I lost your address and have written you two letters which I will now mail. Mary knew the address all the time. A Merry Christmas means a Happy Marriage.

John and Mary.

34. *Champion,* starring Kirk Douglas. My friendship with Carl began the day we met at Fort Capra in the spring of 1943 and didn't end until his death in 1984. He gave my name and Herbie Baker's to characters in each of his scripts, including *The Bridge on the River Kwai,* which, because of the blacklist, was credited to the author of the book. Just before his death Carl learned that he was finally going to get his Oscar. It was presented to his widow at a special ceremony at the Academy.

John's story, "Christmas Is a Sad Season for the Poor," in the December 1949 issue of The New Yorker, *revolved around Charlie, an elevator man in a Sutton Place apartment building not unlike 400 East Fifty-Ninth Street, where John descended to the lobby in just such a conveyance each morning, walked down to the basement, shut himself in a windowless storage room, stripped to his boxer shorts, and spent the day hunched over a portable Underwood writing short stories that distracted him from his novel but fed, clothed, and sheltered his family.*

In his Christmas story he saw Charlie as "a prisoner, confined eight hours a day to a six-by-eight elevator cage, which was confined, in turn to a sixteen-story shaft." In his journal he also saw himself as a prisoner, one who was trying to escape from jail by digging a tunnel with a teaspoon.

"Oh, I think if I could only taste a little success!" he wrote, and in the same paragraph made an an abrupt transition: "M[ary] in the morning, asleep, looking like the girl I fell in love with. Her round arms lie outside the covers. Her brown hair is loose. The abiding quality of seriousness and pureness."

The 1950s

❧❀❧

"Down to see Lennie who is lending me his car for the summer," John noted in his journal on May 27, 1950, his thirty-eighth birthday. "Financially this is a good arrangement, sentimentally there is nothing to lose, but I am tired of borrowing and hedging, of living like a bum. Towards the end of the night I felt like killing myself, I have so little to pass on to my children."

At one point the following spring the two young Cheevers were bathing by candlelight because their father was unable to pay the electricity bill. A few months later, thanks in part to a Guggenheim Foundation grant, they were living in a cottage on a suburban estate where, their grandfather reported in his monthly family bulletin, "Sue can ride her bicycle all over the grounds and Ben can be out of doors without a leash."

In 1955 John looked forward to the first Christmas "in some years that has not been distinguished by the bouncing of checks. Mary will have a typewriter and the children will have a television set and I will put a ten dollar bill in the collection plate at All Saints where, as I said my prayers this morning, I could hear the noise of a rat's tooth in the baseboard. Very loud, persistent and unintimidated by the Gloria. And so long as we can hear both the rat's tooth and the Gloria how can we go wrong?"[1]

1. In "The Housebreaker of Shady Hill," John's narrator has a dizzy spell in church and then "I heard, in the baseboard on my right, a rat's tooth working like an auger in the hard oak. 'Holy, Holy, Holy,' I said very loudly, hoping to frighten the rat. 'Lord God of hosts, Heaven and earth are FULL

When Paramount bought the film rights to "The Housebreaker of Shady Hill" in 1956, John bundled his family off to Italy, where he read galleys on his first novel, got word of his election to the National Institute of Arts and Letters, and registered the birth of his son Federico. When he came home, he won the National Book Award for The Wapshot Chronicle *and, again in need of money, began to draw on his Italian year for new stories while Mary prowled the Westchester countryside, looking for a house they couldn't afford to buy.*

"I wanted it so badly," she later told Scott Donaldson. "I was tired of living in someone else's playpen."

No 1950 letters survive, but we saw the Cheevers that summer when we flew East, visited Gooney Lodge, and took in the Princeton opening of Legend of Sarah, *the final collaboration of Jimmy Gow and Arnaud d'Usseau. We also bought a Pontiac and for the first time in our thirteen years together Harriett and I drove home in a brand-new car.*

400 East 59th Street
January 4th, 1951

Dear John,

When you and Harriet returned to the coast this fall we went into a slump. Wherever I went—Sardi's, the Algonquin, 21—people would hail me and ask: "Heard from John?" Then they would take out of their pockets a dog-eared letter from you and read me a few bon mots. It happened everywhere. Louis Untermeyer read to me from your correspondence at the Saint

---

of Thy Glory!' The small congregation muttered its amens with a sound like a footstep, and the rat went on scraping away at the baseboard. And then— perhaps because I was absorbed in the noise of the rat's tooth, or because the smell of dampness and straw was soporific—when I looked up from the shelter I had made of my hands, I saw the rector drinking from the chalice and realized that I had missed Communion."

Regis. Howard Maier read it to me in the 43rd Street Chockfullofnuts. I overheard Don Ettlinger quoting you at Au Canarie D'Or. And I think it was Don who bruited about the fact that *I* didn't have a letter. Presently the telephone went dead. Lord & Taylors began to dun me and the only invitation I received was to a private sale of stoves at Lewis and Congers. When your long-delayed letter finally did come it was too late for the holiday parties and when I tried to read it at the Algonquin several people referred to me as a Johnny-come-lately.[2] However the die is cast; and I find that a quiet life suits me. Now and then the Ettlingers drop in to use our toilet—they park their Dynaflow convertible in a lot across the street—and through these visits we get a glimpse of the world in which your top-drawer correspondents live. The last times they came up here to urinate, Katrina was wearing a mink coat that was so long it was dragging on the floor and they had just been to a party given by the Angier Biddle Dukes or maybe it was the Duke and Duchess of Angier Biddle. Anyhow the Duke and Duchess of Windsor had been there also the Countess Eleanor Paalfy. That's what Don said. But I don't go much for all this European royalty . . .

We spent Christmas in New York this year for the first time and we had our own Christmas tree, our own popcorn balls, and our own bills for hootch, breakage, and reupholstery.

2. I heartily concur in Ben Cheever's caveat about his father: "He found occasion to express admiration for the letter-writing skills of just about everybody who wrote him. There are letters to Don Ettlinger about what a great letter writer he is. There are letters to Phil Boyer about his brilliant letters. There are letters to John Weaver about people pulling out letters from him and reading them in public. There are even letters to my grandfather, Milton Charles Winternitz, praising him for the writing of something called The Bulletin, a compendium of family news that he regularly circulated through the mail, a compendium that his own daughter recalls as deadly dull. Doubtless many of the people my father corresponded with were superb writers, but my father's talent for admiration must in some cases have exceeded the talents of those whom he was flattering."

I gave Mary a pair of gold ear-rings and a Dodge sedan and she gave me a ten dollar gift certificate for Brooks Brothers hat department. The only hat they had at Brooks Brothers for ten dollars was a beret which I bought, thinking that we might go to Europe for a year, but Mary said that she would rather go to Westchester so I rented for her a remodeled tool-house in a place called Scarborough which is near Ossining where The Big House is. We are going to move out there in June. This is not a basement. There are four bedrooms and a living room, all above ground . . .

Love,
John

On May 28, the day after John's thirty-ninth birthday, the Cheevers moved into a small house on the estate of Frank A. Vanderlip. It had formerly been occupied by friend and New Yorker *colleague Jack Kahn. "A lot of people live in garages in Westchester," John explained to Malcolm Cowley.*

400 East 59th Street,
February 2 [1951]

Dear John,

Everybody here thought your letter was wonderful and the only reason I haven't answered sooner was because I was so busy reading it. The beginning did give me a little trouble and I wondered where the hell you got off, calling yourself the second most sensitive writer in the United States. I guess your subscription to Botego Oscura must have run out. Spigelgass said that *I* was the most sensitive writer in the United States.[3] He didn't give any second or third prizes or honorable mentions, that I remember. Of course that was in 1944 and I lost the prize to

3. In their first meeting, as John told the story, Major Spigelgass had laid great stress on John's sensitivity and his "childlike sense of wonder." The phrase became one of our running gags and continues to be solemnly echoed by critics and doctoral candidates.

Speed Lampkin in a pillow fight the following April. But as I say I thought your letter was wonderful, all but the beginning. I read it everywhere and when Don and Katrina came in to take a leak on their way to Ben Sonnenberg's[4] I read it to them. Just because I had a good letter and he didn't have one he kept interrupting me. He kept asking me if I didn't want a cigaret and could he have another drink and then telling Katrina that her underwear straps were showing. Mary thought your letter was a masterpiece and it's hard to get compliments from that corner. She never reads my letters. Whenever I write her a letter she cuts off the signature and sends it to the hand-writing analyst at the Daily News. She throws the rest of it away.

It looks from the morning papers as if Lennie was going to be business manager of a hit and I guess that's good news.[5] I saw Laurette Maier at a cocktail party and she said that Howard, just like Eisenhower, had been sent over to Europe to take a look. Mary spends a lot of time getting ready to move to Scarborough and we went out and took another look at the house again. I think that it used to be a garage. When we tell people we're moving out of town it doesn't seem to sadden them any. "Who's going to get the apartment?" is what they say. It's only forty minutes on the train and we hope you and Harriet will come out and visit us.

John

"For the first time in my life," John wrote in his journal, "I've borrowed a thousand dollars from the bank and bought a new automobile. In the distance this looks like trouble." He had also received word of a favorable decision on his application for a Guggenheim Fellowship. *"Now all I have to do is to take a physical examination,"* he wrote Mary's parents, *"but I've seen a few Guggenheim Fellows and don't*

4. Don says he never met Benjamin Sonnenberg (1901–78), president of Publicity Consultants.
5. A revival of Mordaunt Shairp's play, *The Green Bay Tree*, which closed after twenty performances.

think their standards of physical fitness are very exacting. I think I'll pass."

400 East 59th Street,

Sunday

[postmarked 29 April 1951]

Dear John,

I was very glad to get your letter because it was only a couple of nights ago that a bunch of us were sitting around the PEN Clubhouse talking about Belles Letters when the subject came up of you as a correspondent. After a few selections had been read by people who had current letters from you one of the members said that the only trouble with you as a correspondent was that you were too good. Another member said that it took him as long to write an answer to a letter of yours as it took him to write a television script. The general feeling was that you should lower your sights for the rank and file and write less brilliant and more homely letters about how you are going to ventilate your television set and why you turned in your Dodge for a Pontiac. Mary is worried about this. The only reason we joined the proud ranks of Dodge owners was because we expected to be marching shoulder to shoulder with you. "If the Weavers have a Dodge," Mary said, "it must be a buy." Before we had even driven our Dodge two thousand miles or paid for more than a third of it I met Lennie Field at the race-track and he told me you'd changed over to a Pontiac. I'd like to know all about this.

On Easter Week Mary thought we ought to take a trip in this Dodge that the Corn Exchange Bank and Trust Company bought and I suggested that we drive down to the Weaver Country. Late one morning we packed some sandwiches and put Susie's cage of rats in the back seat and headed for Front Royal. It was a longer trip than we had planned and we spent the first night in a motel outside Baltimore near the Calvert Whiskey Factory. Early in the morning we drove into Washington and had breakfast at a Hotte Shoppe and I showed the children the Washington Monument. Then we started for Virginia. It was a nice day in the spring and after driving for about an hour we went through a cut in some mountains and there it was; the Weaver Country! It was just like we'd read about in the stories. There were even the same kind of stone walls. We thought the people would be kindly like the people in the stories. The first place we stopped to ask directions was a place called Carter Hall that had a sign out in front of it saying when it was built so I expected it would be open to the public. It wasn't. Then we passed a house that had a sign H. B. Weaver in front of it but I could tell from the pictures that it wasn't your house.[6] Then we stopped and asked a lady on the road for directions. She was kindly although she looked more like a New York woman than a country woman to me. "Turn right and stay with Willy Dupont's fence," she told us. We did this and pretty soon we came to a stone house that didn't look like the pictures of your house either but I left Mary and the kids in the car and rang the bell. A butler with a trick vest opened the door and in a big room behind him there must have been about twenty-five or thirty people drinking martinis. I went in, and took a martini off a tray, thinking that maybe it was your brother's house, but it wasn't. I got out of there with no damage to anything but my feelings and we drove along until we came to a restaurant called the Fox's Head. This was the most expensive restaurant I've ever been in to and as you well know I've been to 21 with Anatol Litvak.[7] Then we drove back through Washington and stopped at the friendly motel again. We have your memories of the Virginia country and it looked just like

6. John had stumbled onto the fox-hunting turf of my older brother, a Washington lawyer.

7. Anatole Litvak, a European film director *(Mayerling)* with a taste for the good life, was a film supervisor and director at Fort Capra. See Joseph McBride, *Frank Capra* (Simon & Schuster, 1992).

your description of it but either we made a wrong turn or the people have changed.

Best,

John

The New York Times *had reported the film sale of a story I'd written for* Collier's.

400 East 59th Street,
May 18th [1951]

Dear John,

. . . Mary hasn't seen the item yet and I hope to Christ she thinks you're John V. Weaver.[8] She still gets Bleriot mixed up with Lindbergh. Things are a little pinched here and I had to hide the check book in the teapot this morning and tell her that I'd lost it. I don't suppose the money will make much of a change in your way of living. It never seems to any more. When Eddie Newhouse sold some stories to Goldwyn this spring I took a bus out to his house in Manuet, thinking that he might have put in a bottle of Calvert's V.O. but plus ca change, plus la meme chose. "Let's go upstairs and knock out a pipe," he said, and that's just what we did. We knocked out a pipe and talked about Lord Chesterfield just like we used to before he struck it rich.

The only news here is that Don is suing CBS for two hundred and fifty thousand dollars which must sound like jujubes to you. Most afternoons now when it's sunny I walk down to the Supreme Court and watch him testify. He's got some nice new suits for the trial and some inconspicuous but memorable neckties. He sits up there on the witness stand with his legs crossed and talks down his nose to Judge Rosenman just like he used to talk to Boris Kaplan.[9] Now and then he flashes

8. John V. A. Weaver (1893–38) was best known for his verse in slang, *In American*.

9. One of our most amiable Astoria officers.

the jury a youthful smile with just a hint of modesty in it and you ought to see them lay back in their swivel chairs. Katrina brings the children to court and wears a little silk handkerchief over her head to give the impression of a family somewhat damaged by a heartless corporation.[10] I think she overdoes her part; but Don is perfect. "No, *sir,* your honor," he says, "you're absolutely mistaken, *sir.*" When he finishes he stamps down from the witness stand with just the mixture of indignation and wronged youth that he used that day he stamped out of the projection room when he discovered that the sound man had scored the V Day or Bright Page of History script with furniture music.

We're moving out to the chicken house in Scarborough a week from Monday—the 28th. Scarborough, N.Y. will be our address I guess for the next ten years. Everybody says it will be nice for the children and I guess it will be nice for the children. Mary doesn't send you her love because she doesn't know I'm writing to you and because she's still looking for the check book. She was pleased to see that you were billed above Paul Horgan[11] in the Book Review section but there's less here than meets the eye because she's got Paul Horgan mixed up with Carl Foreman. My love to Harriet. And my sincere congratulations to you both.

John

"I've been able to work here," John wrote Josie Herbst (July 17), "and the only things I miss in the city are ugliness, noise, and an intermittent sense of disaster. I miss these intensely. Our neighbors are all kind and gentle people; and what we miss in them is a strain of contention, obscenity, and grief. What I'd like is a good quarrel."

10. "It was above and beyond the call of friendship for John to have made the trip to the courthouse for the two days I was on the stand," Don says, "but, of course, Katrina didn't bring the children to the trial." Don won the suit, but the judge ruled for limited damages.

11. Lieutenant Horgan had served at Fort Capra.

Scarborough,
New York
[postmarked 16 June 1951]

Dear John,

Your letter in it's cheerful red-white-and-blue envelope
was the first letter that we received at this address. It was here
the day after we moved and it sure made us feel at home. I think
of you both often but I think mostly of Harriet and I wonder
what she and Consumers Union would make out of this move.
I'll try to describe our circumstances truthfully since, as you
know, I have always wanted to hold our correspondence to a
homely level of exchanged recipes and market-tips. We are
living in what was built as a small factory in 1919 by Frank A.
Vanderlip. It is on a corner of his estate—an obscure corner,
happily—because after the armistice it fell into disuse and became an eyesore. In 1939 when his daughter Virginia married it
was turned into a honeymoon cottage. A bedroom and kitchen
were added to it in 1941 when his daughter Narcissa was unable
to find servants to staff her large house in Tarrytown. Two more
bedrooms were added to it in 1943 when his daughter Carlotta's
marriage went blooey and the house, or factory, and an acre of
land was deeded to Carlotta as a sort of booby prize. All these
alterations were made under the supervision of a gardener
named Angelo Palombo whose home is in Perugia and who has
made the facade of the house a duplicate of the church there.
We rent it from Carlotta at one hundred and fifty bucks a
month, not including heat, light, water, repairs and baksheesh.
Because the living room once housed two drop-forges it is big
and the first thing Mary did was to go to a 59th Street auction
gallery and bid in three hundred dollars for a Weber concert
grand piano which has the legs of a Steinway and which is full
of cigaret butts and moths. "It is just what that corner *needed*,"
Mary keeps saying. In the opposite corner we have a maid
named Milgrig, believe it or not, who comes at fifty bucks a
week. She sleeps in, and what is more important eats in. The
house is named Beechtwig (the big house is Beechwood) and it

is behind the manorial garages and right beside the manorial garbage pail but from the front door we have a nice view of one of the manorial lawns and the manorial swimming pool. This swimming pool is so big that it has a ground swell and makes waves in a northeast wind. However when the wind does come from the northeast Angelo Palombo puts a cylindrical stove into it called an Acme Swimming Pool Heater and overnight it gets just as cozy as Carl Foreman's pool. The swimming pool is all made out of Carrara marble and the Prince of Wales once swam in it. Milgrig can't mix a martini. The house is unfurnished and has two baths. What about it, Harriet?

We haven't been here long enough to find out much about the neighborhood but I do know that Westchester county is one hell of a place to try and kite checks. The only people who have been out from New York were Ellis Marcus[12] and his wife and their lovely children. I've sent directions to the D'Usseaus and the Fields, etc. but I expect they've been tied up in the price war. It's on the junction of route #9 and Scarborough Station Road (right across the road from the Presbyterian Church) and if you come east next fall or the year after that I'll buy you round trip tickets from 125th Street.

Love,

John

Scarborough,
December 20th [1951]

Dear John,

I haven't written because I thought you and Harriet came East for the World Series and didn't call us and my feelings were so deeply hurt that I didn't write anybody or anything for almost a month. Then Lennie called and said that you hadn't come in for the ball games but the Foreman-Kramer row[13] had started by

12. An Astoria alumnus.

13. Carl Foreman and Stanley Kramer parted company after Carl was subpoenaed by the House Committee on Un-American Activities in the late

then and I didn't want to take any chances writing to somebody who might end up in a lie detector machine. Also the Fields had told me some very dubious stories about your new Way of Life. They said you had developed a penchant for being tickled in the back of the knee, that you drank champagne in the middle of the day and that at one party you slipped on a plate of salmon and went through a plate-glass window. That's what they said.

Our pleasures here are simple and wholesome. When it snows the children pour maple-syrup into it and eat it with a spoon. It doesn't add up to a balanced diet, but it's better than some Guggenheim Fellows are doing for their young.[14] Milgrig, the maid, has long since departed, and while the telephone rang fitfully for a while after we had settled here, it seems to have succumbed to the mysterious silence of the deep woods. I am taking piano lessons so that some use will be made of the beautiful parlor grand. I can play a piece called Au Pays des Orangers. Mary is a leading soprano in the church choir.[15] Susie has a little newspaper route.

Merry Christmas!

John

---

summer of 1951. He was offered absolution (and the freedom to continue working) if he would name men and women who had already been named a dozen times. "You would do them no harm," he was told. "But," he pointed out, "I would destroy myself." He completed *High Noon* and went into self-imposed exile in England.

14. "I sometimes feel guilty about taking a Guggenheim from people whose needs are greater than mine," John wrote Josie Herbst, "but I'm determined to finish this bloody book and I don't care where the cash comes from. It is a difficult task, God knows and I think it becomes more difficult every day, but I think that the difficulties only increase our responsibilities and if we don't illuminate the crises we are living through, whoever will. We mean to be prophets and why should we settle for anything else?"

15. "Mary sings soprano in the church choir and I'm a trustee of the local private school," John wrote Malcolm Cowley (March 24); "but all of this is front and the only two stories that I've written about the neighborhood involved a voyeur and a homocidal piano teacher. I hope to cheer up."

[postmarked 5 February 1952]

Dear John,

We worried about you during the flood but as I recall you live on a knoll or rise of ground and I hope you are all right. I bought a copy of LIFE magazine with the flood pictures in it but I didn't recognize anybody I knew. Your agent wrote me a kind letter but he didn't say anything about the flood so I guess everything is all right.

The big news here is that Teddy Mills has come home to the Ivy-League country; back to the east where all the good secondary schools and colleges and all the first-class people live. He gave a big party to celebrate his severance from the congestion, vulgarity and smog of Illinois and Mary and I got invited to it. We expected, of course, to be disinvited, but nothing of the sort happened and when the time came we put on our best clothes and drove down to Riverdale where he has rented a big house. Teddy looked fine and I was glad to see him and Joan looked fine and I was even gladder to see her. Shep Traube was there and he didn't seem glad to see anybody and sat in a corner eating peanuts. He's gotten to be quite a dirty feeder. Teddy took Mary aside and told her that television was the Coming Medium. He said that drama and fiction and poetry and all that was so much shit. He said that he had written a letter to Tennessee Williams, Thomas Mann, Robert Sherwood, T. S. Eliot and Herman Wouk urging them to climb out of the shitpile and get aboard television while Teddy could promise them a good front seat. Mary got black in the face and asked me to take her home and I did take her home but she's since showed signs of improvement and I hope to have the Mills here for dinner soon. I will write.

Otherwise life is humdrum. We've had some wonderful ice-skating and I can play Invitation To The Waltz on the piano. I play the top part and my teacher plays the bottom part.

As ever,

John

Scarborough,
April 24th [1952]

Dear John,

I haven't written you since Jimmy's death[16] because it seemed at first that it would be a harder blow for you and Harriet than it was for us and because I didn't have a damned thing to say. We spent an evening with the D'Usseaus and we didn't mention Jimmy; and that's about the way it is. I still don't have a damned thing to say . . .

I think that I've had a good winter so far as work went and the spring here is slow and pleasant. The Hudson is at the foot of our street and they've put up shad nets opposite the post office—humble details that promise to separate this town from the bulk of white-gloved Westchester, but the promise is usually broken. It's a rich, dull, tree-shaded community and even in this baronial demesne you can feel the atmosphere of privacy diminishing, day by day. In making—or trying to make—our plans for the summer I've thought of writing Henry Lewis[17] but I haven't written him because I'm damned if I think he can get me a job. I keep feeling that His Optimism is His Business and that once my name was mentioned at the studios you would be able to hear a pin drop. I don't know.

What are your plans for coming East? We haven't seen Ruth or Lennie since the leaves turned yellow in the autumn. When Ellis and Dorothy Marcus moved out to the coast we went into town to say goodbye to them at a party where there were a lot of Signal Corps faces. A big, fat, drunken lady came up to me and said: "Jesus Christ. Here's the Aspiring Writer again." We went home then because Mary had to sing in the choir the next day. She sends her love.

John

16. Jimmy Gow's troublesome heart gave out on February 11, 1952. He died in his sleep at forty-four.

17. My Hollywood agent.

Scarborough,
May 13th [1952]

Dear John,

. . . My plans for writing to Henry Lewis are still vague, I guess. I've just finished a long story and if I can sell it, it will keep the family in food and sneakers for the summer months and allow me to refresh the illusion that I can finish a novel. I'll send them off to New Hampshire and remain here. We would both like to see you very much and if you won't come east I guess we'll have to go out to California sooner or later.

I've had lunch at Canarie D'Or a few times recently. The menu is the same and Robert asks for you and M. Ettlinger and speaks of "the good old times." At least *his* memories of the Signal Corps are sunny . . .

John

Some of us, John and myself included, measured the success of a regimental evening by the number of times Ruth Field stood on her head.

Scarborough
July 7th [1952]

Dear John,

Well first the Fields came out here for dinner and Ruth stood on her head twice. They said they were going to Fire Island for the summer and Mary said we would like to visit them. There was a lot of hemming and hawing and downright discomfort and they said all right and we set a date. Next Saturday morning Mary washed and ironed my white Irish linen pants and off we started. I had never been to Fire Island but I had read in Gibbs[18] that you take a ferry to get there so we went to a place called Bay View where it said on the road maps that you get the ferry. At Bay View there were six ferries for Fire Island, all going in different directions. We didn't know which one to

18. Wolcott Gibbs had written about Fire Island for *The New Yorker*.

take so we went into a bar and had a drink and missed all six boats. Three hours later when the boats had returned we flipped a coin and decided to take one to Ocean Beach. It sounded to me like the kind of place where the Fields might be. It was a long trip and when we got to Ocean Beach there weren't any Fields. I told Mary not to worry and that I would straighten everything out. I went to the Post Office, but that was closed. Then I went to the Western Union office, but that was closed. Then I found a public telephone and I called Sardi's because I thought maybe they would know Lennie's address but all I could get was an old waiter who kept saying: "Hesa ona Fire Island." Mary was sitting on a suitcase in front of the drugstore. Then I found a policeman and told him I was lost. "Look," he said, "I can't worry about you. A little three-year-old girl has been lost all afternoon. I have to find her first." Mary began to cry. It was getting dark. I went to a rooming house to see if we could get a place to sleep but all the rooms were taken. Then I went to a boat-livery to see if I could hire a boat to take us back to the mainland, but the livery was closed. By this time Mary had dried her tears, crossed her legs and was making eyes at strangers. I dragged her into a bar and bought her a Rum Zowie which seems to be the vin de pays. They let you take home the mug. I asked the bartender if he had ever heard of Lennie Field. "Sure," he said, "I know him well. He lives in a white house with red trim right at the corner of Neptune Avenue and Sea-weed Lane." Off we went and we found Neptune Avenue but there wasn't any house with red trim and Mary was just about to go off with a fat man who had a bicycle when the door of a brown house without any trim opened and out came Lennie. We followed him in to where a lot of people were drinking cocktails and where everyone said to me: "I've heard a lot about you John!" To Mary they all said: "You must be Harriet!"

It was like this for the rest of the visit which ended suddenly when Lennie had to go to Minneapolis. I tried to tell your story about the tomato factory and the best of your Star material but none of it went over although everybody said they liked Harriet.

As ever,
John

Scarborough,
December 17th [1952]

Dear John,

A man named Ezra Stone[19] called up a couple of months ago and asked if I wanted to try and work for television again. I said sure, sure, because poor little Benjy is dressed in rags. Well this man gave me an idea for a television script over the telephone and I worked it out. I worked Saturdays and Sundays just like Don Ettlinger. Well then when I finished this script I took it into New York and Ezra Stone said: "Hullo, Hullo! Enzio Pinza[20] wants to be remembered to you and how is Harriet?" Then he told me to go home and that he would telephone me, but he never did.

Mary sends her love.
Best,
John

My younger brother, Bill, was working as an associate editor at Collier's. *He later defected to Italy. He comes home periodically to share his awesome knowledge of opera with the Metropolitan's radio audience and to sign contracts for English translations, which have included works by, among others, Alberto Moravia, Elsa Morante, Italo Calvino, and Umberto Eco.*

19. The radio voice of Henry Aldrich. He was developing a television series, *"Life with Father and Mother."*
20. I had written a dramatic sketch for an Ezio Pinza television show Ted Mills produced for NBC in Los Angeles.

Dear John,

A couple of days ago I went in for lunch to a restaurant called Le Mirliton. There were plenty of empty tables down-stairs, but the head-waiter made me go upstairs and who should I see there but William F. Weaver! He commenced to manipu-late his napkin wildly but I recognized him—even when he pulled his napkin down over his head—and I went right over and shook his hand. He seemed to have been drinking cock-tails—at least there was an empty glass by his plate and he was eating the filet of sole de bonne femme. That's $2.75 with the pate maison or potage du jour. It's no Owl Drugstore. I hoped to have a long chat with him, but when I next looked, he had gone.

We don't get into town much and this glimpse of the literary world is the only face-to-face experience I've had for some time, but I'm not altogether out of touch. I have a collec-tion of short stories[21] coming out next month and I've been

21. *The Enormous Radio and Other Stories* was not well received, as John noted in a letter to Josie Herbst: "Something happened here a few days ago that might interest you. Do you remember giving Ben a small bronze boar from Florence—Browning. Well Ben got very fond of Browning. He went one afternoon to play with another little boy—the son of a banker—and took with him his water-pistol and Browning. When he came home he was tired. He remembered in the middle of supper that he had forgotten his water pistol and began to cry. Mary said that she would go back and get it. When she returned to the bankers she was invited in for a cocktail and told that the water pistol could not be found. 'Well,' she said, picking Browning up from the coffee table, 'perhaps this will console him.' 'That,' said the banker, snatching Browning out of Mary's hand, 'is mine.' 'Really,' Mary said, 'where did you get him?' 'I'm not sure,' the banker said, his face getting redder and redder with acquisitiveness and guilt, 'but I think that it was given to me by my mother.' Goodbye Browning.

"I wasn't able to figure out from your letter whether my collection of stories pleased or annoyed you, but I seem to have been over-sensitive on this

sending the galleys around to old, tender-hearted, soft-brained friends. No manuscript has ever had such a curious reception. Everybody who reads the book takes sick. "I would probably have enjoyed the stories more," one writes, "if I had not had all my teeth removed on Thursday." "I was disappointed in the stories," another writes, "but perhaps you can account for this by the fact that I just came down with arthritis." "Loefflers Syndrome is what the doctors call my condition," a third writes, "and this has made it impossible for me to enjoy your stories." God, it's depressing. I'd send you a copy if I felt sure you were immune to chicken-pox and whooping-cough. To get a kind word for the jacket I may have to fall back on old Spigelgass: THE MOST SENSITIVE, etc.

Mary is fine. The idea that I stink has always been at the back of her mind. She turned into an Extrovert the day we settled in Westchester and she takes me out to a lot of dinners, parties, word-games, and dances. She says its good for me. I wish to hell you'd both come east for a day or two.

    Love,

      John

---

score for six weeks; but the reviews did open up for me the immensity of the territory that has been conquered by optimism in the last ten years. With my forces regrouped this seems to be an appalling conquest and while it does not surprise me to find that the banker who stole Browning finds the stories morbid, it does surprise me to find the self-designated intellectuals urging one to cheerup, cheerup and take the world for what it appears to be. It has never appeared so fair as it does here—never were the trains so splendid, never were the parties so well-staffed, never were there so many smiling faces—and yet it seems to be a tragic community. Now and then the minister pays me a call and we speak softly of pessimism and mortality as if they—like the black boots the minister wears and the stale smell of his clericals—were all things of the past. Oh I know how poorly I do—it seems sometimes that my own dismay pervades the stories—and it would not matter, it would help, if one were enjoined to do better, but it does not lead anywhere to be told to smile."

*Henry Lewis had just sold M-G-M an original story written by
Lennie Field's older brother, Danny, who lived in Beverly Hills.*

Scarborough,
Friday
[postmarked 27 March 1953]

Dear John,

Could you send me Henry Lewis's address, if that is the
name of the agent who has been working for you and Danny
Field. I thought I'd send him a copy of the book.

I haven't written sooner because I've been so busy giving
readings of your letter. The Ettlingers came over and heard it,
although Don kept trying to get it out of my hands. They were
fairly troublesome guests. They got a flat tire in Peekskill on the
way here and had to take a taxi which set me back ten bucks. Then
when they decided to go home at three in the morning I had to
drive them to Peekskill and loan them another ten. I haven't heard
from them since and I'm getting damned sick and tired of eating
lentils. I was hooked to give a reading at a large gathering at the
Fields but I got influenza. I showed it around at the Hellmans one
night and afterwards a young lady asked me if you were the father
of William Fense Weaver. She said that she worked at Colliers and
that she loved W. F. W. "He's the up-beat member of our staff,"
she said, snapping her fingers. "He's our ray of sunshine. If he goes
back to Italy I don't know what we'll do." I told her that you were
a ray of sunshine in Astoria for years and it's a lot harder to shine
there than on Upper Fifth Avenue.

Mary sends her love,
John

Scarborough,
May 5th [1953]

Dear John,

My finger is in an ashtray.[22] My Mother wrote to say that
if she'd known I was going to be photographed with an ashtray

22. In the photograph on the dust jacket of *The Enormous Radio.*

she would have sent me a lovelier-looking ashtray. She thought that was a common-looking ashtray. The photograph was very successful and I've received two proposals of marriage from ladies in Virginia. The book hasn't done very well. I sent the Ettlingers a copy but they didn't even thank me. We nearly caught up with them one night on 45th Street after seeing a play called Picnic but we lost them in the lobby of the Paramount Building.[23] Picnic is not a very good play and it has a drinking scene in it which is not as good as the drinking scene in your play.

Mary threw away your letter with Henry Lewis's address in it and would you address the enclosed letter to him. It seems to be the only way I can outwit Mary. She sends her love and we're both looking forward to the day when we see you in the east. We went down to Clark County a couple of weeks ago to drink some of that lime-water and walk in the boxwood alleys at dusk, but every man, woman and child in the valley has gone to England to get a front seat for the coronation. We spent the night in a Motel and came home.

> Love,
> John

> Tree Tops,
> Bristol,
> New Hampshire
> Tuesday
> [postmarked 28 July 1953]

Dear John:

. . . I was very glad to hear about the Fields' visit because we glimpsed them before they left and while we didn't see Ruth's pants or anything like that they sure looked lively. I remembered how on their last visit you slipped on the sturgeon

23. "John and Mary didn't 'nearly catch up' with us at Picnic," Don says. "The four of us went together."

and broke somebody's picture window and naturally I was anxious. Did you drink champagne in the morning like you did last time? Did you go swimming without bathing suits? I've written Don to see if he got a fuller account and I'll go down to New York soon and cross-question the Fields. I feel sort of out of things up here.

We settled down here two or three weeks ago—I can't remember how long it's been. I was only going to stay a day or two because both Boris Kaplan and Ira Steiner[24] wanted me to write television shows for them but they haven't written or called so I'm just waiting. I've bought a Hohner Marine Band harmonica and I'm learning how to play the Skater's Waltz. Susie is at a camp about fifty miles north of here. She was in a play on Saturday and we went up to see her but all the big parts went to girls with speech difficulties and Susie only had a few lines. She can ride horseback (forty dollars extra) swim a quarter of a mile free style, undress under water, clean a toilet and make a nice balsalm pillow. I seem to miss her.

Mary is studying the Pelagian heresy and Ben is collecting frogs. They both send their love.

John

Harriett and I had passed through New York when we decided to blow the proceeds of an unexpected movie sale on our first trans-Atlantic crossing. We were met in London by Carl Foreman, who had joined a colony of blacklisted writers, actors, and directors in self-imposed exile, and for the next ten months we drove across the British Isles, Europe, and North Africa.

Scarborough,
October 28th [1953]

Dear John,

The important thing of course was to see you both and to see you both looking so well. I don't know how, in the crude

24. A talent agent, who helped found Ashley-Steiner Famous Artists, forerunner of International Creative Management.

cultural atmosphere and the industrial overcast of Southern California, you manage to preserve so much; but there it was. I was very sorry that you didn't get over here to see our house and I hope you don't think that we live in someplace like Scarsdale. It was also a shame that you didn't get to hear me play the Moonlight Sonata on the piano and I had hoped that you would ask me to autograph the copy of The Enormous Radio that I sent you. I had worked out a nice limerick with Roman references that begins: There was a young lady named Harriet/Who liked to get fucked in a charriot.

As soon as you left I set into motion my plans to dog you through Europe. I wrote a story for Colliers—that would pay the passage—and asked the New Yorker for a year's drawing account. Colliers was civil enough when they sent the story back—they were plaintive—but as for the New Yorker, I've never seen so many people claim to be stricken with acute indigestion. I was taken to lunch (Vol-au-vent $1.75—coffee—no dessert—) and put on the return train to Scarborough. However when you're in Florence I wish you'd look at real estate. I still think that I'm going to eat my Thanksgiving dinner on a ship that's heading for Genoa. Mary puts no stock in these plans. She's just bought a large, expensive dog and accepted the chairwomanship of the committee in charge of decorations for the New Year's Eve dance. It's going to be a Bal Masque. The decor is heaven. If I have to go I'm going to go as the late Warren G. Harding who was recently elevated—along with George Mortimer Pullman. Sometimes you must feel out of touch over there.

Arnaud's play[25] got five good reviews—two raves—and should be doing good business. I had lunch with Lennie yesterday who seemed in good health until a night club singer named Janice Page came and sat at the table next to us. Then he got all

25. Arnaud d'Usseau had collaborated with Dorothy Parker on *Ladies of the Corridor*.

white around the mouth, big dark bags formed under his eyes, and he didn't quit squirming for a long time. He seemed pleased with his job, apprehensive about his cross-country trip and I should say, unaccustomed to night work.[26]

Mary sends her love and could you find out for me what Botteghe Oscura is paying these days and any other market tips.

John

Scarborough,
November 20th [1953]

Dear John,

It was very good to get your letter from Rome here and what with one thing and another I realize how difficult it must be to get a letter off under the circumstances. I would not like to see you bent over a writing desk when you could be strolling up and down the Spanish stairs. There has never been a more punctilious correspondent than you and I think of you as The Last of the Letter-Writers—the darling of the Cranes. Letter-writing has always seemed to me to be a fine, if idle, art and I hate to see the twilight overtake it. Most of the people I write to these days make copies of what they send me and file what they receive. This takes all the fun out of it. It's like pressing blood-wort in the family Bible. A good letter should be like a daisy in the field, charming for the minute, not much to smell, soon dead.

I don't know what the newspaper situation is in Rome or what coverage you had on the Truman–Harry Dexter White fracas.[27] On the evening when Truman spoke most of us letter-

26. Lennie was general manager of a *Porgy and Bess* company.

27. On the night of Monday, November 16, Truman took to the airwaves to denounce Attorney General Herbert Brownell's accusation that, as president, he had knowingly moved an alleged Soviet spy in the State Department to an even "more sensitive" position with the International Monetary Fund. Harry Dexter White had been dead five years at the time of this attack, which a *New York Times* reporter described as "squalid" when he asked President Eisenhower about it at a press conference. Eisenhower

writers listened to him. We expected candor and got an expedient speech. When Brownell spoke he snarled; when he lacked evidence he screamed. I went to a cocktail party that afternoon—mostly of letter-writing types, all of whom were posing as the German intelligentsia in 1933. I have never seen so many crocodile tears or heard voices so hushed with despair. But I cannot go along with them. They irritate me. It seems that I have served my time in domesday. I went to the party alone, hoping to pick up a pretty woman with lace drawers. I was not successful, but I am not discouraged.

The autumn was lovely here and I kept asking my much-traveled wife if it was ever so brilliant in France, Tuscany, Rome. She kept assuring me that nothing in the world was so brilliant. In this way I master my envy and think how sad it is that John and Harriet Weaver were not here for the North American autumn; the Indian summer. My plans to travel seem burned out. I thought I saw a boat ticket a week or so ago when I was walking along a bridle path on the Rockefeller demesne. An elderly, well-dressed woman was dumped at my feet by a fractious horse. I got the horse by the bridle and saved the lady from getting her skull cracked. Then I tethered the horse and tended the lady until other help came. She thanked me without asking my name.

The plans for the New Year's Eve party are raging. I can't go as Warren Harding, it seems. All the hosts have to wear a uniform, a pink Brooks shirt, white shorts, wings and silver stuff in your hair. No shit. Maybe it's New Year's Eve that I'll spend on the Roma, heading this time for Naples.

Keep me posted on Botega Oscura. Tell Harriet that I will continue to polish the limerick.

As ever,

John

---

ducked the question, but in the fall of 1990, when the incident was revived by the publication of a book on the KGB, Anthony Lewis described it as "one of the low points of the McCarthy era" and agreed with his 1953 colleague: "Tony Leviero had the right adjective: 'squalid.' "

Scarborough,
December first [1953]

Dear John,

I liked your description of the Appian Way and the plain very much but why would you compare—unfavorably—an American institution like the barbershop with something in Rome, beats me. For 450 lire I can open a door on Spring Street in Ossining (a bell rings) and step into a place that smells like a Sunday morning cat-house. The barber greets me loudly. He is a kind of unofficial mayor and everybody who walks by his window (with its card announcing a free lecture on Christian Science) waves to him. "Watch the Fords go by," he shouts. He has a Ford himself. "Thirty-one thousand miles and I haven't spent a penny on her," he says. "I'm going to buy her a new radio for Christmas." Now and then his wife, a pallid old woman who seems to have lost her place to the Ford, parts a soiled cretonne curtain at the rear, behind which she lives, and enters the store long enough to sweep up the curls. Vesuvian clouds of smoke arise from a standard ashtray in the corner, ornamented with a pressed-steel woman doing a scarf dance. The few chairs are sprung and the copies of Life, Look and Marriage Comics have all seen better days. Flies breed and nest among the brushes and combs in a contraption called "The Sterilizer." The calendars on the wall would put lead into any pencil. Here I sit, in an upholstered chair, surrounded by the smell of spit, violets and old hair, discussing the insides of automobiles and women while a twenty-five piece combo plays the new arrangement of Adios Muchachos and the barber keeps shouting "Watch the Fords go by!" I only hope you won't let your hair grow too long or get into the habit of greasing it . . .

Mary says if I don't stop writing you and start writing short stories she's going to make me apply for a job with the department of sanitation. She says I shouldn't think about going to Europe; I should think about keeping out of small claims court.

As ever

John

On February 2, 1954, after picking our way across a bumpy North African desert track we shared with a scattering of camels and their Berber owners, Harriett and I awakened to find ourselves snowbound in Bou Saada, an Algerian winter resort. Two days later, on my forty-second birthday, the road was cleared and we took off for Algiers. "Drove through drifts & new snow," I wrote in the journal I'd begun a month earlier in Sicily, "but I had a bad chest cold just starting. Last 40 miles or so, no snow."

When we checked into a small French colonial hotel, I protested its exorbitant nightly rate. "Chauffage is extra," the desk clerk explained. Too sick to pursue the matter, I signed the register and gave him our passports. I had specified "room and bath" and that, we discovered, was precisely what we had been given, a room and a tub. Harriett put me to bed and kept her winter coat on, waiting for the first indications of "chauffage." Finally, she checked the radiator and found it was not connected to anything. She picked it up and put it out in the hall. "Why?" the front desk called to ask and Harriett explained, "I thought it might absorb some warmth out there." Then she took my temperature (101 degrees) and called room service to order hot soup. "No kitchen," she was told.

She disappeared for about an hour and came back with a bowl of onion soup and a birthday present, the first Paris-Herald I'd seen since leaving Tunis. She poured a dollop of Bourbon for each of us and while I read the paper, she slipped into pajamas and a white terry cloth robe, fumbled through her overnight bag for a roll of toilet paper, and left.

"We are surrounded by U.S. air force officers (heavily bemedalled)," I recorded next morning. "H asked what she thought was one of them if his room was warm. He said, 'Mais oui,' and H said, 'Oh, I thought you were an American,' whereupon he enveloped her in his arms & led her into the room & when she protested, he said, 'But I'm French.'"

Scarborough,
Early in April
[1954]

Dear John,

Your letter about the radiator, etc. was so wonderful that
it put me into a broody frame of mind. We have very little news
and nothing involving snow storms, deserts and clandestine
love. The poignant North American spring is a bust. No lilacs,
no gentle rains, no sense of awakening. It is cold here, dry,
overcast and depressing. We have had dinner with Ted Mills,
but what kind of news is that? He bought a 45 room manor
house near here with a conservatory, elevator, a tower and a
winding drive, illuminated with milky glass globes. The Dick
Simons were there, a couple named Buxton and a photographer
with big wet, blue eyes who is planning to make movies on a
shoe-string. I expect Teddy is in on this. We had cocktails in the
library which is right off the conservatory and then walked
about half a mile to the dinning room where we had sea-food
au gratin and store ice cream. Joan said how thankless it was to
ask "creative people" to your house. Dick Simon agreed with
her but said there were exceptions. "Tolstoy," he said, leering
at me. "Tolstoy and I would have a great deal to talk about."
Teddy was telling Mary how much he liked you and Harriet and
how sorry he was about the misunderstanding. Neither of us
knows about the misunderstanding so there wasn't much point
to this. It had something to do with Pinza. He said your script
for Pinza had made television history; and so why any misunderstanding?[28] Much later in the evening Teddy took us for a tour
of the house. He insisted on showing us the servants' (2) rooms,
although the servants were in bed. "They don't mind," he said.

The day after that we went to the Ettlingers for lunch.

28. The "misunderstanding" was my fault. It sprang from Ted's failure
to invite me to the party he threw for Pinza and the cast after the NBC show
was aired. Never having worked as a television writer, I was not accustomed
to being treated as one.

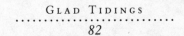

They seemed fine—particularly Katrina. We drank a good deal and were still at the table when night fell. There was some sodden plan for us to spend the night but I trussed Mary up in her coat and got her away. Mary, in your absence, has turned into quite a comical character through her zeal for the League of Women Voters.[29] She gets up early in the morning, investigates county institutions, speaks on the reform of the primary system and nails signs onto trees, telling the ladies how to reach the meeting place. They meet four or five times a week and they are meeting at our house today. I am hiding in a neighbor's attic. And as I sit here, among the old trunks and dress forms and think of you in sunny Spain I can't help but be struck by the divergence of our paths. Give my love to Harriet.

> As ever,
> John

> Scarborough,
> Friday
> [postmarked 3 September 1954]

Dear John,

It was very good to hear from you. I hadn't known where you were. Henry Lewis called and said you were coming home. "I'm at the Hotel Pee-Lahza," he said. I waited. Finally I wrote Lennie who came up from Boston to tell me Ruth had broken her foot and that you were back in California. Lennie looked fine although I'm not very perceptive about people I've known that long. If he'd worn a red wig, arrived in a wheelchair or been

---

29. The middle-aged writer poking fun at his wife's civic activities housed a frightened schoolboy lashing out at a painful memory: "When I was eleven," John recalled in a letter to Tanya Litvinov, "I was attacked by a virulent strain of tuberculosis. A few days after the crisis my mother covered me with a blanket, gave me a pile of clean rags in which I might bleed and went off to chairman some committee for the General Welfare. As a healthy man I expect I should be grateful to be alive and to have had so conscientious a parent, but what I would like to forget is the empty house and the fear of death."

let down through a hole in the ceiling I wouldn't be the man to observe it . . . I don't see how you can expect people to listen to your travel adventures if you're going to sneak through the east like a regular weasel. We would have been very happy to hear about your travels and personally I'd also like to hear your cousin tell about how all the dishes in the Caronia got broken. I expect you'd like to hear about our travels. We went to Tree tops and then to Wellfleet and then came home and now in the evenings I voyage around in my Morris chair, smoking Harvard pipe mixture and reading Eca de Queiroz. Paul Engle called from the University of Iowa on Wednesday and asked if I wouldn't like to teach there this year. I said that I would and then he hung up. The telephone hasn't rung since. Mary thinks he was looking for Jean Stafford and that the magazine gave him the wrong number.[30]

Mary and the children are fine. Susie has a permanent wave. Sixteen dollars. Westchester is just about the same. One of our richest and most prominent neighbors blew in last night with a tomato that happened to be shaped like a prick. Oh, Ho, Ho, Ho. I'm not irritable but I do get bored. My love to Harriet.

As ever,
John

Scarborough,
Wednesday
[postmarked 15 September 1954]

Dear John,
I enjoyed your story in Harper's very much and it was good to see you back in this modest eastern country.

30. John told Bill Maxwell he expected "to get a letter on Monday saying that Winifred Grapeshot, whose wealth of teaching experience and whose many publications on the theory of beauty give her precedence, has bagged the job."

The job in Iowa blew up in my face. I think they were looking for Roald Dahl.

Best,

John

The story was "The Day the Pig Fell in the Well."

[postmarked 1 November 1954]

Dear John,

It was very good to hear from you and I'm glad you liked the story. The mail wasn't very encouraging and all of the cheap-seats wrote in to say that the material was all mixed up and that they didn't know which summer was which. And one of the editors of the magazine came up to me at a party and said angrily that the story was a line over and held up production for a whole day. This was one of the lesser editors. William Shawn, the number 1 editor came out last week to have lunch with the Kahns. Jack telephoned and ordered me to hurry over and say hello to the Boss. I put on my best pants and went over and when the conversation flagged Jack suggested that we play some touch football. Shawn was on my team and on the third play I threw a wobbly pass in his direction. He tried to catch it, slipped and went down, crashing and tinkling like a tray of dishes. I don't know whether he's out of the hospital yet or not and I haven't dared telephone to find out.

The Brickens called and said they were having a reunion at Mrs. Erlanger's tomorrow.[31] I may go, and if I do I'll make a report. I see Buster Mills on the train now and then, but my connection with the television world is slender since we don't have a set. Both of the children consider their lives to be utterly blighted by bohemianism. I saw Kay Jackson[32] who spoke of you

31. Jules and Patsy Bricken were friends from the Astoria years. Mrs. Alene (Kick) Erlanger was Patsy's mother.

32. Katherine Gauss Jackson was an editor at *Harper's* magazine.

and met a woman at a party who had met Bill in Florence. "I'm worried about him," she said. She didn't say why. Mary is still very active in The League of Women Voters and I still have to get up early in the morning and nail signs onto trees saying: "LWV This Way." This is hard on me because I drink so much. I would like to write a book or take a trip or build a house; but I don't.

But all is well here. Mary blooms and the children too and while I rail against the suburbs I don't think I would have been as happy any place else. We do, as always, wish you would come east, but if you won't stir we may drive to California next summer. Mary sends her best; and thanks again for mentioning the story.

As ever,
John

[postmarked 5 November 1954]

Dear John,

I got already to go to the Bricken's party last night but it was raining very hard and Mary pointed out that there was a grease-spot on my suit so I drank some martinis here and listened to the election returns. I feel guilty about missing what must have been a reunion at the regimental level and God knows what galaxies of stars and soldiers I missed. I guess that Herbie played and Gipsy Rose Lee danced, etc. but I wasn't there. The Times is still in suspense this morning about the election returns but this neighborhood—there are seven registered Democrats—is very quiet.[33]

My good friends George and Helene Biddle are coming out to the Huntington Hartford retreat or sanctuary for the winter and I told them to call you. I don't know where the place

33. Westchester County Republicans retained their seats in the state legislature and the House of Representatives, but the final tally installed a Democrat, Averell Harriman, in the governor's mansion.

is but George seems to think that it's close to Los Angeles and he plans to run in and out. He's coming out with the Van Wyck Brookses. I only mention this in case you have some homework to catch up on.

I'm sorry about the Bricken's party.

As ever,

John

Scarborough, N.Y.

Sunday

[postmarked 15 May 1955]

Dear John,

Late yesterday afternoon a white car with a lilac-colored carapace turned in the driveway and out stepped James Pollak,[34] the author of The Golden Egg. "I've come to make you rich, chum," he said. I suggested nervously that we walk down to the swimming pool but he said that his shoes were killing him and so we sat down in the living room. Mary scuttled into the broom closet and shut the door. I asked my unexpected guest if he would like a drink but he made a gesture and said: "I've had *that*, chum," evoking weeks on Skid Row, AA meetings in Parish house basements and much manly travail. I poured myself some gin, feeling like a little child, and asked about you. "Oh you mean that kid who used to work in the library?" he said. He told me he had just flown in from California with Celeste Holme's dog, spoke of the brilliant future that awaited me in television and then told me several anecdotes about people I don't know. These were all told in the Present or Caesarian tense. "So while I'm standing there Janie picks up this diamond necklace and jumps into this . . ." Like that. Then he said he had to take Celeste Holme to the theatre and he drove away. Mary stayed in the broom closet until twilight . . .

We have no news of you from any quarter. Don told me

34. An Astoria alumnus.

the news about Lennie and Ruth and I wonder if you've seen him.[35] The Ettlingers have a Jaguar. Katrina puts her hair in a scarf and Don puts his in a beret and they race up and down the West or Wrong banks of the Hudson River, killing chickens.

As ever,

John

Scarborough, N.Y.
March 23rd [1956]

Dear John,

At dusky dark the phone rang and a voice—gruff, but cheerful exclaimed: "I'll bet that's old honest John." It was Teddy Mills, of course, and he wanted me to come in town and talk over a TV show with Louis de Rochmont.[36] I said that I seldom came to town except to give the class at Barnard.[37] Teddy said that if I would come down from Barnard he would buy me a drink and drive me home in his convertible. I agreed. It fell on a very rainy night and the bus I took at 117th Street was leaky. Teddy's office is on Broadway in the 40's—plushy but not, somehow, substantial. There was no trace or mention of Louis de Rochmont. Teddy, with his feet on his desk, chatted for awhile about Maggie and Carl—divorced. Then he gave me a prospectus to read. His prose is still pure Army-Navy Screen Magazine—high-flown and grating—and while I was reading this the telephone rang. "I'm tied up right now, Laddy," Teddy said, "but I'll meet you in about twenty minutes. Yes, Laddy, no, Laddy, etc." I began to snort or at least to breathe very heavily. "I'm afraid your drink and your ride are out of the question," Teddy said sadly. He still tips his head upsidedown and studies his fingernails. Well I won't go into the rest of the

35. The Fields had split up.

36. Motion picture director and producer (*The House on 92nd Street, Lost Boundaries.*).

37. On Monday and Wednesday afternoons John made his way to Columbia's sister college on 117th Street to instruct young women in story writing.

interview because it was acrimonious and bitter and I joggled home in a sprung-rump local that didn't get me back to Scarborough until after eight. I'll keep you posted if I hear from him again.

I told Mary that you didn't want to have supper with the children and I don't blame you for not coming out again, but I was very sorry not to see you. I had lunch with Lennie who said you were writing with Colliers again which is something I wish I could do.[38] I went up to Yaddo for a week and read a terrible story by Bill in a magazine which comes all to pieces when you shake it. It may just have been the magazine; but what kind of a thing is that? We miss you both very much and hope you'll come east again soon.

As ever,

John

Henry Lewis had just sold "The Housebreaker of Shady Hill" to M-G-M. His files indicate a payment of $25,000.

Scarborough,
Thursday,
[postmarked 3 May 1956]

Dear John,

It was very good, it was wonderful to get your wire this morning and it brought the first note of reality into the proceedings. Mary doesn't believe that the story's been bought for that much money and she keeps buying cheap meat-cuts such as tongue and shoulder-steak. But you *know* how things are in Hollywood, she says. Susie seems to believe me but she's not much interested except in who's going to be in the movie. The dog seems to believe me but she has eight puppies who live in

38. My story, "The New Chairs," appeared in the August 17 issue of *Collier's*. The new fiction editor then gave me a drawing account and put me to work on a serial. The day after I sent in the first installment I heard on the radio that the magazine had folded.

this little room where I am supposed to work and who are now old enough to unlace my shoes and bite me in the ankles. The reason I told the dog[39] about it was because when Henry Lewis called there was no one here but Ben and me and the dog. Mary and Susie had gone to see a movie called The Little Kidnappers. I don't believe that children Ben's age should be told about money and so that left me with the dog. After I had told the dog Ben wanted me to read him a chapter from Winnie the Phoo and so I read him the chapter called How Piglet Meets a Heffalump. Then I came downstairs and drank a pint of whisky. Then a neighbor called to tell me that my annual salary as secretary of the Fire Department—a very high post—would be $37.50.[40] I told him but he seemed suspicious and left at once. Of course I was drunk. Then Mary came home, received the news sniffily, and went upstairs to sleep. This made me cross so I drank more whisky and sat broodily on the sofa thinking how with this money I could have prostitutes of all kinds, dancing to my whip. Now that we have your wire we all feel better.

It couldn't have come at a nicer time. I think I can see the end of a book, I don't have a short story in my head and there's nothing in the bank. In this way I can finish the book and perhaps go abroad for a year. However Mary says she won't go

39. "Daddy spoke to all our dogs, and I suspect they all spoke back to him," Ben recalls, and in a letter to his Iowa protégé, Allan Gurganus (author of The Oldest Living Confederate Widow Tells All), John explained that "the Cheevers are spiritual canines. The day after Mother died I was sitting in the library with my old black Labrador. She had never lost a rabies tag in her life and had a long rope of tags hanging from her chain collar. It looked like a necklace Mother used to wear. I spoke to her. She raised her head very high and spoke to me. The message was quite clear. 'John,' she asked, 'can't you try to be a little neater?' Mother had made the switch in less than twenty-four hours. Shortly after that I dreamed that I was brought before a canine tribunal who would decide whether or not I could become a dog. They decided in my favor."

40. John had signed on as a volunteer firefighter with the Scarborough Fire Department ("a brotherhood of 29 manly, hard-drinking, courageous fellows").

abroad if she's pregnant which she may well be and as I say, she goes on buying shoulder-steaks.

Love,

John

[postmarked 7 May 1956]

Dear John,

Your letter helped a great deal and tonight we are having roast beef for dinner, although I think *she* plans to stretch it over three meals. I have bought an electric egg-beater, a quart of Jack Daniels and the children had frozen custard for dessert at lunch. It seems that we might go to Rome in the fall. There are a couple of villas attached to the Academy there and we might get one of these if I play my cards right which I never do. Do you know what they're like or what part of town they're in? The Warrens promise to be helpful[41] but the last time I had lunch with Eleanor I forgot to bring any money and we had to eat a sandwich on 56th Street. But the most important thing is for me to finish this book which is called The Wapshot Chronicle. I've laid so many eggs that I can't be sure I won't drop another.

On the cheerful side there was a back-porch fire in Briarcliff last night. It's the kind of fire that I like to help extinguish. I rode on the engine and nearly fell off. This is very dangerous. We have a house in Maine and a sailboat for July. We would love to see you there if you came east any earlier. I have asked Henry to have my money spread over three years which ought to keep me from doing anything unusually dumb. And I wish very much that I had been with you and not here, with the dog and I look forward to seeing you in the fall, if not sooner and my sincere thanks for making the whole thing somehow seem authentic. I can smell the roast beef.

Best,

John

41. Robert Penn Warren and his wife, Eleanor Clark, were living in Italy at this time.

Friendship, Maine
June 30th [1956]

Dear John,

About six weeks ago Henry Lewis sent a wire reading MGM THREATENS TO CANCEL ALL NEGOTIATIONS UNLESS, etc. Neither of us mentioned Town House, but it was all I could think of. Very gloomy. I haven't known what to think since then but there was a letter from Henry yesterday saying that he had mailed my check to Scarborough and if it isn't lost in the mail I guess we're all set. Mary's booked passage on a small boat to Rotterdam but I'd rather take a small boat to Naples and I think we'll settle in Rome. If Bill is there could you tell him? I need some kind of advice. The Warrens are in Grossetto and write me that the American Academy will help me to find an apartment but I want to know about clean barber shops, etc. I wish—hope—that you and Harriet are going to be there.

Before coming down here, which was a week ago, I finished a novel, at least I think I did. I gave it to a typing agency and haven't seen it since and I spend most of my time here going to the post office and looking for my manuscript or sitting in this spare bedroom writing myself congratulatory letters (The Greatest thing since War and Peace) or letters of discouragement (Cass Canfield[42] and I think you may have the beginnings of something here but we feel it would be best if you put this behind you and made a fresh start). I wish it would come. Friendship is a small lobster fishing village. I had expected lanterns swinging in the wind and singing in taverns but actually it's a good deal like Iowa or Nebraska by the sea. We'll be here until the first of August when Mary and the children go over to Tree Tops and when I think I'll go down to a New York hotel, drink martinis before lunch, buy boat tickets and go to Berlitz school. I haven't seen or heard from Lennie since early in the winter but I hope you're still planning to stay with him in September and I'll see

42. Chairman of Harper's executive committee and editorial board, 1955–62.

you then. We won't sail until October and it would be wonderful if we could all go over together.

As ever,

John

Friendship, Maine
August 2nd [1956]

Dear John,

You must be giving bottle parties or else your hootch bill would be big enough to send you and Harriet to Italia and what is a gynecologist doing at a party for Lennie or is he married again? I haven't seen him since fall although I tried to call him in New York last week. A telephone service kept telling me that he had gone for the evening and after dropping about ten dollars this way—I stay now only in fancy hotels where it costs about a dollar to make a local call—I got the voice to admit that he was out of town. It seems to me that you're frittering away your fortune[43] and your youth in entertainments.

Many thanks for Bill's address and I will write him. We will be ready for you in September—more than ready. I've had my bum reconstructed and am much livelier than I was last year. You mustn't worry about the children. When I fall down they just step over me. We leave here on Monday for N.H. and I then return to my pleasures and studies in New York.

Best,

John

43. The reference is ironical in view of a letter I had just written my agent: "As you know, I have no outside income. I depend entirely on my earnings from writing and, for the last three years, I have not been able to earn a living from the magazines. And when I think of doing a book I remember the year I spent on *Another Such Victory* and the $1,000 advance I received, and never another cent."

Via del Plebiscito 107
November 24th [1956]

Dear John,

I called Bill a few days ago and a lady answered briskly in Italian and said that Il Senore Bill would return subito. This was your mother who seems to have adapted herself as quickly to Rome as I expect she has adapted herself to other cities and circumstances. She and Bill came here for drinks and they both seemed very well and spry. We had already met at St. Peter's and at Bill's. So the Roman branch of your family is thriving and your Mother tells us that your news is good and we all wish you would join us.

Bill or your Mother will write you about this place.[44] I won't try. It makes for thin ice financially and we have a great furnace here on the third floor and a Fachino who carries coal upstairs on his head all day long and a porter who makes the fire three times a day and a maid who keeps giving us presents—she just gave Mary a compact that plays La vie en rose—and the porter's wife gives Ben toys and Italian comics and the maid in the pensione where we used to stay comes to visit us and brings things and I worry. I worry anyhow. We seem to be central and can reach the Forum in a few minutes and I buy my gin near the Pantheon and take my exercise on the steps of Santa Maria Arecoeli.

Mary sends her best. The children have been homesick, but they seem over this. My best to Harriet and to you.

John

44. The salon in the Cheevers' apartment in the Palazzo Doria struck Bill as "a splendid place for signing treaties." Mother thought it looked "just like the Library of Congress."

Dear John,

. . . There aren't any small rooms in this place—it isn't a place anyhow—it's a palace. I often think of Harriet and how she would disapprove of the arrangement and I often think she would be right. The two maids we have are not enough to get food to the table warm and the porter seems to be working for us full-time. He carries coal upstairs on his head. It is one of the warmest apartments in Rome but aeieeee, aeieeee, non economico. I go to school to learn Italian and to keep myself from saying things like: The Museum, she is called? Also: do not fall this machine while people wish to mirror with me. This about the telephone. Mary is much better but she's not anything like as good as she thinks she is. We've had french fried broccoli every night for the last week all because of some bug in her vocabulary.

Bill called this morning and seems to be fine. We'll see him on Sunday. At this point the city seems to be fifty percent excitement, forty percent excellence and ten percent downright dreary. The dreariness is war news,[45] smog in the morning, the dim lights in the palazzos, the bad gin and the flotsam at cocktail parties. We went to a reception for Red Warren last week and I haven't been so uncomfortable since they discontinued the old 59th Street cross-town trolley cars. God knows it's lovely when the sun shines, and we look forward to

45. England and France had taken up arms to block Egypt's move to nationalize the Suez Canal and Israeli soldiers had occupied the Sinai. "The city seems mercurial," John wrote Phil and Mimi Boyer (November 29), "and while it is lovely in the sun with the fountains sparkling it looks in the rain like that old movie-shot: European Capitol On Eve of War. Everyone carries a wet umbrella, there are anxious crowds around every newsstand, the consulate ante-rooms are full of Egyptian evacuees asking for news or mail and the atmosphere of anxiety and gloom is dense."

seeing you here as soon as possible and everyone sends their best.

John

P.S. I'm very glad you liked the Wapshot piece and I hope you'll like the book. I'll send you a copy or I'll ask Mike Bessie[46] to send you one although he may forget. I got the galleys yesterday addressed to J. Cheevers, via del Televico.

Via del Plebiscito 107
February 24th [1957]

Dear John,

It says in the Rome Daily American that the Dodgers are going to move to Los Angeles and I wonder if this will make any difference in your plans. I should think you might want to come to Italy sooner. Next week would be a good time. I've bought boat tickets for the second of September and I suppose we can meet in New York before you sail but it does seem to me all wrong that we should not be here together. And next autumn here will be very crowded. The Suez invasion sent most of the travelers home but now they are beginning to return in large numbers and Rome feels and looks a little like Saratoga, getting ready for the meet. There are large signs at every intersection pointing the way to the sights and the English classes at the Berlitz School where I go are over-subscribed. You hear nothing but English as far down as the Tritone and the Corso. In preparation for all of this I've bought yellow-plush shoes and a green jacket. I wear a funny hat, piss in doorways and speak nothing but Italian but I'm still always trailed by someone trying to sell me a lousey fountain pen or a phoney Swiss watch.

Mary is so close to having the baby that we don't move around much any more. The doctor doesn't like her to travel and neither do the men who guard the National Treasure. We

46. "Miss Wapshot," an excerpt from *The Wapshot Chronicle* (Harper's), had appeared in *The New Yorker* (September 22). Michael Bessie was the book's editor.

went to Tivoli last week and she was very unpopular. I've been to Florence and Naples but most of our tourismo will have to wait for the baby. Bill writes from Anticoli that he has finished a novel. There's one man around here who works. I try to write in the morning but usually drink some whisky on my balcony at one. After lunch I take a nap and what happens to the rest of the day wouldn't bear looking into. The reason I can't write here is because the ceiling is too far away from the top of my head. It's like trying to write in an open field and I never could do that.

Mary sends her love to you both and I do hope you get over before September.

As ever,
John

"I hope to go without strong drink before lunch but if M has our baby today I think I will ask an indulgence," John wrote in his journal as Mary's time drew near, and on March 10, 1957, the day after his son's birth, John woke up "filled with good wishes for him: courage, love, virility, a healthy sense of self and workable arrangements with God."

"I walked the streets while Mary was in labor and the city, with all it's stone angels, seemed pitiless and cruel," he recalled in a letter to Tanya Litvinov eleven years later. "I went to the zoo for a Campari and found myself surrounded by hyenas, buzzards, wolves and grisley bears. Then I climbed up on the roof of St. Peters, but all the prophets had their backs to me. In the hospital waiting room you could hear the screaming of peacocks from the Villa Sciarra. Then a nun in white said: complimenti, signore, lei ha uno filio robousto. *So I have."*

Via del Plebiscito 107
March 23rd [1957]

Dear John,

It's always good to hear from you even when the news isn't good such as our not meeting here but when we meet in New York in September perhaps we can work out some plans for easing ourselves into the International Set. Our best news is that

Mary had a boy a week ago Wednesday. He is fine—quite handsome and not much trouble—and Rome is a fine place to have a baby. Nuns are better than nurses and not so expensive and Mary had a balcony with a view of Rome. You might think that with a fine son, a novel, a palace, a bank account and a sunny day I would be a contented man but between you and me I have a terrible hangover and feel very covetous and forlorn.

Bill was here for dinner last night and seemed well. Josie Herbst was also here and took a great—a conspicuous—shine to him and kept saying loudly: "Oh I want to see more of *you*." I hope Bill likes her. He left early because he had to go to Naples today and seems to be a very temperate or slow drinker. The Blumes and Lucy Moorehead[47] were also here if you should be interested. We had fish soup. It was our sixteenth wedding anniversary but the Blumes have been married for twenty-six years so this took a lot of wind out of our sails. I bought Mary a gold watch which cost one hell of a lot of money. Mary says the baby is my present. His name used to be Frederick but there being no K in the alphabet here I had to change it to Federico. He is listed as a citizen of Rome in the books of the Comune and will have double citizenship until he's twenty-one.

I do not cut any ice with the princess Caetani but I had tea with Prince Doria and Donna Orieta last week. The cook says the only reason they asked me was so that I would not be able to complain about the green brocade sofa which is coming to pieces. I had a big slug of whisky before I went to the tea-party but I'm afraid I overdid it. Anyhow I now talk loudly about the old Prince and try to give the impression that we are old friends. But my Italian orientation goes slowly and I will obviously not have learned the Bella lingua when we

47. Peter Blume, the Russian-born artist, had married Grace Douglas Gibbs Craton on March 9, 1931. Lucy Moorehead's husband, Alan, was an Australian writer for whom John had the highest personal and professional regard.

leave. This morning I heard myself say to the maid: "Please do not undress, you egg."

Mary, Federico, etc. send their best.

As ever,

John

In his Roman journal John recorded a dream in which he found himself in the White House: "It is after supper in a bedroom that I have seen on postcards. Ike and Mamie are alone. Mamie is reading the Washington Star. *Ike is reading* The Wapshot Chronicle.*"*

Via del Plebiscito 107
April 30th [1957]

Dear John,

I'm so glad you liked the book and I'm sorry that I didn't send you a copy. I could blame Mike but I guess the fault is mine. As for Mike he now signs his letters Simon Michael Bessie and if you ask him about advertising the cat gets his tongue. There just isn't going to be any advertising. And to hell with it.

We saw Bill at a cocktail party in Parioli right after Easter. It was a real stinker: excellent food and liquor and a roomful of burned fuses. The hostess had a dress with a tail on it which led to endless jolification. Mary left early to da la papina a Federico and I drove home in my new Fiat. Wrong gear all the way. The parties around here are terrible. I've never seen such a collection of bums and in the circles we move in there aren't any pretty women at all. But we went to Venice for the holiday which I liked tremendously. The first day I took a look at Harry's bar just to see how disgusting it was. The second day I went in to make sure. It was very disgusting. There was a lady sitting on one bar stool and a poodle on another and they were both eating shrimp sandwiches. I had several drinks. I took Mary back the next day to show her how disgusting it was and we stayed until closing. The next day we went to the suburban beach in Torcello and the next day we came home.

Give my best to the Ettlingers and tell them to write. And my love to Harriet.

As ever,

John

The Cheevers stayed at La Rocca, a vast dilapidated stone fortress overlooking the Mediterranean in Port'Ercole. "When we arrived here we found that the signorina had rented the place out as a movie set," John wrote the Blumes. "There were two light generators in our yard and a small company of about forty-five people wandering around, acting, eating sandwiches and relieving themselves. Then Mary got empetigo off the toilet seat, Ben found a scorpian under his bed and thirty-nine old shoes in the thistles by his door and it seemed that we were not cut out for La Rocca. But we were. Mary is cured and the movie people went yesterday and it is the most beautiful place I have ever seen. The sea is purple, the fisherman are golden and throw their nets off our beach and pull them in hand over hand, singing, full of silver fish. Ernesta then cooks the fish which are very good. On Saturday nights an accordian plays for dancing in the village and wild horses couldn't keep Mary and Susie away."

A place not unlike La Rocca was described in John's New Yorker story, "The Golden Age" (September 26, 1959).

La Rocca
Porto Ercole
Provincia di Grossetto
Italia
[postmarked 27 July 1957]

Dear John,

I'm very sore at Lennie. What kind of thing is that? To come to Europe when your old, old, old friends are practically RUNNING the place and not even send them a card. Think of how useful we would be to them with our fluent Italian, our familiarity with the nobility, our knowledge of restaurants and other gathering places and our gin. Basta coli.

We sail from Naples on the second and will be home, I think, on the twelfth of September and look forward very much to seeing you. I don't know what the date is now but I'm sure the time will go quickly from now until when we sail. We have rented this—a big sixteenth century ruin on the sea—for the summer and we have ramparts and towers and moats and draw-bridges and not quite enough pots to piss in. It's very good excepting about the pots. Bill went off to Austria and Germany early in the month. He's very busy organizing Gion-Carlo's opera festival for next year and I guess it would be downright unbrotherly of you not to come over and see it although I wish you'd wait until we come back which we plan to do in 58. However we'll talk this over when we see you in September.

As ever,

John

A handwritten note from Florence on a phallic postcard.

Dear John,

There is going to be a party in Scarborough on the four-teenth of September which we hope you can make.

Best.

John

We attended the Cheevers' party and did not break with precedent by leaving in a state approaching sobriety.

Scarborough, N. Y.

January 2 [1958]

Dear John,

You were very sober as our guests go and very, very civil, both of you. The last time I put Eleanor Warren on the 2:17 she turned around and hissed "Procrustes" at me. Alan Moorhead came out for the weekend and missed all the trains. I had to get Susie out of bed and put her in the cot in Ben's room and

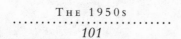

then put Alan in Susie's bed which is hot and smells funny. Iole[48] woke Alan up at seven for early church, thinking he was Susie. He looked awful when I took him down to the early train.

I still can't find a place to work and so do little or nothing. The telephone rang a few days ago and the operator said: Long Distance, Mr. Henry Lewis calling Mr. John Cheevers. I asked her to wait a minute and got a cigaret and a drink and sat down to take the news calmly but Henry was only calling from New York and only wanted to wish us a Happy New Year. He said you were both very well and that he had had lunch with Lennie and then I wished him a Happy New Year and that was all.

Best.

John

When The Wapshot Chronicle *won the 1958 National Book Award for fiction, John had at least two friends among the judges, Bill Maxwell and Francis Steegmuller. He also had an unwavering third vote from our friend Elizabeth Ann McMurray Johnson. The other winners were Robert Penn Warren for poetry* (Promises: Poems 1954–56) *and Catherine Drinker Bowen for nonfiction* (The Lion and the Throne).

"The book was difficult and very pleasant to write," John said in his acceptance remarks. "As I approached the end I had bronchitis but I went on working, telling myself each morning that I did not care what physical or mental disasters overtook me so long as I could finish. When the book was done all these promises seemed due and I began to limp, to cough, to wheeze and to tremble. I went at once to a doctor who told me I was in splendid condition so presumably a novel is not as difficult to write as it appears to be at the time."

48. Iole Felici went to work for the Cheevers in Rome, fell in love with Federico (Picci, she called him) and, as Ben notes, "has remained an active force in all of our lives."

Scarborough
Saturday
[postmarked 15 March 1958]

Dear John,

Just in case you should ever get a National Book Award I think I can give you some good advice. First you have to have at least three good friends among the judges and then you have to have strong nerves, a commodious bladder and a good supply of bourbon. On Monday I made six whattheycall tapes. You go into these hot little studios where there is a man with small eyes and a big voice, a card table, two folding chairs, a dusty piano and a bullfiddle. Then the sound engineer comes out from behind the glass partition and tells you about his stomach. They always do this. Then they give you a time signal, your tongue swells up to twice its normal size and the man with the little eyes asks you in a booming voice what you think about the American reading public. After six of these I was so tired I couldn't sleep at all and on Tuesday morning I sneaked a little bourbon about half-past ten. Then Mary revealed to me that she had bought a new dress which cost one hundred dollars. She said it was cheaper to buy a new dress where she didn't have to wear a hat than to buy a hat to wear with her other dress. We drove into New York and I went to Parlor B, Mezzanine C at the Commodore where there were quite a lot of people penned in by velvet ropes. I saw Lewis Gannett trying to get away but Betty Smith and Ishbel Ross held him down. I expect he had to go to the bathroom just like me. I was jumping. Then Clifton Fadiman said he was going to give us a plaque and a thousand dollars but all he gave us was a plaque. Then they took this away from us. Then Fadiman gave us the plaque again and they took it away again. Then we pretended to autograph books for John K. M. Macaffrey and Fadiman gave us the plaque again and took it away again. Then I went to the bathroom. Then we went downstairs where there were more people. It cost ten dollars to get in. Fadiman gave the plaque and a check to Red Warren.

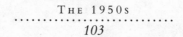

Then Red made a ten minute speech about the poem as structure and structure as the poem and sat down in a chair with a
sign on it saying POETRY WINNER. Then Katherine Bowen made
a speech but I didn't listen to this because I was afraid I would
forget my own speech. Then I made a speech and sat down in
a chair that said FICTION WINNER and Randall Jarrell, who had
just washed his beard, made a long speech, the gist of which was
that Bennet Cerf is a shit, that South Pacific is shitty and that
people who look at the sixty-four thousand dollar question are
virtual cocksuckers. This went on for forty-five minutes and the
Random House contingent coughed all the way through it.
Then some screens were removed and there was one of those
bars made of a trestle table covered with a bedsheet and a couple
of hundred highball glasses each containing two ice cubes and a
teaspoon of whisky. Bert Rouche asked me how you were.
Knox Burger asked me how you were. Then we went to Toots
Shors where there was one of those buffets they had for movie
previews. Smoked butt, baked beans, and one old turkey. All the
publishers got drunk and sang Down By The Old Millstream.
Then we went back to the hotel where there were some friends
drinking in my room. They did this until about two. Then early
in the morning I went to the Dave Garroway studio which is
really a store window on Fifty-second street and outside there
were about four hundred women milling around and holding
up signs saying: HELLO MAMA. DORIS. SEND MONEY. GLADYS.
HELP. IDA. I was asked to wait in a green room where there was
a chimpanzee drinking coffee, a man with a long beard and a
lady in Arab costume practising a song. She said the song was in
Arabic and it was about how the little raindrops fill up the big
well. Then she went up and sang her song and then they said it
was time for me to go up but it took two strong men pushing
and pulling to get me into the studio and everybody on the street
shouted: It's Gary Moore. I sat down at a baize-covered table
and quivered like a bowlfull of chicken fat for fifteen minutes
and then I drove Mary home. Mary took the check away from

me and Ben hung the plaque up in his clubhouse which is in the woods and is made of two packing crates so I may not be any richer but I sure am a hell of a lot more nervous.

Love,

Jean Stratton Porter[49]

Scarborough
Monday
[postmarked 2 June 1958]

Dear John,

. . . I saw Louis Untermeyer who said you were reading a dirty letter of mine to mixed company but I don't suppose there's any truth in this. I also saw Marilyn Monroe and have written many poems to her about how she is like a ray of sunlight in a subway tunnel. Did you know that if a publisher owes you one thousand dollars in March they can put it on the April statement and pay you in December? They can.

As ever,

John

Scarborough
[postmarked 15th July 1958]

Dear Harriet,

Why write to John all the time I said to myself. Who the hell is he? All he ever does is the sand-papering and I'll bet he couldn't tell me where to buy bartop or thread a venitian blind if his life depended on it. That's at least what Mary says of me. With the big children gone off to camp and the maid never giving us even one little peek at the baby Mary has taken up carpentry, the re-threading of venitian blinds and the re-finish-

49. Berton Roueché, a *New Yorker* writer, had been a *Kansas City Star* colleague in the late 1930s. Knox Burger was fiction editor of *Collier's* before setting up shop as a literary agent. Dave Garroway often made use of the chimpanzee J. Fred Muggs on NBC's "Today Show." John *did* bear a slight resemblance to quiz-show host Garry Moore. The typed signature is John's spelling of Gene(va) Stratton Porter, author of sentimental romances.

ing of table-tops. I do the sand-papering, not because it makes her sneeze but because she thinks it's tiresome. I'm ready, she says. Hurry up, she says.

When I'm done with the sand-papering for the day I spend the rest of the time brooding around the house, trying to think up some witty, trenchant but childlike double-entendre to write in the front of the two books you sent on. I haven't come up with anything yet and I may just write LOVE in them and let it go.[50] That's about all anybody ever writes in my books.

I guess Lennie is with you now and tell him to call me when he gets back so that I can get a true account of the festivities; the broken windows and naked swimming-pool parties. Things are fairly dim here. We had guests on Wednesday and I told one of my dearest neighbors that since he had drunk up all my liquor, tracked dog-shit all over my rugs and made dirty passes at my wife he could get the hell out. He did. Mary says I drink too much but I don't think she drinks nearly enough. Give my best to John when you see him.

Love,

John

On August 28 I wrote Lennie Field: "Please alert the Cheevers & Ettlingers that we will probably be around next month. They may want to prepare the children with a series of lectures explaining the mores of Southern California." He passed the word on to John.

Scarborough

Saturday

[postmarked 6 September 1958]

Dear John,

That is all very good news and this is just to say so and that we will keep the ice-cubes warm. We warmed up quite a few

50. He signed *The Enormous Radio* for Harriett and *The Wapshot Chronicle* for me with another of his standby inscriptions: "In memory of an unforgettable experience."

ice-cubes last night when Mike Bessie came to dinner and it is a terrible exertion this morning for me to hit the typewriter keys. Publishers drive me to drink. All of them. We also had dinner with Lennie on Tuesday at his new establishment. Very elegant, I thought. Almonds in the string beans and sparkling wine, but the toilet had a baulky flush. It seems that Mary flunked Lennie's girl friend at Sarah Lawrence and that I once screwed Peter Matson's aunt.[51] Small world.

    Love,
      John

Scarborough
Monday
[postmarked 8 December 1958]

Dear John,

The books went off to you on Thursday, all suitably in-scribed, and I'm very sorry to have been so slow about this but I haven't been in town since I last saw you. No one in town asked me to come in and I kept thinking that if I stayed home I might get something done. What I done got was a rotten headcold. It's the first I've had in years and I think it's very interesting but Mary's love of me does not seem to include my infirmities. She seems lost in some race memory where primitive men, once they began to sniffle, stripped themselves naked, lay down in the snow and let themselves be eaten by crows.

I had lunch with Lennie on Thursday and also went there for a drink. Alan Rivkin[52] was holed up in the guest room and there were a couple of chatty, young ladies on the sofa. A colored house boy passed the cashew nuts. The conversation was all about how funny Lennie Spigelgass's play is.[53] Lennie was

51. Lennie's older daughter, Mary Ruth, had married Peter Matson, a literary agent.

52. A Minneapolis friend of Lennie's and civilian writer-producer at Fort Capra.

53. The Spigelgass play, *Majority of One,* starred Gertrude Berg.

very pleasant and let me help myself to his gin bottle which I needed because I had to lecture at Columbia. This was the usual. They made me use the service entrance at the Faculty Club, they wouldn't let me into the auditorium because I didn't have a ticket and when I finally flailed my way up to the lectern I knocked over the water glass and opened my remarks with an apostrophe to the pystery and massion of life

As ever,

John

Scarborough,
New York
December 30th [1958]

Dear John,

I do hope the books reached you in time. This has been on my mind. For all I know they may be bumbling drunkenly around some midwestern postoffice or even gathering dust at Harper Bros. They should have gone out on the third but perhaps it was too late.

My cold had the common decency to turn into something as manly and straightforward as virus pneumonia and when the doctor came to take me to the hospital Mary could hardly overlook the fact that I seemed peaked although she tried. The doctor thought I had tuberculosis but neither Mary nor the kiddies were deceived for a moment. I'll be sprung on Friday but I'm not quite sure where I'll go.

A happy New Year to you, Harriet and Lennie.

Best,

John

"Harriet is one of the wonders of our day" John wrote my editor at Rinehart after reading the galleys of As I Live and Breathe. *There were some illustrations and the book was priced at $3.95. John's* Housebreaker *went for $3 and* Some People, Places *for $3.50.*

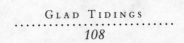

Scarborough
February 4th [1959]

Dear John,

I'm very glad the books got off to you in time but instead of you're paying for them why don't you, next Christmas, send me inscribed copies of your book for me to give away. I realize that this arrangement might get us into hot water and that your book may be a five or six dollar book with illustrations but I think we can straighten it out somehow. I'm very happy to hear that the book is done and I'm sure it will be a success. You can't miss on this one.

I had lunch with Lennie on Monday and I am always very happy to get my back against the wall at Sardi's, to smell the lady-dust and the origano and feel the gin flow over my kidneys. Lennie is always good and gentle company. I went to Saratoga for two weeks after leaving the hospital and I still feel a little feeble and peculiar. Did I write you that I went for a walk here one splendid afternoon and was picked up by a policeman on a charge of vagrancy?

Love,
John

Scarborough
Saturday
[postmarked 14 February 1959]

Dear John,

I don't quite know what to make of your letter but the gist or drift of it seems to be that I can't give away your book for Christmas. I said that if it cost four and one half or five fifty I'd pay the difference but I don't suppose you believed me. And anyhow Don and Lennie aren't the only people I know. I know Myrna Loy and Baroness Blixen and Carson McCullers and Thornton Wilder and Baroness Blixen and Wysten Auden and the Baroness Blixen and James T. Farrell. I also knew Prince Doria before he died although he was not much of a reader. I also know Francis Steegmuller, Leonard Spigelgass, Dorothy

Parker, Morrie Werner, Cabel Greet, Irwin Shaw. Martha Gell-horn, Dawn Adams, Louise Bogan, Glenway Wescott and don't forget that Henry Fonda is supposed to have bought a copy of my book. Don't forget that.

Tell Phyllis Kirk[54] that the Five-Forty something was done on TV. It came right after Mary Martin's first appearance as Peter Pan. I mean it was the same hookup with all the little kiddies still in their bathrobes and fuzzy slippers and it was one of the most clear-cut disasters the medium has ever experienced. Susie wouldn't go back to school for ten days. As for Spigelgass there's a great deal of talk about his play here and they've already cast the National company: Sophie Tucker and Burgess Meredith. In order to talk about the play you have to lapse into a false Yiddish accent and there is a scene where Gertrude Berg gets wet that is so funny nobody can talk about it. I suppose I could buy tickets for it and give them away at Christmas.

Best,

John

[postmarked 13 March 1959]

Dear John,

I also know Archibald MacLeish, Victor Gollancz, Hilary Rubenstein and John and Harriet Weaver, but I haven't heard from Weaver and I'm very anxious to know how the book is going. I feel, somehow, as if it were my own chicken but this may be just another facet of my deep suspicion of publishers, enthusiastic or otherwise. I recently had lunch with Mike Bessie and told him if I broke my arse writing stories for the next three months I might be able to take six weeks off this summer to think about a novel. "I am indeed pleased, to hear this," he said, "and while I know it's the sort of thing publishers are not supposed to tell authors I *think* Harpers might be able to give you a little money if you need it badly." I had a drink with him

---

54. An actress interested in making a film adaptation of John's story, "The Five-Forty-Eight."

a few nights later. He told me two funny stories in French and then patiently translated them for me. I haven't been so miffed since I got the shrimp fork.[55] And after that I had dinner with Victor Gollancz[56] who had just had dinner with Cass Canfield. "It's the most correct house in New York," he said of the Canfields. "A short cocktail hour, black tie, cigars afterwards, all that sort of thing and you never find any writers at his table who are not both gifted and gentlemen. But then," he added archly, "of course you must know that." Aw shit.

It is snowing here, shin-deep and very bad driving. I do want to hear about your book.

Best,

John

Scarborough
April 14th [1959]

Dear John,

I've had a story rejected by Botteghe Oscure and took my brother to the hospital on Monday in the last stages of alcoholic malnutrition. I now have to support two families and so I wrote a long story with this in mind and Mary read it today and said that it was terrible. Lennie called to say that he was having a party on Thursday but I go to Saratoga on Wednesday in order to write a million stories and put everyone on Easy Street. Right now my brother lives on Stonehenge Lane and we live on Station Road.

As ever,

John

55. One evening during his brief tour of duty at Fort Capra in the spring of 1945 John dropped by the Roosevelt Hotel and, to his astonishment, was served a creditable martini. Encouraged by evidence that missionaries had been at work in the area, he downed another and proceeded to order dinner. When the waiter served his shrimp cocktail, he pointed to the silver at the left side of John's plate and said, "Use the little fork."

56. The English publisher of *The Enormous Radio* had also acquired *The Wapshot Chronicle*.

John had agreed to attend a writers' congress in Germany and planned to walk through the Brenner Pass with his mountain-climbing friends, Louis and Christl Hechenbleikner. "They came for dinner on Saturday," he had reported some months earlier in a letter to George Biddle, "and asked such questions as: 'You haff nose-bleeding at twelve thousand feet?' I said I didn't want, under any circumstances, to go above nine thousand feet. 'Mit ropes, is easy,' they said. I said I didn't want to climb with ropes. 'Not,' they asked, 'mit liddle ropes?' If crossing the Brenner means crampons and pitons I may take a train but I'm sure there must be a decent pass."

Carlton Hotel
Frankfurt am Main
Am Hauptbahnhof 18
Telefon 339061-7
Fernschreiber 412618

Saturday
[postmarked 25 July 1959]

Dear John,

My schedule goes like this: 12:30 Uhr. Fruhstuck gegeben vom Prasidium der Industrie und Handleskammer. Cocktail party auf Einladung des S. Fisher Verlages. 17 Uhr. Weinprobe in Kloster Eberbach. 20 Uhr Empfang des Hessichen Minister-prasidenten in Wiesbaden, Kurhaus.[57] What the hell. It started out as a high-flown literary discussion group but as soon as we got the idea that the wine was free all hell broke loose. The French and the English are the worst but I'm no Alice-sit-by-the-fire when the corks start popping. It was not polite at the weinprobe to drink less than fourteen glasses of wine and I think of myself as an unofficial ambassador and bound to be polite.

57. John's German spelling was about as idiosyncratic as his English. This was the schedule: "12:30 P.M. Breakfast given by the Board of Trade and Chamber of Commerce. Cocktail party hosted by S. Fischer, Publishers. 5:00 P.M. Wine tasting in Kloster Eberbach. 8:00 P.M. Reception of the president of Hesse, in the Kurhaus, Wiesbaden."

Oh well, I'll see you in September and if the truth is ever revealed to me I'll know what I'm doing here. We never did go to the Readers Digest for lunch because I had a cold and I still don't know whether or not they took Harriet. I had a letter from Susie yesterday (who enjoyed the book tremendously) asking if the Digest had taken it.[58] How should I know, here on the banks of the Main. I go to Innsbruck and then Kitsbuhel tomorrow and plan to walk from there to Cortina but if they have wein-probes and empfangs in Kitsbuhel I'll never make it. I get down to Rome on the twelfth but I guess Bill will be in the alps and I'll see the Weavers in New York in September.

> Best,
> John

A handwritten postcard from Frankfurt am Main.

> n.d.
> [postmarked 27 July 1959]

Dear John,

I can't write very well so there's no point in my trying to phrase a pithy message. I've been here a week and go to Innsbruck tomorrow. The wine here is very good and my publisher is very free with the wine. Letter follows.

> John

Lennie Field had married a San Francisco widow, Virginia Clayburgh Meltzer.

> American Academy
> Porta San Pancrazio
> Roma
> August 17th [1959]

Dear John,

I was going down the Grand Canal in one of those vapporettos when I happened to look out at the terrace of the Gritti

58. The *Digest* did not buy *As I Live and Breathe*.

Palace and saw Lennie sitting there drinking coffee. I began to wave my arms and yell: "Lennieee, Lenieee," and he finally recognized me. I couldn't get off the boat until San Marco's but then I ran back to the Gritti and Virginia came down and we went to the Lido and in the very next cabana was Nancy Mitford and Victor Cunard. Swam in the same water with them and everything. Nancy had her own boat so we went into Venice separately. I missed John Galsworthy but I haven't missed everything.

Lennie and Virginia went to London on Tuesday and I came down to Rome the next day. I think Bill is out of town but I'll see if I can't get his number and call him. I do not see much of Rome because I spend most of my time washing my clothes but I think Harriet would be proud of me excepting when I washed my best shirt with a package of cigarets in the pocket. I washed everything in Innsbruck but then it rained like hell and I had to go to Kitzbuhel wet. I didn't dry out really until I got south of the Brenner but then I was nice and dry in Venice and I'm dry here excepting for the Frascati which is in season.

As ever,
John

Dr. Winternitz had died October 3 and John wrote Josie Herbst: "I have a hole in the seat of my pants and not enough money for last month's bills. I needn't have a hole in the seat of my pants because I have just inherited my father-in-law's wardrobe but he is ashes and I can't bring myself to open the package and try on the pants so my underwear shows . . ."

Scarborough
Monday
[postmarked 2 November 1959]

Dear John,
And we were sorry not to have seen more of you but it seems to have been an ill-starred autumn. First there was Mary's

poor father's painful and protracted departure from this vale of tears. Then a member of my family went on the financial skids and at the moment I have nine dependents. This is one hell of a burden for my childlike sense of wonder. Then Sam brained Iole, our Italian cook,[59] with a gas range. He claims he did it in self-defense. She was biting his ear and I seem to be implicated because it was I who bought the teeth. Anyhow she is too spiritually upset to work. In the meantime all the quarterlies have opened fire, not on my writing, but on my person. In the Hudson Review I am toothless. In the Partisan Review I have false teeth and greying hair. In the Kenyon Review I am hairless. I don't know why my prose should evoke such a denuded figure. I not only have all my hair and all my teeth but I am part-owner of the cook's teeth.

I haven't seen Lennie since we got dried out. I don't think I've been into New York since then. I have three stories still to go on the deadline and an increasing, a swelling indifference to the short story as a form. The only story I seem to want to write is a long story called The Death of The Short Story. I also suffer from post-nasal drip, gas on the stomach and a sore pecker.

Love,

John

Scarborough
26th
[December 1959]

Dear John and Harriet,

It is a wonderful present and I wanted to wire you yesterday when I opened it but Mary said that would be improvident

---

59. Iole had married Sam Masullo, who worked on the Vanderlip estate. "Our Italian maid is gone," John reported in a letter to George Biddle (November 13). "Her husband beat her quite severely, claiming to be jealous of our baby and our milkman. Mary always thought the milkman was in love with her. I am in love with Mrs. Arthur Miller. But in any case the maid is gone." John made use of Iole's wedding in "Clementina" (*The New Yorker,* May 7, 1960).

and kept an eye on the telephone. I have never seen such a beautiful book—neither has Mary nor Susie—it was the nicest present I got, the least expected and it excited in me a volcanic turmoil of Christmas emotion. It also bolsters my pose as a linguist. I keep the translation hidden in a copy of Life magazine and sneak looks at it but when anyone steps into the room I seem to be reading French. A very merry Christmas to you.

We had the usual and the older I grow the stranger and more bewildering it seems. The baby got so damned many things—trucks, trains, oil derricks, an artificial shrimp bed and a musical toilet seat—that I began to wonder gloomily, if our native misconception of innocence doesn't begin early in life and early on Christmas morning. The Ettlingers asked us for lunch and I told them I would have to consult the children. The children all said they wanted to have Christmas lunch at home so I accepted the Ettlingers invitation and drove a fairly uncooperative family across the river. "Who wants to spend Christmas afternoon watching you two get drunk?" lisped the baby. Well he did. The Ettlingers were fine although the future of Don's play seems unsettled and this is a sensitive area. Mary drove Susie to the Nantucket plane this morning at five A.M. but they went to Idlewild and the plane leaves from LaGuardia and Mary had a knock-down fight with a coin-changing machine in the lady's toilet and they are both sulking around the house.

Love,
    John

The 1960s

❧❧❧

"The air seems to have gone out of my tires," John wrote in the spring of 1960, on the eve of his forty-eighth birthday, and two years later, when he returned to Yaddo, hoping to finish his second novel, he dreamed he was "a Good Humor man, ringing a small bell and urging people to try the seven flavors of discouragement. There are, between you and me, more than seven."

The harsh taste of discouragement was still on his tongue when he wrote his scholarly California friend, Fred Bracher (November 2, 1962):

Let us think for a moment about Mr. X, a conscientious and brilliant novelist whose works were like lamps in the dark but who had received no recognition. He was seized, at the age of sixty with a penchant for exhibitionism. He hid himself in a clump of bushes in Central Park, dropped his trousers down around his knees and sprang out at his prey who happened to be a police woman. He was given a suspended sentence but the New York Times carried the story and the disgrace was so galling that he began to drink. After being drunk for about a week he got very disputatious at a party and tipped over a sideboard containing a collection of Crown Derby. His hostess sued him for ten thousand dollars and the newspapers carried the story. (Novelist breaks ten thousand dollars worth of dishes.) He went on drinking and in a drunken rage beat his gentle and loving wife into insensibility. She was taken to the hospital with multiple sprains and abrasions and he was remanded to Bellevue for observation. When he finally left the hospital he found that he was famous. Irving Howe put him at the very helm of American literature. Maxwell Geismar incorporated him into the stream of vital writing. Arthur Meisner paid him a sober and considered tribute in the Times and he did not have to wait long before Leslie Fiedler was heard from. He drank himself to death and now his shy and handsome face looks out at me from every bookstore on Fifth Avenue.

In the first half of this new decade, thanks to a brief writing stint in Hollywood, John bought the handsome Hudson Valley home where he would spend the rest of his life. He brought out his second novel and two new collections of short stories, sold the film rights to his two novels and to a stunning new story, "The Swimmer." He spent a glorious ten days in the Soviet Union with John and Mary Updike, fell in love with a movie actress, and in the early spring of 1964 his shy and handsome face looked out from the cover of Time *at commuters swarming past Grand Central's newsstands.*

By the end of the decade his health had begun to fail and, he confessed, "the spirits of the gin bottle seem to have complete mastery over my comings and goings." In the meantime, however, he had received "a letter from the Nobel prize people who want to take a look at me and see if I can walk backwards."

Scarborough
Wednesday
[postmarked 6 January 1960]

Dear John,

The book still excites my childlike sense of wonder and I like the text as well as the pictures; especially the piece by Camus on what it is that I cherche and Sartre on Venice which makes my own imagery seem very concrete. I think you're right about the return of quizz shows and I know you're right about the telephone. Some day it will ring; and that way lies salvation. I've always known this. When I was a boy, walking home from school, I was always convinced that the U.S. Maratime commission had called to say that I had won the trip through the Panama Canal for having colored the neatest map. I never approach the house today without a soaring conviction that someone has called—Louis B. Mayer or the arcangel Gabriel—with some piece of deliverance and when Mary tells me that no one has called I think she must be either subversive or deaf. Tell Harriet that a friend of our's once got behind the exhaust pipe of a bus on the Corso and the fumes consumed both her stockings, most of her rayon dress and made a big hole in her girdle.

Best,

John

Scarborough
May 24th [1960]

Dear John,

I haven't seen or talked with Lennie or anyone else for so damned long that I feel terribly out of touch. I suppose Lennie's gone to Europe. God knows. I roughed out a big piece of a novel but now the air seems to have gone out of my tires and I will go alone to Nantucket on the first of June and hope this will perk me up. Mary and the children come down at the end of the month. A week or so ago it looked as though we might move to Saratoga. The town is a distressed area and real-estate is very cheap. I drove the whole family north to look at houses and they seemed quite enthusiastic but on Sunday I found Mary weeping into the dishpan and when I asked what was the matter she said it was because she never, never, never wants to live in Saratoga. I'm quite pissy about my disappointment. It's the sort of thing one learns in New England. Life is a casting off, and all that shit. But confronted with the houses around here (which

Mary wants to buy) I feel exactly like a plant confronted with a pot that will do it's roots no good.

We are all well although Susie is not as docile as she might be, considering all the dough I've spent in giving her a genteel education. She gets all red in the face when she talks about the Summit fracas—its a very subversive shade of red. Ben is fine and big and we go fishing together and Iole has taught the baby to piss against the wall of the house. He won't do it anywhere else and so I guess we'll have to go back to Italy. I am taking Mary to San Francisco in the last of October for some kind of literary blow-out[1] and then if you are home we will come down and see you. My love to Harriet.

As ever,
John

Lennie Field and Caroline Burke Swann presented Brendan Behan's play, The Hostage, *at the Cort Theater on September 21.*

Scarborough
Some Tuesday
[postmarked 13 September 1960]

Dear John,

I saw Lennie last week for the first time I think since spring and he is fine. We had lunch with Behan and I'm sure the show will be a great success because otherwise why would Vincent come to the table practically on his hands and knees and why should Lennie Lyons[2] embrace me? Also Behan had canneloni (What the fuck, he asked, is this fucking canneloni) and they gave him a special one, full of minced chicken, much better than

1. John was scheduled to participate with Philip Roth and James Baldwin in a symposium, "Writing in America Today," sponsored by *Esquire,* which was about to publish "The Death of Justina."

2. Vincent Sardi usually stopped by Lennie's table. Leonard Lyons was a gossip columnist famed for his ability to foul up the punchline of the latest story making the rounds of the local fleshpots.

anything we ever get. On Saturday Ginny brought Behan out for a swim. Now that I'm off the sauce—he said—I'm more interested in farney. What is farney—asked Mrs. Vanderlip. Farney, Mam, said Behan, is an abbreviation of farnication. I like him tremendously and I'm sure the play will be a great success. Lennie's sterling qualities were never so apparent. He is kind, unhurried and pleasant as ever.

Mary and I are trying to buy a house which is a source of tension and also very embarrassing because no bank will give me a mortgage. The reasons are that I am self-employed or unemployed and also that I am old. The house is beautiful, the price is modest and the banks are cruel. I thought Henry might stir up a job for me but his promises seem to be pure gossamer. I am impatient with him but please don't say so, he seems so defenseless. Mary isn't coming with me to San Francisco—we're saving for the house—and I'm not sure that I'll come down to Los Angeles. I'm bored with the whole thing. What can I tell the beards at Berkeley. Love all around.

John

I had written John to invite him to look in on us when he came to California. Once I got his letter I called immediately to point out that on his return flight from San Francisco he could, at no additional expense, be routed through Los Angeles, where I would meet him and whisk him off to our guest house.

Scarborough
Tuesday
[postmarked 27 September 1960]

Dear John,

You are kind, sweet, generous, helpful, encouraging, hospitable, witty and friendly and as soon as I get in touch with Esquire and find how much it will cost to get to Los Angeles I'll write. I'd love to see you both. I had lunch with Henry yesterday and after lunch we telephoned Jerry Wald. I said Hello Mr.

Wald,[3] it's nice to talk with you. He said it was nice to talk with me too. Then Henry called someone else in California. It was lots of fun. Then I came home and Henry went to Philadelphia to see the Unsinkable Molly[4] and I do hope it's a great success. Henry was nervous.

I haven't seen Lennie since his opening but he seems to be doing allright. I decided to write a story a week from now until Christmas but I wrote two and pooped. I also have a cold. Negotiations for the house still go on but I expect we'll get it sooner or later.[5] I still haven't figured out what to say in San Francisco and if you have any suggestions I would appreciate them. I told the editor of Esquire that I thought I might open by observing that the secret of a good prose style is a stiff prick but he turned green and pretended not to have heard me so I guess that's out.

Love,
John

3. A film producer at 20th Century–Fox, who wanted to talk to John about writing a screen treatment of D. H. Lawrence's novel, *The Lost Girl*.

4. Henry Lewis also represented Richard Morris, the author of a new musical comedy, *The Unsinkable Molly Brown*.

5. "One of our rich neighbors offered to underwrite the folly and all I have to do now is to write a short story a week for the next twenty years and turn out plays and novels in the evenings," John wrote Malcolm Cowley (September 26); "and having been exposed all my life to the possibility of emotional disaster I now find myself exposed to the possibility of financial catastrophe. But it is exciting to think of having a place of our own. Neither of us sleep much these days. I scythe the orchard—at three in the morning—and Mary tosses and turns as she rearranges the furniture." The "rich neighbors" who agreed to cosign the mortgage were Dudley and Virginia Vanderlip Schoales. The sticking point was the down payment, for which John was casting about when he set out for California.

Scarborough
Thursday
[postmarked 12 October 1960]

Dear John,

Esquire says that I leave San Francisco at 2 pm on October 23rd by United Airlines #582 and arrive in Los Angeles at 3:42 pm. Is that allright with you. Then I leave for home on the morning of the 26th. I have to come home and take care of the baby so that Mary can go to Vermont and see Susie.

Love,
John

Scarborough
Thursday
[postmarked 27 October 1960]

Dear John,

I enjoyed the flight back very much, although I don't seem able to find any decent writing paper. I saw Pikes Peak, Boulder, Denver and the pilot was a very playful fellow who spoke of his part of the cabin as the sharp end of the plane. The temperature in Denver, he said, is seventy-five. Seven (pause) five. I sat with a little toy salesman who makes the trip to L.A. four times a year. Everybody on the plane said L.A. I had the same lunch I had on the way out: goulash with a noodle fence on the other side of which lay some corn and lima beans. Nobody eats the strudle. I liked best of all flying into the night. At two-fifteen the clouds were all red and purple and I asked the stewardess to bring me some ice. She was very nice about it but there was some snickering from a couple across the aisle when I poured a drink. At three by my wrist-watch they were washing up the supper dishes in Forest Hills. Mary met me here. The damned baby had fallen asleep and I still haven't spoken to him but Ben was fine and Susie called. Mary leaves tomorrow morning for Vermont and I get back into my apron.

The only real complaint I have to make about your hospitality is that it seemed to be of such pure strain that I took advantage of it, poured too many stories into your ears and drank more than my share of liquor. You must know how much it meant to me to see you in your own house, your own fine climate. Here, it seems late in the autumn. All the leaves are off the trees outside my window and I am very restless. If it all falls through I will still have my souvenir copy of the Virgin and the Gipsy[6] and my memories of standing on your terrace smelling shell-fish and hearing your pleasant voices.

As ever,
John

Scarborough
Tuesday
[postmarked 1 November 1960]

Dear John,

Henry called on the stroke of midnight on All Hallows Eve. I don't know whether or not this was significant. I was all shook-up from giving away candy to children in disguise. Both Mary and I were sound asleep when the phone woke us up and neither of us could figure out where we were or with whom we were sleeping which I suppose is some sort of moral reflection. Anyhow when we came unscrambled it seems that Henry said I should leave on Monday and if it really was Henry on the phone and not some disembodied spirit that is what I will do. It is an immense consolation to both of us to think that you will be on the hill above the hotel.[7] It makes the city seem amiable to me and Mary feels that your kind presence will guide me away from violent drunkenness and disgusting venereal embroilments.

I am delighted. It will give me enough freedom to break my long-standing contract and we can move gracefully into the

6. Jerry Wald had given John a copy of the D. H. Lawrence novel with PROPERTY OF AMERICAN RED CROSS stamped across the flyleaf.

7. We had arranged for John to stay at the Chateau Marmont, within walking distance.

new house. On Saturday our 1959 twenty-seven hundred dollar Studebaker Lark fell utterly to pieces in the outskirts of Williamstown, Mass. Mary continued on to Woodstock by taxi (thirty-five dollars) and a farm-hand put the car together at a cost of two hundred dollars. He seems to have been a Ford partisan and used all Ford parts which gnash and grind and smoke and will have to be replaced (another two hundred) with Studebaker lights and vitals. This would have staggered us if it hadn't been for dear Henry. I am also grateful to you on another count because nothing but your kind invitation would ever have got me down to Hollywood.

Mary reports that Susie is very happy at school. She has been going to school since she was two and this is the first good one we've found. Picci went out last night disguised as a rabbit and made a big haul. Ben went as a tiger. A friend of Ben's, who has always seemed to me on the delicate side, showed up at the door in high-heeled shoes and an old evening dress, rouged to the ears and blooming. I, who hope to be so generous on these matters, was rigid with indignation. I gave him only a small handful of chicken-feed. My shoes are killing me, he said and drifted off. I broke with the Asia people yesterday afternoon. Goddamit, they said, Jesus Christ, etc. It was very unpleasant. They pointed out that if I traveled tourist and ate rice I could take home fourteen hundred and I had to point out that this is not enough to support my family for nine weeks. I'll see you very soon.

As ever,
John

Nixon's campaign elicited one of John's rare political responses.

Scarborough
Tuesday
[postmarked 8 November 1960]

Dear John,
This is a wild stab at catching you but it is election day and I am just sitting around with sweaty palms, worrying. Did you

catch him yesterday on the telethon. I think he looks like Raymond Massey with the mumps. Mary claims that he's had the mumps and they've damaged his apparatus. Iole says he has a bocca storta and a viso non allegro, non mais. Even gentle Benjamin can't look at him for long; and he seems to me the candidate of criminals, wall-eyed baby-sitters, embittered widows, seriously impoverished debutantes, and native fascists. In this last hour it seems to me that I can pick out the faces on the street who will vote for him. In order to conceal my sympathies I am dressed entirely in clothing left to me by my conservative father-in-law—Peal shoes, a polka-dot bow-tie and of course the vicuna. It is a brilliant, still day and I've had to leave off the umbrella.

I called Henry who seems to be allright. Business is evidently wonderful—ticket-scalping is going on—and they must be set for a year or two.[8] He still hasn't [sent] the plane tickets and I will feel better when we have these. I've not been able to do any work this week but I suppose that's only natural. I look forward to seeing you very soon and seem not so much to be going to Hollywood as going to the Weavers which is fine with me.

As ever,

John

John decided to return to New York by train. Before depositing him at Union Station we had gathered some fruit and nuts at the Farmers Market for Mary and the children.

8. *The Unsinkable Molly Brown* had a good run and was made into a film starring Debbie Reynolds.

Somewhere
[postmarked 27 December 1960]

Dear John and Harriet,

This is on the Olivetti and I am not accountable for the typing. I guess you will have told everybody by now about how I lost my peanuts in the chopper at the Farmers Market but I do not care. After leaving you I went into that bar at the station you mentioned and met a nice girl who was going to Chicago. I filled her up but when it was time to get on the train she got on something called Il Capitan. I think there are only five people on this train, counting the hiders. It is deluxe with a dome car and a turquoise room where you are encouraged to give cocktail parties. I have been trying to make friends but I have not had any success. It is just like The Losers.[9] Yesterday I think we were held up by Indians. I was sitting around beararse, drinking gin and reading about Cranmer so I did not get out to see but we were stopped in a snowy pass for about an hour. I have eaten one orange, two pears and two tangerines. I do not eat the parsley in the dinning-car because I know that this is a terrible aphrodisiac so I have not had much trouble on that score. I think that Belloc must have been a Jesuit and that I am getting a paunch. I have finished Belloc and am now reading Snow who is no good. From time to time I look at the pictures in Susie's book.

I think often of you both and that I do not possess and cannot cultivate anything like your grace and your kindness and that when you come to visit us you will not only have to put up

9. A neighborhood bar where John had been eighty-sixed (denied service because of intoxication).

with a bad, bad bathroom picture but with a basically surly, untruthful and confused host. My love to you both.

John

Scarborough
December 22nd [1960]

Dear John,

In a burst of sentiment I got the children all lined up in front of the telephone last night, preped them all in how to thank you for the fruit and nuts but nobody answered on Hillside Avenue and I guess you must have been out, repairing the damage done to your social fences by this broken-down bore. Everyone is very grateful, everything made the trip wonderfully and I expect you will get some letters after Christmas. We were late getting into Chicago and by the time I got across town the New York train was loading and I didn't have a chance to call your friend.[10] The train approached New York by a sneaky route and did not come near Harmon but I got a cab at Penn Station—and had him drive me home. At first everyone thought the fruit was a present from Daddy but I told the truth.

This part of the world is buried in snow and very cold. Mary and everybody is fine and grateful to you for keeping Daddy clean. Saks called and accused me of taking the perfume home but I was very sarcastic and I hope Harriet gets the stuff and with my love.[11] I had lunch with Bill Maxwell yesterday and said everything I felt about their payments and have a peace offering in the mail this morning. I take it that the Rome Project fell through and you must put all the blame for this onto me for

10. John had gone back to New York by rail at a time when hogs could cross the country without having to change trains in Chicago but not passengers, no matter how solvent.

11. I had accompanied John to Saks in Beverly Hills, where he bought perfume for Harriett that had not been delivered and an expensive cameo watch for Mary that, as he reported in a subsequent letter, didn't work.

having written such a random and disjointed book.[12] The temptation to return to Hollywood is much stronger here—because of the domestic bills, I guess—than it was there. I will decide on New Year's eve.[13] I will report on what Santa Claus brings and my love to you both.

John

On the Cheevers' Christmas card, under a picture of the snow-covered house on Cedar Lane, to which they would soon be moving, Mary scribbled this note:

[December 1960]

and it's all thanks to
John and Harriet
because John Cheever
couldn't have gone to
Hollywood unless they
had been there to
take care of him!
Love
Mary

The Masters School
Dobbs Ferry, New York

Scarborough
Thursday
[postmarked 31 December 1960]

Dear John,

This pretty paper is accountable to Susie who is so loyal to her new school that she won't use it for anything. I checked in

---

12. An Italian film producer had expressed interest in a letter I'd written Henry Lewis outlining a proposed film treatment of *The Wapshot Chronicle*.

13. Wald had offered him two thousand dollars a week to write the screenplay. He decided not to take the money.

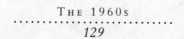

with Lennie yesterday, hoping to find him full of malicious misinformation about my trip but he seemed to have none and we spent most of the time singing the praises of your kindness, your hospitality and the comforts of your guest house. Lennie's show closes on the seventh with half the investment lost but he doesn't seem depressed and I don't think we should worry too much about his bank account. He has put off his trip to Nassau but not because of a cash shortage. I have never felt so at home in Sardi's and talked very loudly about Jerry and Corinne and large sums of money. I don't actually say that I know Howard Hughes and Corinne Griffiths but the story is taking that direction. Mary's watch doesn't work so after lunch I went to Saks to have a bracing little dust-up. The opening gun was fired by a fat lady with lavander eyebrows who looked at the watch with scorn and said: "That's costume jewelry and not returnable." I rallied vigerously and was subdued by a female section manager. She was quite nice and I showed her how when you lift up the lady's face there is a tiny watch and that it is all marked 14 k. She took me to another lady in the precious jewelry department who said you didn't buy that *here* and I said I sure didn't and there was some more sparring so the section manager took me up to the eighth floor where they have a special office for difficult cases. Thank God you urged me to keep the documents because I think they might have washed their hands of the whole thing but it all turned out pleasantly and I went banging up Fifth Avenue, feeling like a grenadier. I'm very sorry I didn't get to fight them over Harriet's perfume and quite hurt that you suspected me of leaving it at Frascati's but one can't be too sensitive, can one?

It all seems worlds away and I guess it is. I've been skating with the children and now we have heavy snow. You can hear chainlinks on the Post Road and if it keeps up at this rate the back roads will be blocked by dark. The closing date for the house is set for January fourth but now it seems there is an error in the title search and there will be another postponement. I will write to Henry as soon as the date for the closing is set and please give him my best. I gave the art book to the Ettlingers and Susie got a guitar instead. Ben hid the peanut butter and can't remember where he put it but we still have oranges and fresh dates.

Love,
John

A handwritten note from twelve-year-old Benjamin Hale Cheever.

January 1, 1961

Dear Mr. and Mrs. Weaver

Thank you ever so much for the peanutbutter. I love it. So does the whole family, as a matter of fact everybody loves it so much I had to hide it where I thought no one would find it and I was lucky enough to find a good place.

We also love all the other fruit and goodies you sent the family we love them all.

Yours truly,
Ben Cheever

Scarborough
Tuesday
[postmarked 3 January 1961]

Dear John,

Our moving date has been postponed again because of an inaccuracy in the title search and God knows when we will make it. Perhaps in another couple of weeks. I was to have seen the lawyer today but Susie got up early this morning and took the car. I had to buy a new car because the old one cost so much to maintain ever since Mary broke the transmission. The new one is whiteish pink like the Falcon.[14] On New Year's we went

14. John had rented a white Falcon in Los Angeles.

to Beechwood because the driving was bad although that's what everyone said. This is something to see. There is a ballroom attached to about half a mile of random parlors. There were about a hundred guests, I guess, most of them about a hundred years old and they stand around looking like old Christmas trees that have lost their needles but not their ornaments. Old Lady Vanderlip sits in a throne chair in the ballroom and practises the meanest game of chopanose I ever saw. She has a wicked and roving eye and claims to be deaf which is nothing but a social ruse. Some people have to wait practically an hour to wish her a happy New Year and then when they get up to her she asks them would they mind stepping into the kitchen and getting a plate of fresh sandwiches. You dance to a phonograph which is operated by a maid and the records are Mr. Vanderlip's favorite records. Mr. Vanderlip died in 1935.[15] I always come in strong and give her a big buss which makes her sputter so that she's off social base long enough to miss the chance of cutting me up the back; but you have to be nimble. I danced a lot and once when I was careening around with Stella Spear[16] I spun her and she commenced to fall backwards. She is not exactly socially ambitious but it wouldn't have done her any good to be stretched out on the ballroom floor. Anyhow when she started to topple I got a good hold on her and ran with her all the way across the ballroom floor until she ended up in a heap on a needlepoint sofa. Then I had to go back and find her shoes which had come off during the Long Glide. It was a lovely party.

Happy New Year,

John

William Weber Johnson was a Time-Life foreign correspondent. His Texas bookseller wife, Liz, was one of the National Book Award fiction judges, who had stood firm for The Wapshot Chronicle.

15. He died in 1937.
16. Stella and Arthur Spear were friends and neighbors.

Scarborough
Wednesday
[postmarked 11 January 1961]

Dear John,

Bill Johnson writes that you have the grippe but are feeling better and I hope this is so. It must be fairly pleasant, lying in bed with the yellow tree in bloom and the city spread out at your feet and I'm sure that Harriet takes very good care of you and does not, like some wives, expect you to go hide in the garage until you feel better. We have the closing for the new house on Friday and I am no longer allowed to answer the telephone after the cocktail hour. This is because the seller called up on Monday night, petulant with drink, and offered to let me have his colored tv rig for ten dollars. I asked if he meant by this that the price of the house would be thirty-seven thousand and ten dollars? He sputtered and his wife could be heard swearing in the background. Then I asked what he would take for the power lawn-mower. He said I couldn't have the power lawn-mower but would I give him five for the tv rig. I skipped this and went on to the aluminum extension ladder and he asked me would I give him fifty cents for the tv rig. It all ended very badly and Mary had to call them back and ask them to dinner so that we will be on speaking terms for the closing. She has also asked the people who have bought the gate-house and I am to pass the crackers and keep my mouth shut.

I wonder how your journal is coming along. I have lost about a hundred pages of the novel and when I go back through my files all I can find is accounts of what I had to eat and drink last year.[17] I think I may have over-documented myself. Also that character with the bit of flounder is still around.[18] I went into the local bookstore today and he [the owner] said: Hello

17. He was working on *The Wapshot Scandal*.

18. As noted in the Introduction, it was on this visit that two of John's code phrases, "Fish Lady" and "Wrinkled Crotch," originated, indicating loneliness and untidiness.

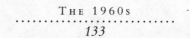

stranger, where have you been? but before I could say anything she was in there asking if he had any valentines. Then I asked him if he had any Peggy Lee[19] records because, etc. but she was right in there again and he didn't hear what I said. I bought a record anyhow and Picci and I play it on the lonely afternoons when Mary goes to New York to buy clothes. My love to Harriet and I hope you feel better.

As ever,
John

Cedar Lane,
Ossining, New York
Wednesday, I think
[postmarked 25 January 1961]

Dear John and Harriet,

Oh my God. First snow on Sunday which meant a post-ponement. Then on Monday the oil burner in the old house went blooey and after having been repaired went blooey again on Tuesday. The vans came on Tuesday and Wednesday and on Wednesday after a big tv lunch and an appalling conversation Mary, Iole, Picci, the dog and I made our final journey. Both the dog and I were so cross that we wouldn't look at anyone. Because of Iole the move was made in two languages and I overheard one of the moving men say it was too bad that wops had bought the Van Cortland Mansion. By Wednesday dusk the library was in operation with its pilasters, 18th century engrav-ings, rich turkey carpets, polite guests, crystal goblets gleaming with Jack Daniels, walls of books and its runty, snaggle-toothed and shook-up host seemed very gracious but did you ever want a library with pilasters?[20] I must have wanted one so why should

19. John had met her at a Hollywood party.
20. "The house is really one of the most beautiful and various domi-ciles I have ever seen," John wrote Peter Blume, "but sitting in the library which has pilasters, I feel very much a bum and think that what I would like most to do is grow a long beard and recite dirty poetry in my underwear at the YMHA. This revery alternates with an imaginery evening party in which

the charming room fill me with such galling indifference? It may be a touch of stir-madness or the fact that my interest in re-arranging furniture is terribly limited. The snow began to fall on Thursday and we are still half-buried and the cold seems like a wall.

The house is beautiful and was a steal at the price. I will feel better when the weather is more clement. I spend most of the time shoveling snow. First I shoveled the outside stairways and paths and terraces and roofs and yesterday I just shoveled random paths all over the place for the pleasure there is in it. I burrow until dusk when the north wind rises and I hit the bar. But soon, as I often tell myself, the valley will be a bowl of grass and flowers, birds in the trees, carp in the ponds, etc. . . .

Affectionately,
John

Cedar Lane,
Ossining
Tuesday
[February 1961]

Dear John,

Zowie. First of all there was the dolorous, the ancient, the Russian cold. Night after night it was ten below which is much colder than this part of the world has been for nearly a century. Half the cars in Westchester wouldn't start, the trains ran late if they ran at all and the kind of jollity one finds in Dickens and Tolstoy when the mercury hits bottom seems to have been lost to the national personality. Everyone was cross. At dusk on Friday it seemed a little warmer—one's nose-hair didn't crisp—and at dusk it began to snow and snowed for thirty hours. It fell so heavily that even in the dark it seemed luminous and when I went to bed on Friday all our paths and drives, our car, our

---

I say things like: President de Gaulle may I present my old friend Peter Blume? However the house is for Mary and the children and I expect that I will someday get used to so much charm."

garbage pails and our yew hedges were buried. On Saturday I dug a path to the gate-cottage and asked them to come down and drink champagne which they did. Sunday was brilliant and so is today but the darkness of the storm was something to live through. It is the time of the wolf, says Iole.

I've lost the Paxton's address and could you send it on again so that when I do go to Harpers I can mail them a book.[21] Also on some idle afternoon could you send me a list of the names and addresses of your friends who might like a copy of the new book. I'll have copies in a month.[22] The house is so comfortable and we are all well.

John

Cedar Lane,
Washington's Birthday [1961]

Dear John,

I am out of paper which accounts for this blue. Many thanks for sending on the addresses and what happy people they will all be. Harpers has begun that charming series of blunders that attends publication. Caskie's new throwaway came to me heavily scented with after-shave lotion and I think this is unfair competition.[23] How Cerf will run with that ball.[24] BANISH UGLY

21. John Paxton, a Kansas City high school classmate of Harriett's, was a carpenter, bricklayer, plumber, electrician, and horticulturist whose high-priced screenplays *(Farewell My Lovely, Crossfire, On the Beach)* enabled him to spend most of his time working on his never-quite-finished Laurel Canyon home.

22. *Some People, Places, and Things That Will Not Appear in My Next Novel.*

23. "It beats hell out of me what Cheever was writing about when he said *Speaking of Holiday* was heavily scented with after-shave lotion," Stinnett said when I showed him this letter, and, tongue in cheek, went on to add: "If Cheever were not so widely known as a temperate man, I would say that perhaps he had a little gin on his breath."

24. John's low opinion of Bennett Cerf goes back to at least 1944, when he remarked over bagels and coffee at Borden's that at dinner the night before Cerf had mentioned his projected "novelization" of a radio program. For this he had let William Faulkner go out of print.

AND DISTASTEFUL HOUSEHOLD ODORS WHILE READING THE NEW NOVEL BY EUDORA WELTY. THIS TANGY AND AUTHENTIC AC-COUNT OF INTERNATIONAL WHIPPING SOCIETIES IS EXCITINGLY PERFUMED. The snow is melting and on Thursday Ben and I shoveled a path to the front door. We had our first week-end guest on Friday. Both boys pumped ship at 3:45 AM. They thump down the stairs, then don't close the door, then don't flush the toilet and half the time they don't hit the pot. I hope this situation will improve before you come to stay with us. A painter is now working in the dinning room and a well-digger has promised to come on Monday. I thought your piece in Holiday looked very well and did a great deal to raise the tone of the magazine.[25] Bruce Catton (I thought) had it down under the radiator. I am having one hell of a time getting back with the novel. I don't seem able to rewrite the section I lost and the rest of it looks like junk. Mary is very happy bumbling around the house and on Sunday night it was warm enough for us to have a window open so we could hear the brook. It is all very nice although I still stand around the place like a fool, pretending never to have seen it before.

As ever,

John

Harry Sions, my Holiday *editor, had come to California to promote a San Francisco issue which contained an article I'd written about a popular night club, the hungry i. When Harry ran low on clean shirts we lent him one that John had left behind.*

25. I had just started writing for *Holiday* and so enjoyed my working relationship with editors Ted Patrick and Harry Sions that this article, "A Capsule History of the Movies," was the first of eight pieces to appear in the magazine that year.

Cedar Lane,
Tuesday
[postmarked 28 February 1961]

Dear John,

Harry Sions sent back the shirt but I am worried about what he did for clean socks and underwear during his stay. I hope he didn't go up to San Francisco in dirty underwear. Do you think I should write him? I knew I should have left the Stretchsox and the Stretchpants I bought at the Thrifty [Drug Store]. I liked your piece on the i very much.

Worriedly,
John

Cedar Lane,
Friday
[postmarked 10 March 1961]

Dear John,

. . . We still have a lingering winter here; another worry. On Wednesday dusk it began to snow and by Thursday morning our driveway was closed again. It melted a little yesterday but today is somber and cold. I have bought a great deal more land than I knew including a thick forest, choked with honeysuckle and dying elms so in the late afternoon now Ben and I spend our time cutting down trees and splitting wood for the fireplace. It is a lot more fun than writing and as for that it is only a question of time before the barking of little foxes and the honking of wild geese begins to louse up my prose.

Mary's step-sister came to look us over on Tuesday. She is an angular young woman with splayed hands, three gold bracelets, a St. Timothy accent and a pitiless laugh, ranging from C sharp to G sharp above C. "It's simply divine," she said. "Of course it looks awfully restauranty, doesn't it, it's the kind of place they're always turning into restaurants, but it is charming. I mean the library is so *small*. I don't suppose you *see* anyone anymore but then I don't suppose you care, you must be busy with the housework." She's the first to make it. My own adjustment comes along slowly. At dusk, lame from wood-cutting, I stand at the long window with a glass of gin, watching the brook course among the laurels and listening to the barking of foxes and the honking of wild geese.

Mary says that I am getting very coarse in my middle-age and that I use words like fart all the time so I have promised not to use the word fart for the rest of Lent. Did I tell you that Harpers was planning to bring the book out here on the tenth and west of Chicago on the 28th, thus cutting down sales on a nation-wide scale. Those farts.

Best,
John

Friday

Dear John,

. . . It snowed last night. Susie is home for her vacation and she is overweight and I am not very nice to her. She has just heard about the House Unamerican Activities Committee and she gets all red in the face and pokes me in the ribs with her finger and asks me what I am going to do about it.

Best,
John

Cedar Lane,
Ossining
Tuesday
[postmarked 15 May 1961]

Dear John,

Mary has mis-laid the spading fork and I have a few minutes at the typewriter. How strange it seems to hit these little keys with my knarled fingers. We have, it seems, three acres of tapis vert, fifty fruit trees, a dark forest, and five gardens and I run around the place all day long. However it's really very pleasant. The house has stairs like a magician's card-shuffle. They fall from the boy's room down to the library, from the library to the guest-room, from the guest-room to the dinning room and there are as many stairs outside as there are in, connecting the gardens and the terraces. There are dark halls and light ones, high-ceilinged and low rooms, a droopy balcony off our bedroom and an attic full of mice. I couldn't have imagined anything better. I got Ben a shot-gun for his birthday and now in the evenings I sit on the gallery banging away at the rats who live at the edge of the duck-pond. I've nicked the ducks twice and blasted a hole through the flowering quince but it keeps the neighbors away.

Mary isn't speaking to me. On Sunday she sang some Handel with something called the Ossining Music Guild and then invited about fifteen members of the chorus back for drinks. There was a steam-fitter, the wife of the dentist, a customs inspector, a plumber, a veterinarian, etc. and I got quite icy. One of the guests introduced himself as Mr. DeWitt. "My name's really LeBlanc," he said. "I'm descended from the Kings of France. You know about them. When Richlieu killed Louis the fourteenth my family went to Holland and changed their name to DeWitt. It means white. LeBlanc. DeWitt." They drank four quarts of whisky, broke the glasses and spilled the ash-trays and I finally took Mary into the pantry and told her if she didn't get them the hell out of the house I was going to load up the shot-gun. As it happened the pantry door was open and they could all hear me so that Mary didn't have to say anything but she hasn't said much of anything since then. Here she comes with the spading fork and I'll get back to work.

Best,
John

In the early spring when Harriett and I were planning a research trip to Las Vegas for Holiday *one of the editors called to ask me to write something to accompany a sheaf of Santa Barbara photographs the art department had in inventory. Instead of sending back a casual, somewhat jaundiced essay on the antics of the rich, as I'd planned and as the editors expected, I submitted a sobering report on the John Birch Society, a right-wing phenomenon that had gone unmentioned in the nation's magazines and newspapers, other than the* Santa Barbara News-Press. *The* Holiday *editors (and their lawyers) were incredulous. Why hadn't they read about this in* The New York Times?

Cedar Lane
[postmarked 14 June 1961]

Dear John,

I liked the Santa Barbara piece very much and have heard a great deal of talk about it here. And I was happy to see that Holiday advertised it. I'm not always sure that they know what they're doing but they seem, in this case, quite clear in the head. Getting in a piece a month must be a task but I think it's great for Holiday.

Wednesday was the institute lunch and it was awful. I was in charge of John Knowles who said: "I never dreamed I'd take a leak with Robert Graves and Frederick March." Graves made a speech on traditional values and was an awful bore. In giving an award to Mark Harris Glenway said: "You have made a *game* of the sport and a sport of the *game!*" Lillian Hellman walked out. John Ciardi fell asleep. Leonard Bernstein kissed Sid Perelman. I kissed Mrs. Edward Stone. Mary asked Edward Stone what he did. Carl VanVechten wore two hearing aids. We had roast beef.

I often wish Harriet were here. I put 150 pounds of Sakrets in the pond walls on Saturday and came away with lacerated hands coated with some kind of adhesive that is just beginning to wear off. Then I tried to cook hamburgers the way Harriet does but I put about an inch of salt in the pan which I guess was too much because they were awful. I also rented an electric floor-waxer which ran away with me and made a hole in the wainscoting. Susie has a job at Macys.

Best,
John

On a trip to Montana for Holiday *I not only flushed a herd of antelope on a back-country road but also checked out a chandelier*

in a Miles City brothel that a traveling salesman had told me about.
On our last night in town when Harriett and I were dining with a
local official and his wife, I mentioned the chandelier and he asked if
I'd like to see it. "My research would otherwise be incomplete," I
said. On the way back to our motel, our host pulled up in front of
what seemed a large, pleasant, middle-class home. He and I went
inside, had a drink, admired the chandelier, and left rather hurriedly
when a customer came in and whispered something to our middle-
aged hostess who called out to her clients, "Any you fellows got
wives in a car out there?"

JOHN CHEEVER
Cedar Lane,
Ossining, N.Y.

Cedar Lane
Friday
[postmarked 30 June 1961]

Dear John,

Oh God, here I sit, listening to the barking of rabid little foxes and swatting the deer-flies after scything the north orchard and the jewel-weed in the meadow and most of the writing I do these days is little lists like ask Mrs. Briant for a load of horse-shit and take in the strawberry crop before dew-fall and tune the piano and bury the dead ducks and shoot the pit-viper in the petunia bed and all the time you go around drinking with whores and counting antelopes and chatting with Buddy Hackett and Michael Arlen.[26] That name does ring a bell. Also I seem suddenly by times fell hand besmote. I lost a clutch of back teeth last week and right after this I thought my prose style had gotten as fuzzy as Waldo Frank's. I was about to hang myself when

26. I had run into Michael J. Arlen, a writer whose work I enjoyed (I had also enjoyed meeting Iris March in his father's novel, *The Green Hat*), at a backlot dinner given by Warner Bros. for a gaggle of visiting journalists. Buddy Hackett was one of the entertainers.

Mary suggested I try on spectacles and sure enough fifty percent magnification seemed to take much of the mould and ear-whiskers off the verbs.

But we take it off the pad from time to time and hot it up. We went for instance to my publishers for dinner. He lives over a ridge in Bedford in a large copy of a Palladian villa. They have 46 head of Hereford show cattle and I got one of the maids (3) giggling when I asked them what they did with the milk. They also had a family of white swans, seen at a bend in the distant stream through a pair of one hundred dollar binoculars that he bought in Tokio when he was last there distributing rubber goods. Everything was wet and grand and when the old fox saw by the look in my eye that I was recalling my last royalty statement he drew me aside and said that the house, the maids, the cows, etc. all belonged to his wife. Jack Fisher[27] who was there wrote Mary a note, asking her to lunch with him in New York and continue their interesting discussion on Angola. I spoke almost entirely in iambic pentameter and we had pigeons to eat.

Susie has her working papers, thank God and goes off to Macy's on Monday at fifty a week. She enters college in September and her room will then be yours.

As ever,

John

On one of our strolls along the Sunset Strip, John had described the nine-tenths-mile stretch of county turf linking Hollywood and Beverly Hills as "the ultimate in a motel civilization." In my Holiday article I attributed the remark to "a New England novelist." Slim Aarons, on assignment in Biarritz, had photographed the Comte de Paris with his wife and two daughters at the Grand Ball in the Hotel du Palais for the same issue.

27. Editor of *Harper's* magazine.

Cedar Lane
Ossining, New York
Saturday
[postmarked 22 July 1961]

Dear John,

I just got the Strip piece and I liked it very much with the exception of the pungent observations of that wet-smack New England novelist. What a gloomy sonofabitch he must be to go sniffing around through so much glamor to find a dun. I wish they'd run photographs but I guess the customers prefer the Comte de Paris. It made me quite homesick.

I cannot work much because people keep interrupting me. "I don't want to disturb you," Mary says, "but I think there must be a fire in the attic." Yesterday noon Ben knocked gently on my door and when I asked him angrily what he wanted he said he'd got his prick stuck in a zipper. I gave the zipper a yank and he let out such a howl that I nearly fainted. The dog began to bark and Picci ran around in circles, wringing his hands and saying, "No Mummy here, no Mummy here." Mummy was in the super-market. I called our doctor but he was out sailing and then I came at Ben with the rose shears, planning to cut off his trousers. He pointed out that even without his trousers his prick would still be caught in the zipper. Then I called the hospital but before I got through to the resident Ben had liberated himself. It's all part of the rich bulk of human experience, I suppose, but I don't seem able to work it into the novel.

As ever,
John

[postmarked 15 September 1961]

Dear John,

I had lunch with Lennie on Tuesday who said you were coming east on the 20th and that you were working on a very tight schedule. We have no plans and any dates that will fit into your schedule will be fine with us. I do sometimes worry about the condition of the house. I sometimes remember the horror

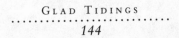

with which Harriet looked into the chaos of my suitcase and I hope she won't think of the house as a sort of suitcase. The linolium is threadbare, there is a big hole in the dinning room rug and some of the wall-paper is stained and peeling but the house, for all its infirmities, is 18th century and given a little gin and a clear evening I find this a solid pleasure in itself.

Susie went off to college[28] on Sunday, taking an enormous bite out of the bank account. We were both quite excited when she registered, but for very different reasons. I slog away at the novel but very slowly and Mary is about to teach freshman English at a junior college in the neighborhood.[29] We all look forward very much to seeing you both and since you must be pressed for time don't bother to write but call us when you know your plans.

As ever,

John

On our visit to New York we had looked in on the Peppermint Lounge at the height of the Twist craze. Around 2:30 A.M. we dropped John off at the Royalton Hotel. He had an appointment later that morning with the Chelsea dentist we had both patronized during the war.

[postmarked 4 November 1961]

Dear John,

Now that you're back in the hills things have quieted down although I still spring to my feet when I hear any loud music in 4/4 time and start twitching my pelvis. When I woke up on Thursday morning in the Royalton I couldn't figure out where the hell I was. It was awful. Of course it was dark. Anyhow I got dressed and went down to Freedman's where a brutal attack was made on my exposed roots . . . Then I went across the street and got a drink and took the next train home but Mary wasn't

28. Pembroke.
29. Briarcliff.

terribly interested in my demonstration of the Twist. "I'm just slamming the door in your face," she said, "so that the smell of cooking won't go all through the house."

> as ever,
> John

We were not threatened by the Bel-Air fire, which broke out November 6.

Cedar Lane
Friday
[postmarked 11 November 1961]

Dear John,

I hope you are allright. I've been going around wringing my hands and studying the fire-map in The Times. It would seem from the maps that you are all right; but it must have been something to live through. I remember Harriet saying she had come to regard fires calmly although I cannot imagine anxiety so easily mastered. Every cloud has it's silver linning and what a blessing it was that I wasn't in the guest room, looting the whisky stores, generating worry and getting under everybody's feet.

> As ever,
> John

The Bel-Air fire swept through Stone Canyon, where our friends Bob and Mary Jane Carson lived. When the alarm sounded they left their new Manza in the garage and took off in their utility car to deliver their cat, Woodley, into the safekeeping of his vet. Heading back home to pick up the Manza and, among other things, the MS. of an almost completed novel, they were turned away by a police cordon. They repaired to Perino's, the city's most distinguished restaurant, and after a leisurely luncheon (with, Bob assured us later, "an appropriate wine"), they dropped in on us. We spent the evening watching the progress of the fire on television.

It was not a "nice fire." It destroyed 484 homes, many of which represented the life savings of middle-class professional families who lived from one paycheck to another. John's adjective sprang from a satirical letter I wrote him at the time. A paragraph survives in an excerpt from a copy of my letter, which fell into the hands of a Saturday Review columnist: "The big fire must, I'm sure, rank as one of the most chic disasters in American history. Refugees at noon were streaming into Perino's and the Polo Lounge in charred Jaguars. The Red Cross set up emergency shelters in Brentwood with army blankets and Campbell's soup, but by then the homeless had taken over Chasen's and La Rue. Next morning their butlers were making their way through the police lines to the fire area, checking wine cellars."

Cedar Lane
Friday
[postmarked 17 November 1961]

Dear John,

I was just sitting around thinking about Harriet's legs when I got your letter about the fire and I'm glad it was such a nice fire. I had worried about the Carson's although I did not know they had a Manza. I wonder if they had one when I was there. We are all well except that I get a lot of letters from ladies telling me not to be so *sad* and *bitter*. If they only knew, as you and Harriet do, what a sunny person I am. Mary had a very bad experience on Friday. She wanted to get some special meat and so she and Iole went to a butcher who speaks Italian. She wore a hat and gloves and everything because Iole is very particular about how her signora looks. Anyhow they were chatting elegantly in Italian and poking their fingers into the sweet-breads and so forth when the head butcher said: "Cut the talk, for Christs sake and give them the fifty-five cent hamburger. They's no meat where they come from. They're just a couplea greenhorns off the boat." Iole didn't understand but Mary was very upset. She kept going around the house saying I'm not just off the boat. The meat was for the Penn Warrens and he talked all about Twelfth Night after figuring out that I had forgotten the play. Also Alan Moorehead was here but he had to go to

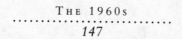

Ketchum and see Mary Hemingway. I had lunch at the club on Wednesday and one drunken old man on crutches called to another drunken old man in a wheel-chair: "Hail, blithe spirit."[30]

My best to you both on Thanksgiving.

As ever,

John

In his collection of his father's letters, Benjamin Cheever clarifies John's dispute with Bill Maxwell over "The Brigadier and the Golf Widow." "Bill told me that the story had two endings. He said he tried a cut to see how that worked. My father was in the city that day, visiting the offices of The New Yorker, *and he saw the truncated story on a desk and assumed that it had been drastically changed without his permission. At first my father thought that he could go along with the change, but he phoned Bill in a fury that night and the story was run at full length."*

An olive-branch note to Maxwell explained John's reference to Salinger. "It was merely the coincidence, providential as I see it now, of reading a piece in which Salinger was compared to Blake, Beethoven and Shakespeare a half hour after my own judgments and gifts had been seriously challenged. I admire Salinger, of course, and I think I know where his giftedness lies and how rare it is. Another reason for my irritability is the fact that I am never content with my own work; that it never quite comes up to the world as I see it. This is not to say that I despair of succeeding; I think I may—but I am touchy."

[postmarked 5 December 1961]

Dear John,

I'm very glad you liked the story and there was a story within the story. When I went in to correct galleys I found that the story had been cut in half and was told that Mr. Shawn

---

30. One day when John and I were lunching at the Century Club he commented on the long waiting period for applicants. "Our members," he explained, "are not dying off at a satisfactory rate."

wanted it this way. I saw trouble ahead and told Bill I'd meet him at the club in half an hour and had a couple of drinks. I kept the conversation, during lunch, on the subject of his wife and children but when we said goodbye he asked about the cut. "Do anything you want," I said and walked over to the station where I bought a copy of Life in which J. D. Salinger was compared to William Blake, Ludwig von Beethoven and William Shakespeare. I went into a slow burn which didn't erupt until nine that evening when I telephoned Bill who happened to be entertaining Elizabeth Bowen and Eudora Welty. "You cut that story," I yelled, "and I'll never write another story for you or anybody else. You can get that Godamned sixth-rate Salinger to write your Godamned short stories but don't expect anything more from me. If you want to slam a door on somebody's genitals find yourself another victim. Etc." Anyhow the magazine had gone to press and they had to remake the whole book and stay up all night but they ran it without the cut.

We went to the Biddles for lunch yesterday and Helene nearly had a fist fight with the butler. When he passed the coffee he forgot the sugar and so she rang and asked him angrily to bring some sugar. So then he brought in a tarnished silver sugar bowl that turned out not to have anything in it but a couple of mouse turds. So then she hit the buzzer hard and he sailed through the swinging door all red in the face and they had a tug of war with the sugar bowl and if I hadn't come between them I think it would have been an interesting match. And after that we went to Jack Kahn's birthday party where I kissed, nose-rubbed and otherwise gentled at least twenty-five ladies and I wonder if this is a bad trait. Ask Harriet. They danced the Twist but I didn't stay. And also tell Harriet that I bought a chain saw. It cost one hundred and sixty-eight dollars. I love it. So does Ben.

Best,

John

A handwritten note on a UNICEF Christmas card.

Dear John and Harriet:

> Mary says that I should
> write you a note not
> knowing that writing notes
> to you is one of my
> principle occupations.

> Merry Christmas
> John and Mary

[postmarked 26 January 1962]

Dear John,

It's been so long since I've heard from you that I wonder how and where you are. The Times this morning says that there was snow on Sunset Strip and so naturally I'm worried . . . I think I may write a piece about my trip across country on a train; all about how I fell down the stairs from the Vistadome and had an erection all across New Mexico and the unfriendly Indian Chief and the lady with pin curls in her hair who ran away when I asked her to join me in an aperitif and the biography of Cranmer and the seizures of melancholy, elation and despair that swept over me as we approached Chicago. Everything. Also Caskie cut me off from the free list after my remarks about Salinger and I don't know if you're keeping up your monthly average.[31] I don't even get Speaking of Holiday anymore.

The Ettlingers came for Christmas lunch. They pulled up in a Lancia and had so many expensive presents that they had to make several trips from the car. We gave them simple things we had made such as apple jelly and pen-wipers. It was very picturesque and extremely pleasant. They seemed in very high spirits.

---

31. Rushing to Salinger's defense in the September 1961 issue of *Speaking of Holiday*, Stinnett aligned himself with "the several hundred thousand other people who think he is perhaps the possessor of the greatest literary talent in the United States today."

I didn't get to say good-bye to Lennie who I now expect is in Asia and I do miss him. Tell Harriet that I am afraid of my chain-saw. When delicate and impressionable guests are calling I'm a regular bull with the engine but when I'm all alone in the woods with the Godamned thing it's a very different story.

As ever,

John

A Hollywood press agent had invited Harriett and me to take a look at Liberace's new digs, providing I promised not to publish my impressions. Next day I not only wrote John, but also my Holiday *editor, Harry Sions. He showed the letter to Caskie Stinnett, who slipped it into* Speaking of Holiday, *where it was picked up by gossip columnists across the country. It was some years before I was back in the press agent's good graces.*

"Everything in Liberace's house is shaped like a piano or Liberace or both," I wrote. "Our host greeted us at the door in a sequin-studded sports jacket, and Harriett was asked to remove her shoes, as the other women had done. She was then given a pair of gold-mesh slippers, with sequins. This was a thoughtful touch Liberace came up with when a woman complained some weeks ago that his carpeting, although beautiful, was treacherous to high heels. The carpeting was woven from a special design in Mexico by forty women who worked around the clock and, on completing the assignment, were put to death under an international trade agreement.

"Martini in hand, we made a tour of the twenty-eight rooms, nine of which are dining rooms and all of which are filled with pictures, busts, bas-reliefs, medallions, etc., featuring the Liberace profile. In the master bedroom, where the bed is placed on a dais, there is a large silver head of Liberace just above the master pillows in case he wakes up and forgets what he looks like. Curiously enough, the busts of Chopin, Beethoven and Bach—even the pre-Columbian fertility gods—all manage to look like Liberace.

"We came downstairs, penetrated a forest of drunken columnists, disk jockeys and candelabra, put our empty glasses down on a shelf in front of a picture of Liberace's Mom, watched a photographer take a

picture of Jimmy Durante hugging two pretty girls, watched Mrs. Du-
rante look at her wristwatch and tell Jimmy it was time to go home,
chatted with a young actor and his wife, noticed that the hi-fi was shaped
like a piano, shook hands with our host, noticed that he surely brushes
after every meal, and left. Our car was delivered by a parking attendant
who looked like Liberace."

[postmarked 14 February 1962]

Dear John,

That was a wonderful letter about Liberace and we both
felt right in the swim. We never go any place where they give
you shoes. Mostly we lose things like rubbers, scarves, gloves
and hockey sticks. And we go out mostly to little dinners to
meet Aldous Huxley's niece or to anniversary and birthday
parties. The Kahns had one last Sunday—skating, cocktails and
dinner. A surprising amount of hooky-tooky went on. I mean
feeling and all and serious versions of the Twist and he said: Just
pretend you're wiping your arse, dear. What he meant to say, of
course, was: Just pretend you're drying your arse. People were
French-kissing all over the place. Old people. Before that we
had Jean Douglas for lunch. She is Salinger's mother-in-law.
"I'm very pleased to meet you," George Biddle said. "I haven't
read Franny and Zooey yet but I've read everything else she's
written." I took George to the end of the room and told him
Salinger was a man. "Well," said George crossly, "I've never
before heard of a man named Hortense." Jean is a friend of Bill's;
and could you send me Bill's address.[32] I think I will go to Rome
in March and I would like to see him.

I think I will go to Rome because I can stay at the Academy
free, the plane fare is low and if I don't get away from here
before the place starts to bloom I won't get away at all. I will go
for two weeks but I will have to wait until the snow falls are

32. Jean Douglas, at the time the Cheevers met her in Rome, was the
wife of an art historian, Langton Douglas. Bill remembers her as "an enjoy-
able, attractive woman, a good hostess."

over. We had a heavy fall on Friday and have a good two feet this morning. You can't get out of the place.

    Best,
        John

                            [postmarked 2 March 1962]
Dear John,

    . . . I still don't know about Rome; I don't know if they'll be any scratch in the sugar-bowl at the end of the week. I think I should get away, because as I tell Mary, scrutiny is my principle occupation and if I don't have anybody to scrutinize but she and the boys I may destroy them. However we have had snow almost every third day of this month and I don't like to leave them with the driveways blocked and the roof groaning under its lovely burden of whiteness. I enjoyed your account of the Roman movie very much because Mother and I can't get to the movies anymore and I liked all that about how he probed her in the Dolomites and Mother and I could imagine the background scenery and all.

    Best,
        John

I had rented an apartment in Washington and set to work expanding my Holiday *article, "The Unglorified Civil Servant," into a book,* The Great Experiment *(Little, Brown 1965).*

                                  Cedar Lane
                        Ossining, New York
              [postmarked 2 May 1962]
Dear John,

    I wrote you first to the hotel address in Washington. Then Lennie called and gave me an apartment address on S Street. I threw away the first letter and wrote a second which was returned to me and now I don't know where the hell you are. We're delighted to know you're somewhere in the east and I do hope you can get out here for a visit. We would love to have you both here anytime and for any length of time. I don't expect you'll be content to sit by the fire listening to me tell about how the clutch went [out] on the chain-saw and about the night I knocked the rim off my child-like sense of wonder. They both went to the shop. I got my child-like sense of wonder back on Thursday but the clutch is still on the bench.

I didn't go to Rome at all; I went instead to a place called Casey Key on the Gulf of Mexico and that was very nice. It has been very hot and cold here and I expect the same in Washington. The wild foxes bark a lot at night and on Saturday a flock of geese went over due south but half an hour later they turned around and flew back due north. They honked both ways. I hope this reaches you and please write and tell me where you are.

As ever,
John

Cedar Lane
Ossining, New York
Friday.
[postmarked 12 June 1962]

Dear John,

It sounds like a wonderful idea for a book and I can't think of anyone better equipped to manage it. I will be very interested in seeing what you do with what always seemed to me to be the surrogate essence of that city. It was, God knows, a long time ago but when I was there I seemed to see manifest power everywhere and never power incarnate. I was a hall bedroom boy and went everywhere but what I remember most keenly was the sense, on my way to some third-rate party, of an especial aloneness in the streets; the first taste of the nomadism I felt so strongly on bad nights on the strip. I was, as you can see, a broody clerk. I got a bad case of crabs from a girl who worked in the archives and who was saving all her money to get her buck-teeth capped. She was a nice girl, the daughter of a small town ward-heeler, one of the legions, but I never felt the same about the archives and anyhow she told me they were full of silverfish. I was much under the influence of Fitzgerald and used to ask cab-drivers to tie my black tie. I thought that was very good. But what I remember mostly, I think, is the city always seemed surrogate[33] and that I first got in it's streets a whiff of that enormous disenchantment that hangs in the streets of most modern cities. Amen.

Summer is in full spate here and it is lovely. Irwin [Shaw] came for lunch and said that we both had got what we wanted: i.e. I got a picturesque old dump and he got a Swiss chalet and a taxfree two million in Geneva.[34] We have all kinds of excitement. George Biddle presented us yesterday with a large Muscovy duck. It is as big as a big swan. As soon as the duck hit the pond the young retriever hit the duck and Ben dove in, fully dressed, and hit the retriever. Then all three of them commenced to go around and around in the water quacking, barking and hollering. I got Ben and the dog out and mixed myself a strong martini although it was only eleven thirty.[35] Lennie seemed fine and said his Thing was all better.[36]

As ever,

John

33. As a State Department poet, Ernest Kroll, expressed it at the time:

How shall you act the natural man in this
Invented city, neither Rome nor home?

34. "I admire and perhaps love Irwin," John wrote in his journal, "but he is so rich and has dined so often with the Duke of Argyle and I am so poor that these differences come between us."

35. "Duck Biddle is well," John later wrote the Biddles from "Cedar Pond." "He seems sage, sentimental, I think, and has a fine grasp of his own limitations. Now and then a wild goose comes to visit. I go down late each afternoon to feed him. He approaches me making a harsh, barking noise like a bronchitic dog and attacks his corn a little like the late Harry Cohen, president of Columbia Pictures. I mean he is not a neat feeder. Then I talk with him for awhile and he walks me part of the way back to the house where we part. He is a very pleasant companion."

36. Lennie was the first of our Astoria luncheon group to be hit by the prostate's reminder of our advancing years.

Cedar Lane, etc.

[postmarked 13 August 1962]

Dear John,

I was very pleased to see your piece on Montana[37] and it seems to me that as always you do a good deal to pick up the tone of that magazine. All is moderately well here although there seems to be no news. We dined with the Ettlingers about a month ago and it was like stepping into the crucial chapters of some extraordinary success story. They are all rich, happy, well-fed, well-staffed, well-dressed and enthusiastically at peace with the world. Don loves his program.[38] Katrina loves Don. The dogs and cats lie in one another's arms amongst the roses.

Mary and the children went to the mountains three weeks ago and Susie is now in Nantucket, leaving me alone with the old dog in this picturesque dump. I've done a lot of work but I do miss having a female around. The novel moves but there is still so much to be done that I feel like a dog worrying a corpse. I shall go to Saratoga as soon as Mary returns and see if I can finish it there. I've had a lot of people in and dined out a lot but it all seems less of a pleasure than a hedge against loneliness.

Give my love to Harriet and a nod to the lights of the city.

As ever,

John

Wednesday

[postmarked 11 October 1962]

Dear John,

I had lunch with Lennie on Tuesday and he reported that his thing was all better. We went to the Biltmore after lunch to leech out the martinis and I got a look at Lennie's thing. It looks the same. On Sunday we went to lunch with the Ettlingers and they seem, enthusiastically to be carrying on their success story. The sponsors love Don. Don loves the show. Katrina loves Don.

37. In the September issue of *Holiday*.
38. A daytime television series, *Love of Life*.

Money rains down gently upon the household and all the guests come in Lancias, Jaguars and Mercedes-Benzes.

I went up to Yaddo on the first of the month to see if I could finish the novel but I didn't and last night I dreamed I was a Good Humor man, ringing a small bell and urging people to try the seven flavors of discouragement. There are, between you and me, more than seven. I thought I had the novel up in the air but I was mistaken. Mary is teaching now and Ben's dog Flora goes off to hunting school on Friday which leaves me alone with the cat. Saturday is Father-Daughter weekend at Susie's college the high point of which will be a Charleston contest and then on Tuesday I will mooch out to the University of Indiana and give a reading. I have never given a reading before but I know what will happen. First I will drink a lot of cocktails to give me nerve for the performance. Then I will have dinner with three deans and their wives and drink a lot of coffee to tone down the drinks. Then half-way through the introduction I will remember that I forgot to piss. I will approach the lectern in a glide-step, squirm through the first story, jig through the second, and positively jump up and down during the third when I will call an unscheduled intermission and streak for the can. I will be talked about in Bloomington for years.

I think of you often and often wish I were standing on your terrace, smelling shell-fish and admiring the lights of the city. My love to Harriet.

Best,

John

[postmarked 3 January 1963]

Dear John,

It was very good to hear from you and I haven't written sooner because there seems almost nothing to report except that the wind came round from the NNW and that the light was exceptionally brilliant. The ground is covered with snow, the temperature is below zero, the pond is frozen and a fox killed the drake. My humble Christmas present to Mary was to paint the kitchen. This is a big room with five doors, four windows and many cabinets. It took almost a week and I decided to give myself a vacation and put cow-manure on the peony hedge. I spent an afternoon at this, thinking what a lucky chap I was to have so many cowflops. This seemed to imply some kind of bind so I went to New York and had lunch with Lennie. It is all very much like this.

Christmas had it's charms although sitting at the breakfast table, arsedeep in wrapping paper and watching a battery operated plush dinosaur push it's way amongst the unpaid for cashmere sweaters and Irish tweeds gave me a distinctly new sensation. We went to the Ettlingers for lunch who were deluxe, fragrant and golden-hearted. The Kahns gave us a brace of tinned pheasant. We retagged the tin and sent it to the Wilsons who sent it to the Lowes who sent it to the Larsens who rushed it to the Boyers who got it back to the Kahns within twenty-four hours. I don't think we've got all the bugs out of it but I see somewhere on the horizon a solution for that holiday.

We are all delighted with your presidency[39] and want you to know that we are all with you in spirit every minute of the day although I wish to hell I knew what the subdividers had in mind and would appreciate it if you would send on some literature. Now I will dispose of the drake, bring in the apple-wood, lay the fires and sand the driveway. Picci is delighted at the thought of a new year and I hope he is right; he usually is.

Love,
John

Until Harriett totted up the expense involved, we had been thinking of moving to a house with a pool or at least with room for one, because of my need for a regimen of daily exercise.

39. I attended meetings of the Federation of Hillside & Canyon Homeowners Association to support Harriett, who was its fire, flood, and landslide expert. Somehow (I must have missed the meeting at which the vote was taken) I had become its president.

Dear John,

I'm very happy to hear you are not going to move. When I cannot sleep at night I imagine that I am 1. fishing a trout stream, 2. skiing a mountain, 3. having dinner with the Weavers above the lights of the city and if you should move to some place I have never seen it would sure fuck up my raveled sleeve of care. Henry is not quite right about the end of the novel being in sight. The end of the novel is completed. So is the beginning. But the middle, aiie, aiie. The middle is wreckage. On the Metamophoses I don't think there are any author's galleys. I wrote them last summer. The New Yorker sprinkled the text with commas and deleted a reference to the scantness of Hermes' fig-leaf but I think that was all. If it seemed disinfected to you the fault would be mine. They did schedule and pull it several times in favor, I suspect, of O'Hara pieces.

The maid stole three of Mary's Plaid Stamp boxes, just the day before Mary was going to White Plains to get her Waring Mixer. I bet that would have made Harriet mad. It made Mary very angry. Lennie appears to be back from Algiers briefly but I haven't seen him and probably won't. This is the time of year when I split the firewood and redistribute the cowflops.

As ever,

John

Harriett had inherited some blue-chip stocks from an uncle.

Cedar Lane
Thursday
[postmarked 2 May 1963]

Dear John,

I'm delighted to know that Harriet has a boodle. I'm sure she will be very nice about it. Mary got a sort of boodle when her grandmother died but I would not describe her conduct as nice. She pretends that she doesn't have a boodle because she's afraid I'll borrow money from her to buy gin. This is allright except that I have to declare her income on the tax returns and her pretense of not having any money is very hard to get around.[40]

I met John Paxton's agent in the Oak Room. A moment earlier I had lost my bridge in an English muffin and appeared to be speaking German . . . It is cold and gloomy here for May and I am still mucking around with the middle of the book. My best to Harriet.

As ever,
John

Cedar Lane
[postmarked 3 July 1963]

Dear John,

You must have seen Lennie by now; and I haven't written sooner because I don't seem to have any glad tidings. I slept—in case of theft or fire—with the book between my legs for several weeks and made all sorts of bargains with the devil, offering him my teeth, my health and my reason if he would help me complete it. There was a fleeting moment of contentment when it was done followed by an engorgement of paranoia. I can't think of the book without getting tremors and when anyone makes the mistake of saying they like it I fly into a rage. I am very sulky and nervous and wish I could see you both. There are some revisions to be done but every time I look at the fucking mss I commence to heave and jitter.

It is very hot and somehow inclement weather has lost it's innocence. The cleaning woman thinks that the heavens are loused up and I'm inclined to agree with her. Ben is canoeing up the Allagash with some expensive Indian guides and Susie is working at Time. She has a red convertible and a boy-friend

40. The tax returns John and Mary signed during the sixties and early seventies reported her annual contributions to household expenses ranged between $8,000 and $15,000.

who wears sneakers, tight pants and has a Bottom-the-Weaver haircut. They read Reich aloud to one another and play junky music. I keep routing them out of one another's bedrooms.[41] At dusk each evening Picci and I go out on the terrace and wish on the evening star. Picci thinks I'm kidding but he's mistaken.

Give my best to Lennie, Henry, the waves at Malibu and the lights below your terrace.

John

Cedar Lane
Friday
[postmarked 6 September 1963]
Dear John,

Lennie tells me you're on a 5 A.M. schedule so I won't expect a reply to this Muskrat Ramble but I thought you might be interested in all the thrilling things that have happened to me and so forth. First I have a new place to work which is the general meeting room of the Veterans of Foreign Wars, Post 10041. I face a sea of folding chairs and am surrounded by seven flags, two gilt eagles, a dozen Garand rifles and many gilt trophies for snappy marching in Loyalty Day parades. Loyalty is Liberty! Over the door there is a sign saying: "No beverages allowed in this room." Over my head there is a sign saying: "One God, One Flag, One Country and One Language." Abastanza questa cosa. The air smells of cigars which may or may not give my prose style a boost. The book at long last is in the works and I have the catalogue copy which describes me as "a master of barbed irony" in describing a world "where brightness no longer falls from the air." I was invited to lunch at my publisher's

41. "He was cool and courtly as long as there was no overt display of affection," Susan wrote in *Home Before Dark*. "Hand-holding, kissing, and even open flirtatiousness made him furious. He liked to invite my boyfriends off with him to go scything in the meadow or work on a felled tree with the chain saw or clear some brush out behind the pine trees. I don't know what happened out there, but they always came back in a rage."

country estate where he recited a paragraph from the book which he had pretty much memorized.[42] I said how charming of him but there was no further discussion of the matter and we mostly discussed Alan Moorehead's giftedness.

Lennie and Gin and Kathy came for lunch and brought the lunch which was nice. I kept calling Gin Ruthy. Bad. Mary was in New Hampshire three weeks and I ate mostly scrambled eggs. Susie stayed with me and worked for Time Inc. In Mary's portfolio there are some short term bonds issued by the First National Bank in Boston. This is Curtis, of course, and I wonder if Harriet has anything like that in her portfolio. I mean if I sell a story to Curtis it will be just like taking money out of the sugar bowl won't it? I'm going to Yaddo on Sunday and I'll be back in time to see you in October.

Best,
John

Cedar Lane
Friday
[18 October 1963]

Dear John,

It was good to hear from you and I'm terribly sorry to know that we won't see you this fall. It means that I won't have to paint the trim and clean up the pine copse for Harriet's inspection; but it would have been a pleasure. I keep hoping that Henry will work out something so that I can come west and get a look at you both over a plate of cracked crab. That would be nice. However Henry writes that the book is a Personal Triumph and by that I think he means that the triumph part of it is very limited.

I saw Lennie on Wednesday sitting in his posh office. He seems fine. All the brass and silver was very highly polished and I wonder if he does this. Mary is teaching Salinger. I am trying

42. *The Wapshot Scandal* was the book, Cass Canfield of Harper & Row the publisher.

to kick tobacco. This is very difficult. It is now 10 am and I am sweating and shaking all over. My love to Harriet.

As ever,

John

JOHN CHEEVER
Cedar Lane
Ossining, New York

Friday
[13 December 1963]

Dear John,

I hope you got your copy of the book and I hope you like it. Susie thought it was terribly depressing . . . The ground here now is covered with snow. Mary is trying to make Christmas cards but she is having trouble with her eyes and is way behind with correcting papers and if you don't get one of her hand-made cards this comes to you with our affectionate best wishes.

As ever,

John

Dodd, Mead had just published my book for young readers, Tad Lincoln: Mischief-Maker in the White House.

JOHN CHEEVER
Cedar Lane
Ossining, New York

Thursday
[postmarked 14 January 1964]

Dear John,

Many thanks for sending the Tad Lincoln book. I read a chapter to Fred last night and he enjoyed it very much and perhaps the long and noble shadow of Lincoln will make him pleasanter in the mornings. I lunched with Don and Lennie yesterday and they both seem fine. Don wore an outer coat with a fur collar and under this a blue blazer with brass buttons. Lennie wore a Roman suit with a Venitian shirt and large gold cufflinks. I wore the dark oxford my father-in-law left me. I had the roastbeef bones.

I announced to Mary and the children a few nights ago that I would go to Rome on Sunday. Then I decided that I could not leave them and announced that I would not leave for Rome on Sunday. They seemed so terribly disappointed that I announced again that I would leave for Rome on Sunday and so I shall. I will be gone two weeks and will look up Bill and report on my return.

Best,

John

I had just finished The Great Experiment: An Intimate View of the Everyday Workings of the Federal Government *(Little, Brown).*

JOHN CHEEVER
Cedar Lane
Ossining, New York

February third
[1964]

Dear John,

I had lunch with Lennie yesterday who said you'd finished your book; and my congratulations and best wishes. I saw Bill in Rome. He was wearing a dinner jacket and going to the ballet. I was wearing damp dacron and going to the dogs. He looked very staid and made me feel disheveled. The Sterlings[43] tell me that he is an exceptionally prosperous and hard working member of the community and he seemed fine as well as staid. I returned on Thursday and one of my first tasks here was to start reading Tad Lincoln aloud for the second time.

Best,

John

43. Tom and Claire Sterling were writers Bill had introduced to John and Mary.

Henry Koerner's portrait of John seated at his typewriter beside a book-lined wall and the family's two pet doves appeared on the cover of the March 27, 1964, issue of Time. *The article, "Ovid in Ossining," was written by Alwyn Lee, with "a major part of the reporting" attributed to Andrew Kopkind.*

JOHN CHEEVER
Cedar Lane
Ossining, New York

Sunday
[1 March 1964]

Dear John,

I got the news from TIME when a portrait painter called from Pittsburgh to say he had been commissioned to do the cover. I called the office and asked them to please stop it; and then took off for Stowe with Ben. An editor and research girl followed us. They followed us right up to the summit of Mt. Mansfield—gale winds and twelve below zero—asking me how tall my mother was and how precisely would I identify my family class-wise. A second editor was flown in from California. When I returned I found that the painter had set up his easel in Susie's bedroom and was painting a picture of one of my blue shirts, draped over a chair-back. Then the telephone began to ring and is still ringing. These are mostly calls from people I used to play marbles with when I was about five. They seem to think I've done something wrong.[44] The two editors and the research

---

44. "Sally Ziegler, a small-town Georgian who lives in the cottage on the hill, has been preparing herself for the TIME interview for a month," John wrote Malcolm Cowley. "On Friday the doorbell rang and she let the man in. 'I don't approve of this kind of sneaky journalism,' she said, 'but the truth is is that I know a lot about him because I can see him from my windows. I mean to say that I know he's a very heavy drinker and I often see him out there at twelve o'clock noon with a martini cocktail in his hand. And he sometimes chases his wife through the orchard in full view of my children. And he almost never wears his bathing-suit when he goes swimming and I've always thought there was something peculiar about men who

girl have been at my side for a week now and have filled four note books with information. Cheever #4 it says. I said if they didn't desist I would go to Europe. They said they would too. They take us out to dinner. I usually have the seafood brochette. Mary has the roast beef. I ask them all about their mothers and they tell me and I think I have them buffaloed but Mary says they've been trained to talk about themselves so that I'll spill my own beans unselfconsciously. I could have hid in the bathroom like Salinger but I don't think that's the way to do it. I'm not sure this is either.

Best,

John

John had flown to Los Angeles to meet Alan J. Pakula and Robert Mulligan, who were buying the film rights to the two Wapshot *novels. It was on this visit that he met Hope Lange, who at this time was Mrs. Pakula.*

JOHN CHEEVER
Cedar Lane
Ossining, New York

Sunday
[12 April 1964]

Dear John and Harriet,

I still feel suspended somewhere between here and there. I don't seem able to connect your pleasant living room to the rooms here. It would seem easier if there were an ocean between us. I find the eastern flight very exciting. I huffed and puffed all the way across the painted desert and began to moan

---

go swimming without their bathing suits. But as I say I don't approve of this kind of gossip and if you'll ask me some suitable questions about his habits I'll try to answer them to the best of my ability.' Then the man said, 'Lady, I'm your Fuller Brush representative.' "

like a dove when I saw the lights go on along the banks of the Cimmaron River. Mary, Ben and the dogs were waiting for me here.

I do wish I could bring our worlds closer together or cultivate some composure as a traveler. I don't want to go down shouting golly gee. All is well.

Love,
John

On John's second 1960 stay in Los Angeles the Chateau Marmont management had installed him in its Mitzi Gaynor Suite, where, he wrote Bill Maxwell, he found himself confronted by "a revolving ten foot papier-mache nude outside my bedroom window." It advertised the Sahara Hotel in Las Vegas.

JOHN CHEEVER
Cedar Lane
Ossining, New York

Wednesday
[postmarked 21 April 1964]

Dear John,

I don't really think that the girl outside the window of the Marmont had anything to do with it but anyhow the Del Webb Corporation that runs the Sahara in Las Vegas has elected me to the American Academy of Achievement and named me CAPTAIN OF ACHIEVEMENT IN LITERATURE. If I go to San Diego in June I'll get a gold plate.

Best,
John

Ben Cheever recalls Hope Lange Pakula coming up the stone steps at Cedar Lane with her husband: "I think Hope called me 'dear,' and may even have kissed me. I was in my early teens at the time, and I complained about it later to my father. 'I never met her before. She doesn't know if I'm a dear or not.' He said that was the way people were in Hollywood, and that it didn't mean anything."

Thursday
[postmarked 14 May 1964]

Dear John,

. . . The Pakulas are now in town and I called her yesterday (Jimmy Stewart) to ask if she didn't wanna go to the zoo. Naturally, it was raining. "Come and have tea with my nieces at the Plaza," she said huskily. (Jean Arthur) You could cut it and sell it to the container corporation. So I ran all the way up Fifth Avenue where her nieces dropped curtsies and ate French pastry and I made goo-goo eyes and listened to the rain. They're expected here for dinner tonight.

I called Marsha[45] and asked her to dinner and she sighed: "Not a prayer, my dear, not a prayer . . ." Holiday very kindly sent on a copy of the issue with your piece on the conventions which I enjoyed very much. I hope you get rested and come east and we'll take a long walk.

Best,
John

JOHN CHEEVER
Cedar Lane
Ossining, New York

June third [1964]

Dear John,

I talked on the phone with Lennie who said you were tired as well you might be. I do hope and pray that you won't be enveloped by the sort of cafard that struck me when I finished the novel. It is shaped like an ectoplasm and smells of that faint perfume they use in cheap handsoap. It is worst in the mornings.

We leave for Italy on Tuesday. The plan is to go directly

45. Marsha Hunt Presnell.

to the Mooreheads in Porto Ercole but we're bound to spend some time in Rome and I shall try to see Bill. We return at the end of the month. My love to Harriet.

Best,

John

JOHN CHEEVER
Cedar Lane
Ossining, New York

July second [1964]

Dear John,

We didn't see Bill in Rome because the Beckers didn't produce him. They did produce a man . . . who is going to build super-markets all over Rome. "Rome needs Minimax," he said and "Minimax needs Rome. Why, Mr. Shiffers I'm going to build a supermarket that will put the Pantheon to shame." I asked him why the fuck he didn't start by embarrassing the Colosium and everyone went to the other side of the room.

I dropped the cafard somewhere in midAtlantic and it didn't catch up with me until ten days later in a room at the Eden-Roma. I caught a train to Sperlonga that afternoon and remained fairly light-hearted. Ben has been admitted to Loomis and I'm going to buy him a dinner jacket if I ever get him out of the briarpatch. At the mention of Brooks Brothers his eyes cross and light up wildly and he hides in the woods. Susie has rented a house in Cambridge with a Chinese girl. I am having difficulty working. I lunched with Lennie on Tuesday and he was fine. My love to Harriet.

Best,

John

Film producer Frank Perry read "The Swimmer" in the July 18 issue of The New Yorker, *and lost no time in calling about the film rights.*

JOHN CHEEVER
Cedar Lane
Ossining, New York
Wednesday
[postmarked 1 August 1964]

Dear John,

I guess The Swimmer will be settled today. I shall have the drainpipes on the house repaired and put a new toilet into the boy's can. Mary goes to New Hampshire tomorrow with my sons and I am as bitter at being left alone as a little child. I have been invited to the Cape, Nantucket, the Thousand Islands and both the French and Italian Rivieras but I shall regret them all and sit here alone with the old Labrador, pissing into the fresh lemonade. They'll be sorry. I shall be taken ill. I don't know the exact nature of my illness but it must be painless, fascinating, near-fatal and cured by the well-springs of my pure and cheerful disposition. While they sport in the mountains I shall be lying in a hospital bed. Won't they be sorry.[46]

I hope boy-chum[47] is well. I had hoped to take boy-chum Field to Russia with me but the Russians say that if I take a boy-chum the Russian writers who are coming here have to bring their boy-chums and so no boy-chums. Lennie is in England and doesn't know and I'm afraid he'll be disappointed. But the whole thing may blow up because of Goldwater. Whatever happens I will go back to Europe in the fall.

Best,

John

46. Maurice Sendak's readers may look on John's imagined punishment of his family as a rewrite of Where the Wild Things Are, but years ago, without ever having read the book or heard of its author, I drew on the same fantasy in a children's story titled I'm Gonna Eat Worms and Die. I withdrew it hurriedly when an editor pointed out the similarity. I also disqualified myself from ever sitting on a jury considering a case involving plagiarism.

47. Robert Presnell, Jr., an erudite Los Angeles screenwriter, married to actress Marsha Hunt.

The Benedict Canyon house had an 180-degree view of the city and from our living room we looked across a draw to Cary Grant's place.

JOHN CHEEVER
Cedar Lane
Ossining, New York

[postmarked 29 August 1964]

Dear John,

You must be very excited about the new house. I can't think of a place more intimately associated with two people than Hillside Avenue. I know that Harriet made the rugs but I've always felt that she spun the grass and roses and I cannot yet see her on another terrace with another view. You must realize that many of us, at the end of an uneasy day, conclude that we can eat crab-meat with the Weavers but if you wander around like nomads we will all be lost. I think I speak for most of your friends when I say that I would appreciate a more exact description and snapshots if possible. The pool sounds splendid but you say nothing about the amenities available to your guests. Will we have a separate apartment. A private bar. Will we be able to hear the laughter of Santa Claus on the easterly winds. I wouldn't count too much on Cary Grant's swill. We had Mrs. Vanderlip's swill in our side yard for eight years and excepting for one rainy evening when she, in grande tenue, discovered two frozen turkeys amongst the coffee grounds and boxed the cook's ears, it offered very little.[48]

48. We rarely saw Cary Grant and never sampled his swill, but we did become friends of his English secretary and his wife. When they had the house to themselves, they used to invite us over for shepherd's pie and spend much of the evening telling stories of their employer's penuriousness. He would order up the Rolls to take our host to a discount store to buy socks marked down from 89 to 67 cents and after a dinner party he counted the empty Champagne bottles. But the morning Harriett walked home with the ink drying on the signature Cary Grant had put at the top

I seem to be in suspense between the publication of a collection of stories next month and a somehow somber and mysterious trip to Russia in October.[49] I don't want to write stories and I'm not ready to expose myself to the exhaltations and pratfalls of another novel. Ben goes to Loomis in the fall and I took him to Brooks and bought him everything in sight, beaming like a foolish swain. Susie was about to leave for the Virgin Islands with a boy-chum when they quarreled. She tore up a two hundred dollar plane-ticket and came here with another boy-chum named Roger. He settled in at once and it was Mary's guess that he would be here until Easter but I gave him a drunken speech on decisiveness and he left at the end of the week with a large packet of roast-beef sandwiches. Another boy-chum named Courtland something is due this morning. They will drive to Miami, fly to Nassau and take the mail-boat to a small island in the Bahamas where I believe they plan to smuggle ammunition into Cuba.

I don't suppose, with the new house, that you will be coming east for sometime and I don't know when you're book comes out.[50] UCLA asked me to lecture but I really don't have anything to say. I do hope to return from Siberia in time to do my Christmas shopping. Please keep me posted on the house. You say that it is neither new nor imposing but you say nothing about the number of bed rooms and baths. My sincere and affectionate best wishes to you both.

As ever,

John

of her petition against a proposed subdivision her shoes never touched the ground.

49. The new collection was *The Brigadier and the Golf Widow* (Harper & Row). On this visit to the USSR John met Tanya Litvinov, who was translating *The Enormous Radio and Other Stories,* and began his friendship with John and Mary Updike.

50. *The Great Experiment* (Little, Brown 1965).

A handwritten beach scene postcard from USSR.

[October 1964]

Dear John and Harriet,

This is just like Beverly Hills only more exclusive. Tell Henry I'm in Yalta.

Best,

John

I had passed through New York on my way to Washington to begin work on a three-part series of Holiday *articles on Chief Justice Earl Warren, which would later be expanded into a book for Little, Brown.*

JOHN CHEEVER
Cedar Lane
Ossining, New York

Armistice Day [1964]

Dear John,

I had lunch with Lennie yesterday and it seems that we might have met on Sunday. Lennie said you were very well dressed and told me about the advance for the Warren book which I think is splendid. It's perhaps just as well that we didn't meet since I was in the throes of a noisy monologue about my interesting trip to Russia which is only just beginning to taper off. I could not believe before I left that I was going and when I was there I could not believe I would ever return. This double state of disbelief has no powers of cancellation and I still wake up in the middle of the night thinking that I am in Baku or Tibilisi. I got my royalties.[51] To do this you sit at a felt-covered table and drink brandy, coffee and eat cakes. Then a man comes in with the boodle and counts it onto the felt. Then you say

51. I had asked about his royalties because of the rubles supposedly set aside for me following the unauthorized publication of *Another Such Victory*.

Bolshoi Spaseba and the publisher gives you a big smelly kiss, right on the bouche. I got so rattled by all this demonstrativeness that I damned near kissed the Ambassador but the first secretary gave my arm a wrench and I ended up romancing the butler who was Chinese. I think it's very strange that our ambassador should have a Chinese butler, don't you?

The vodka and the caviar were very good and that's the place where they really appreciate a childlike sense of wonder. I went swimming a lot and learned some songs about how birch trees have hair like maidens which nobody wants to hear me sing. As soon as I got to Berlin everybody said how happy I must be but I wasn't happy at all. Shaggy Old Mother Russia seemed to be the girl for me. I'm delighted to be back with Mary and the children but I feel much more lost than I ever did on leaving Italy.[52]

    Best,

      John

I had fallen from a ladder while trimming a tree at our new home in Benedict Canyon and shattered my right wrist. For a while it was touch and go as to whether I would regain its use. I did.

December first [1964]

Dear John:

Firstly I'm very sorry to hear about your arm or hand. There is some question in Sardi's about which it is. Nextly I am very pleased to have the book. I found it comprehensive, brilliantly organized and best of all sassy. I got it the day before I went to Washington for my debriefing and was able to use almost all the information in the State Department chapter. Thirdly there was a conversation with Susie at the breakfast table

52. "Nothing untoward has happened excepting in church on Sunday where I went for Holy Communion," he wrote Tanya Litvinov. "After the Agnus Dei I had a paroxysm of coughing and was unable to take the sacrament. 'He's been to Russia,' someone said, and so I have."

on Thanksgiving morning. "Someone," she said, "thinks I should save your letters." "I hope you won't, my dear," I said pissily. I was at the other end of the table trying to write a letter. "I can't see any point in saving your letters," she said. "I can see saving John Weavers letters because they're so good but your letters are sort of drivel."

I'm still on the Russian hook and took Chaykovsky[53] and his wife to the theatre last night. When we went through the usual demonstration on the BMT platform we agreed it was extremely painful for Russians and Americans to part because one never knew what would happen by morning. I then returned to Sardi's where Lennie and Gin were discussing your break. Lennie said Eva said it was your hand. I said you were trimming the Christmas tree, very drunk, and got a multiple break in the arm. Gin said crossly that you were pruning a tree, a tree she knows very well, and fell from a high ladder.[54] I left their table for the Shaws where I chatted with Irwin about how if you have a yacht with twin diesels you don't get much work done but you have very concentrated reveries.

Best,

John

December 29th [1964]

Dear John,

I had no idea the break was that grave or that threatening. It is very like me to wonder if drinking with the left hand is any inconvenience. I shall be here in February and the State Department does not ever want to send me anywhere again. I got minus points for my excessive childlike sense of wonder and I can't remember whether or not I wrote you about sliding down the bannister at the Writers Union. I lunched with Lennie and

53. Alexandr B. Chakovsky, the affable, pipe-smoking, thirty-one-year-old editor of *Literaturna Gazeta*.
54. Virginia Field was right. A friend of the former owners of our new house, she knew the tree well. Eva was Lennie's Beverly Hills sister-in-law.

Kathy yesterday who are fine. Lennie and Gin go off to Jamaica tomorrow. I'm still far from settled after my trip and there are a great many people who do not care to hear about it. I always give them a chance. I mean I always wear my fur hat but yesterday for instance Frances Lindley told me about how her son came home from Andover and went to a dance in a rented tuxedo and then asked about Mary and the children and then asked if I'd been doing anything exciting and so then I pulled on my fur hat and said no, I hadn't been doing anything exciting at all and went away.[55] There's a great deal of this sort of thing.

Best,
John

Tuesday
[postmarked 19 January 1965]

Dear John,

The fact that you couldn't write letters excited in me the unholy glee of a long-winded bore who talks someone into a corner at a cocktail party. It seemed, at long last, that I could do my impersonation of Yevtushenko, my soft-shoe routine, my detailed description (hoot-hoot) of the midnight train from Moscow to Leningrad. I had a marvelous feeling that you were quite helpless and would have to hear about my dogs, my cats, my experiences in extra-sensory perception[56] and my rapture for life. I missed a great chance.

55. John had met Frances Lindley, his editor on *The Wapshot Scandal,* at Yaddo in 1934, when she was married to Lloyd (Pete) Collins.

56. "A writer is born with it," John told a young woman at a dinner party in Beverly Hills when she asked if he had ESP. "What am I thinking about right now?" she asked. John took a paper box of matches from his pocket, scribbled the words, "Grass and violets," and passed it across the table to her. She was visibly shaken. She had been thinking about a walk through the woods on a spring day. In telling the story to Harriett at breakfast next morning, John said he had promptly taken shelter in the bathroom, where he waited until he was sure the conversation had veered away from ESP.

I wonder how long you'll be in Washington.[57] I'm supposed to give a reading there in March. Black tie. Mary bought me some court pumps which are a size too big and fall off when I dance the frug but I think I can make the lectern if I keep my toes curled up. You'll definitely need a hat. I can loan you a fur one. Mine is genuine bear with earflaps although I've twice put the cat on by accident; and Fred claims that I throw the hat out the door every night and stuff the cat into the hat-shelf. This is not true. He has a serpent's tooth, that boy. Anyhow I'll see you here or in Washington or New York and I'm delighted and pleased and relieved that your arm is healing.

As ever,

John

We had moved to our new home without having sold the old one.

JOHN CHEEVER
Cedar Lane
Ossining, N.Y.

Saturday
[postmarked 13 February 1965]

Dear John,

I wish you'd straighten out your real estate holdings so I could come out and visit you. It's very disconcerting for your friends in the east to imagine you spread between two properties. I go to Yaddo on Monday and will perform in Washington on the 27th which means that you will miss seeing me slide up to the lectern in my court pumps. That's too bad. However I will return on the twenty-second and see you here or there. I wouldn't count too much on Little Brown. I mean I'd bring some money. Simon and Schuster invited Louis Kronenberger

57. I was preparing to head East to continue research on the Earl Warren book.

to lunch and took him to Sterns. You can't tell. Delacourt is having the restaurant of The Four Seasons transformed into summer to celebrate the publication of Irwin Shaw's new novel but when Elizabeth Spencer came to New York Magraw Hill put her up at the YWCA. You can't tell what they'll do.

Irwin Shaw broke his arm or did I tell you. I got bursitis in the left hip from a coasting accident but it's all better. The coasting's been great but Fred hates it and we have father-son fights about whether or not he's a *real* boy. He likes Goldfinger best. Susie wrote a brilliant attack on Henry James.[58] I write nothing at all.

Best,
John

J O H N   C H E E V E R
Cedar Lane
Ossining, N.Y.

March sixteenth [1965]

Dear John,

. . . It's too bad we didn't meet in Washington because there was an opening at the Cocheran Art Gallery the night I performed and you wouldn't have had any trouble getting seats. Katherine Anne Porter called and said: Angelchile, you're jess where I was five years ago and do be keerful. Scotty Fitzgerald got to the

58. It may have reflected sentiments her father expressed in a letter to Tanya Litvinov: "I perused most of James when I was eighteen and was intoxicated by the innuendoes, the circumlocutions, the pools of light and the high-flown speeches delivered at dusk. Five years ago I bought the complete works and settled down to read it again. It was appalling . . . I could not imagine why he had spent so much time rigging the scenery, arranging the flowers and brewing the tea. I could hear his heavy breathing behind the walls of all those wonderfully beautiful, beautiful rooms. I felt as if I were caught at some unsuitable occupation such as embroidery. (My sort of novelist walks boldly onstage, belches, picks his teeth with a matchstick and sneaks a drink of whisky from the bottle hidden in the fireplace). But the work seemed to me to have so little moral urgency, so little ardor that I gave up with volume five. This is still heresy here and if I said as much at my club I would be dropped."

reception after I'd left. Mary took Fred to see the Spirit of St. Louis and Friendship 7 and I walked to the National Gallery where I had such a seizure of vertigo that I couldn't go down the marble stairs without screaming. I hung around the rotounda for about an hour, wondering how in hell I was ever going to get out of the place but finally I found an elevator and descended.

Then I drove to Providence and performed at Brown-Pembroke where there was an academic procession with organ music and where Susie hid in the balcony, swept by paroxysims of embarrassment and pride. She's quite nice and has got herself a job teaching secondary school English in Colorado but she wants to go to Chile for the summer and get the bugs out of her skiing. Ben is in Hatii with a French school-chum and is in love with a girl named Janice Maloney. When I asked him about the Chaffee prom he said he was thinking about Janice all the time so he didn't feel like dancing tight with the Chaffee girls which disappointed them. Janice goes to Oxford. Yesterday there was a telephone interview with six universities in six states. This is a stunt the Ford Foundation has set up and I don't think much of it. They keep saying well now lets switch over to Texas and people ask you why you're so unfair to homosexuals and psychiatrists and the dogs kept barking and Fred kept asking if he couldn't look at tv and I could hear Mary and my chum Art Spear giggling on the other line and having drunk so much for lunch I had to piss something terrible and you don't get paid. That Ford Foundation is a bunch of skins. Also I had to set my brother up in a bookstore in Westport which he calls the eagle i. I have to keep writing checks to the eagle i. The lawyer says its just like as if I was a cockroach.[59] I

59. In *archy and mehitabel* (doubleday, doran; 1927) Don Marquis tells how he came upon a "gigantic cockroach jumping about upon the keys" of his typewriter. The cockroach, archy, was unable to manage capital letters, so he wrote lowercase poems to mehitabel, a cat who had once been cleopatra and liked to point out that "there s a dance in the old dame yet." archy was also unable to handle apostrophes.

wonder what you've decided about the houses and please report.

    Best,

      John

Our new house in Benedict Canyon lay within the city limits of Los Angeles, but mail was delivered only if it was addressed to us in "Beverly Hills."

JOHN CHEEVER
Cedar Lane
Ossining, New York
Tuesday

                        [postmarked 11 May 1965]

Dear John,

    The address bugs me but I'm glad you're settled although it seems like a hell of a long way off. Anyhow you sound happy. Alice Pearce has millions of affluent aunts and she is also personally affluent.[60] I did not know she had a husband. We are all fairly well although I am confused. I took Mary to Chicago on the train Monday night where I talked about the beauties of literature. Mary flew back on Thursday and I took the Twentieth Century Friday night, carrying a lot of nice, serious books . . . I didn't even go to the club car. Well the engine took fire somewhere east of Gary and in the confusion I got horribly mixed up with a broad from Evanston who was drinking rusty nails. This went on until three when the conductor told us we couldn't play strippoker in the observation car. He was wrong about the game.

    Everything is in bloom here and it's floral as hell. I get the Howells medal next week which is very embarrassing because the only reason I get it is because Saul Bellow and Ralph Ellison had a fight and Ralph wouldn't let them give the thing

---

60. We had sold our Hillside Avenue house to Alice Pearce, an actress who had gone to school with Mary Cheever.

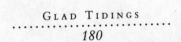

to Saul.[61] Anyhow Harpers had the book bound in rich leather and gilded the pages and that's nice.

> Best,
>
> John

It was more difficult for Louis Untermeyer and John than for Harriett and me to give up 8242 Hillside Avenue.

JOHN CHEEVER
Cedar Lane
Ossining, N.Y.

Tuesday
[postmarked 25 May 1965]

Dear John,

My last letter was so pissy that I must apologize; but I am having difficulty working and I find this depressing. I saw the Untermeyers at the wingding on Wednesday and they both looked very well. This is more than I can say for most of my friends there. You can't shake hands impulsively at that party because most people are holding in their right hand either a crutch or a stick. Anyhow we talked about the charms of 8242; about the fact that we are getting a little too old to change. You must know the move was a blow to us all. However Louis seemed composed and I shall take him as a model.

I felt crushed on Wednesday morning and took some gin before starting into town. The secretary took one look at me and said: "Every single year, someone has to be carried out feet first." My medal was, quite naturally, lost and I had to pose for

---

61. "I wanted passionately to regret the Howells Medal," John wrote George Biddle, "but it would have meant offending at least twenty-seven people. To accept it will make as many people or more very angry but it seemed in the end better to nettle than to insult my associates. I have to make an acceptance speech at that dead hour in the proceedings when everyone's bladder, including my own, is about to burst and Deems Taylor appears to have died."

photographers with Walter Lippmann's medal. He was very nice about this. Lewis Mumford, who seems to be losing his marbles, ended lunch by ringing a cowbell. He then opened the ceremony with an attack on American foreign policy. Tom Benton and Henry Cowles marched off the platform and Phyllis McGinley hissed and booed. Marianne Moore wrote: "I love Daddy-bird" on little slips of paper and distributed them up and down the aisles. Then we were addressed on the subject of American Literature during the Administration of Thomas Jefferson and everyone fell asleep. Then there was a pee-break and after this I got my medal which is solid gold, as big as a saucer and weighs a pound. I was very pleased.

We had dinner with the Ettlingers on Saturday and they are splendid. Their pool is empty because of the water-shortage. Susie graduates from college on the seventh and then goes to Tuskeegee to teach for a month. After this she will teach in Colorado. Ben is on the LaCrosse team and has been elected to the student council and I am insane with pride.[62]

   Best,
   John

"There has been a great deal of dispute about whether or not American intellectuals should accept the invitation of a President whose foreign policy they detest," John wrote Tanya (June 15). "I accepted."

62. "We visited Ben at his school last weekend and saw a La Crosse game," John wrote Tanya (May 1). "This is a marvellous sport invented by the Indians. The school is small, a little like one of the English public schools, a definite rear-guard action on the part of the American upper-class but the playing fields are green, the trees are massive, the voices of the ladies are musical, the food is ghastly and the boys are privileged and while it may be a scene from the past, it is a charming scene. Ben, I'm happy to say, does not take it seriously. Susie, at the other end of things, will teach at a Negro University in Alabama this summer."

JOHN CHEEVER
Cedar Lane
Ossining, N.Y.

[postmarked 16 June 1965]

Dear John,

First Phil Roth called and said Robert Lowell wanted to know if I would go to the White House if I were asked and I said I had been asked to the White House for Tuesday and I had accepted. Roth said I had been asked to the wrong party. On Sunday when we went to Providence for Susie's commencement I ran into Sid Perelman who was getting an honorary degree and he said guess what?[63] I'm going to the White House on Tuesday. So I said let's meet at the Hilton and get stoned so we met at the Hilton and got stoned and walked to the White House. Everybody else came in cars. Then I bumped into Mrs. Johnson and she said: He's late, but this isn't the first time. Then the band played Hail to the Chief and he came down the hall and a sharp dresser named Valente pushed me into the music room where I found John and Mary Updike.[64] So I kissed Mary

63. Susan graduated from Pembroke, a women's college affiliated with Brown University, S. J. Perelman's alma mater, which was chartered in 1764 and opened as Rhode Island College the following year. John described the ceremonies in a letter to Essie Lee, whose husband had written the *Time* cover article: "The university was founded in 1760 and a great many rites and arcane ceremonies have accumulated over the years. There were mace-bearers, chain-bearers, staff-bearers and in the middle of it all S. J. Perelman floundering around in what appeared to be a black bathrobe, his mortar awry. He was moving towards an honorary L.L.D. It was a slow process and they didn't get around to him until after lunch but I stayed to see him elevated and he carried it off very well. He is now known as Sidney Joseph Perelman L.L.D. since Dr. Perelman makes everyone think of a dentist."

64. Cheever and Updike arrived in the USSR in 1964 with copies of their latest books, *The Brigadier and the Golf Widow* and *Centaur*, to hand out in exchange for the gifts heaped on them by their Soviet colleagues and admirers. At the American Embassy, Cheever boasted, he un-

Updike and told Mrs. Johnson that Updike carried autographed copies of his works with him wherever he went in Russia and sure enough he had three with him at the party. He gives away paperbacks. Then the President made a sad speech and gave gold-plated medals to a lot of high school kids and I went back into the Rose Room and danced with Mary Updike. The Frug. You weren't supposed to dance. Then Jason Robarts said that if he didn't get a drink he was going to take the next shuttle and a newspaper woman showed us where the bar was. There was plenty to drink but with the buffet all we got was bug-juice. The buffet was on the lawn and I had supper with Marianne Moore and John O'Hara and John Glenn and Stan Musial. When it began to get dark there was more music and then Updike got up on a platform and read from his works. Sid Perelman and Howard K. Smith and I left. Then on Wednesday I flew home in time to say good-bye to Susie who is going to teach English at Tuskeegee for a month. Then Ben returned on Friday and told me about the day he was elected to the Student Council. He was playing LaCrosse and some men came running across

---

loaded eight *Brigadiers* to Updike's six *Centaurs*. On the train to Leningrad, he wrote Fred Exley, "he [Updike] tried to throw my books out of the window, but his lovely wife Mary intervened. She not only saved the books; she read one. She had to hide it under her bed pillow and claim to be sick. She said he would kill her if he knew." When Scott Donaldson asked Mary Updike (who had by then remarried) about this "joyous disporting of literary rivalry," she wrote back: "Once in a while on the Russian trip the three of us were left alone, unescorted, for a breakfast or a visit to the Hermitage, and then we behaved like children let out of school, comparing notes, griping about the system, talking to the bug, gossiping, feeling homesick and missing our children. Cheever was very funny, relaxed, more emphatic and more revealing. It was then that he and JHU began talking in earnest about writing and I felt some of the rivalry you describe. . . . Little of what they said had to do with me other than simple showing off and most of it was invented to amuse and entertain us on our way, as is the description of books being thrown out the train window or hidden under the bed pillow: a germ of truth contained in a whirlwind of fantasy."

the field just before dark and picked him up on their shoulders and carried him back to the gym. Pow.

John

JOHN CHEEVER
Cedar Lane
Ossining, N.Y.

The Day Before Thanksgiving
[postmarked 24 November 1965]

Dear John,

It has been much too long since I've heard from you and the fact that I have no news at all does not seem to constrain me from writing. The TIMES only carries disaster news from your part of the world and how do I know that you haven't been consumed by a tinder-fire or washed away in a flood. Lennie describes your house as so spacious and elegant that I think of you and Harriet as mere shadows, moving through the vastness of the rooms. Would you like to know that Susie is happy in Colorado? That Ben has developed a thick neck, a boxer's squint and high cheek-bones? Or that our neighbor Charlie Brieant ran for town-supervisor and by way of a campaign distributed five thousand pot-holders printed with "Brieant is Cool." He was defeated by a plurality of fourteen hundred and is so convinced that he is the victim of a communist plot that I don't wear my fur hat when I walk Fred to the bus-stop these cold mornings. I am becoming one of those old bores whose literary work is a chronicle of every fallen leaf, ice in the bird bath, cumulus-cirrus in the Northeast, rabbits in the Mangle-Wurzel, gin in the pantry.

The work goes slowly and since this is mostly on my mind I suppose it is mostly what I have in the way of news. I think that I am not quite ready to write such and such a scene and so I write letters to Yevtushenko, the Moorehead's parrot, the Becker's beagle and the Sterling's cat. I throw the letters away at noon and drink some gin. The New Yorker summarily rejected the only story I've written this year and the Post summarily bought it for so large a sum that I got a three hundred dollar suit and a cherry-red Ghia convertible.[65] Mrs. Vanderlip lies dying and the family is gathering to quarrel over the assets but it hardly seems a story worth telling, mostly because I liked the old lady.[66] Ben returns this afternoon and when I meet him at Stamford my head will swim at the first glimpse of his manly handsomeness. Five minutes later I will tell him to sit up straight and offer to give him the money for a haircut.

Mary is well and happy. So is Fred. The cat is fine, the old dog is lame, the yellow-bitch threw a litter of eight in August and there are rabbits in the Mangle-Wurzel as usual. I hope this

65. The story was "The Geometry of Love," the purchase price $3,000.

66. "She operated the Infirmary for forty years, founded the Cosmopolitan Club (for governesses) and negotiated the truce between Turkey and Armenia," John wrote in his journal March 6, 1966, the day after she died at eighty-seven and received mixed notices in the obituary columns. "Her enemies said she was a ruthless climber and for some reason her enemies yesterday seemed to have the field. She operated her cotillion for forty years but the Astors and Vanderbilts always came out somewhere else. The cotillion was indescribably vulgar—a sort of vaudeville where the debutantes wore maribu muffs and waved rented ostrich feather fans. Her most favored daughter—Narcissa—told me that when she went to her Mother with a problem she shouted: 'How dare you approach me like this? Make an appointment with my secretary if you want to see me.' Of the columns in her garden she said: 'I bought them during some depression. The limestone quarries were without work and I got them quite cheap.' I found her there one rainy afternoon, collecting moss specimens for one of her grandchildren. 'I was feeling impatient and angry,' she said, 'but the moss and the rain have done wonders.' During a football game she came slowly down the lawn, walking with two sticks and wearing an enormous hat she had found in the attic. 'I love bright colors and movement,' she said. 'I love to see the sparks fall out of the brakebox of a train. When I was a child we had horse-cars or I suppose one could call them mule-cars since they were drawn by mules. By jumping on the back platform you could lift the shafts into the air. My how I loved to do that.' She gave a demonstration of the tango when she was eighty. She had committed the elaborate footwork to memory and seemed winsome and graceful."

finds you both well, prosperous, dry, creative and in possession
of that fine degree of concentration and intellectual tranquility
that seems, for the moment, to have escaped your old
Buddy,

John

*Mary Cheever had never met Tanya Litvinov, but had read her
letters and thought "she must be one of the finest women alive," she
wrote Josie Herbst. "Imagine Virginia Woolf forced into the role of
heroic patriotism, and you'll have some idea of her." She quoted two
sentences from a recent letter: "We are more cheerful about things of late.
There seems to be a mustard-seed of public opinion, and who knows but
it may develop."*

J O H N   C H E E V E R
Cedar Lane
Ossining, N.Y.

Wednesday
[postmarked 22 March 1966]

Dear John,

You sound very serene and it was good to hear from you.
No one writes me but the Russians and since Sinyavsky and
Daniel were jugged their letters have degenerated into a series
of barometric double-meanings. "Oh what a dreadful wind
blew yesterday," writes Litvinova, meaning seven years at hard
labor. I have a smattering of fan mail but I have learned to handle
this warily. A man named Exley wrote to say that he liked the
stories. I thanked him briefly. He then called collect from Miami
and asked me to post five hundred dollars bail. He had just
smashed up a saloon and knew I would understand.[67] Neiman-

67. John continued to correspond with Frederick Exley. When he died
in 1992 at the age of sixty-three, *Newsweek* noted: "His three 'fictional
memoirs'—from 'A Fan's Notes' to 'Last Notes from Home'—recorded his
alcoholism, mental hospitalizations, and two divorces. His failure, wrote a
critic, 'accounts for his success' " (June 29, 1992).

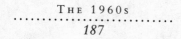

Marcus wrote to say that since I was such a lovely person they were sending me an Easter egg to decorate for display in their window. I also hear now and then from the Famous People's Eye-Glass Institute. This is in North Dakota.

I saw Lennie's play at a preview.[68] It did seem a mixed bag but it is running and a great deal of credit goes to Lennie for having got it together. I also dined with the Ettlingers who seemed jolly. I got over my block by telling everyone at a large party that I was blocked. I have never seen such spontaneous joy. Even Lillian Hellman cheered up. The book moves slowly but now and then it gives a shudder and inches forward.[69] Susie flew in from Aspen and Ben from Loomis on Friday. I had always hoped that Susie would be like one of those young women who advertise girdles; but she is instead a most strong-minded and contentious young woman. Ben is now religious. We have the usual now: Geese at dawn, fly-hatches, etc. All is well.

> Best,
> John

JOHN CHEEVER
Cedar Lane
Ossining, N.Y.

May 10th [1966]

Dear John,

It was great to hear from you and to hear that everything's going so well. I've seen Lennie once since the show closed and he doesn't seem to have taken a staggering financial loss . . .

The Perrys and Lancaster are planning to shoot the Swimmer in Westport in June.[70] I've written the Bishop of Connecti-

---

68. *Bags Full,* written by Jerry Chodorov and directed by George S. Kaufman, opened March 6; closed April 2.

69. *Bullet Park.*

70. "They've asked me to play the part of a stumbling drunk and I have refused," John wrote Tanya. "I want to play Hamlet."

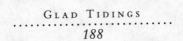
GLAD TIDINGS
188

cut and asked him to quit praying for rain. I've bought Mary an electric typewriter—American—but it makes a noise like a buzz-saw and writes a legalistic prose and I'm much more comfortable with this engine, heaped as it is with dandruff and fallen hair. Susie will return to Tuskeegee for the summer. One of her best friends was murdered last winter and I do worry. Ben will work with negroes here. I think their zeal may be traced to the fact that my old cousins—Mary and Ann Thompson—were Natick Indians. I do want the children to be zealous and visionary but I seem to want them to accomplish this innocuously.

I fight the booze, work on the book, catalogue the songbirds, cut the grass, trim the pines and remain,

Yours,

John

"Burt Lancaster is fifty-two, lithe, comely and somewhat disfigured by surgical incisions and he looks both young and old, masterful and tearful," John wrote Tanya, and spoke well of Eleanor Perry's screenplay which "followed the line and the sense of the story precisely. There are no flashbacks, no explanations for his mysterious journey and it ends in an empty house in a thunderstorm."

[postmarked 11 July 1966]

Dear John,

I'm sorry about this paper but I don't seem able to accustom myself to the correct stationary used by mature men anymore than I have been able to accustom myself to Mary's electric typewriter which makes so loud a buzzing sound that it's like having a flea in your ear. Anyhow I thought you'd like to know about Burt and me and so forth. The picture seems to be shaping up very nicely and Irving Lazar[71] tried to get me on the telephone yesterday but I was down in Westport with Burt. Burt's skin is getting very tough because he's in the water so much.

71. A prominent Hollywood agent.

Burt wants me to be in the picture. They want me to play the part of a booze-fighter who's passed out on a rubber raft. "You ought to get in the movies, Cheever," Burt said, "because they let you keep the clothes. We've only been shooting eight days and I already got three bathing trunks and two bathrobes." He's doing a wonderful job although he hates water and didn't know how to swim. The UCLA coach is on the set. They use his feet for the flutter kick. He's very sexy and commanding in the girl scenes but half the time he looks as if he were going to cry which is just right for the part. Eleanor Perry said that I looked just like Burt only shorter of course and that did it. I need some new teeth to point up the resemblance but I'm working on my Lancaster walk and I've developed a cute quick sweet sad smile. Mary doesn't speak to me. Burt thinks Norman Mailer is bitter. Burt thinks Norman Mailer is washed up. Burt doesn't eat anything but cream cheese. I eat things like Pate en croute which are prepared by Genevieve[72] who comes out to Westport whenever the Perry's cook leaves. The Perry's cook leaves twice a week. Genevieve says things like oolala but she's a very lively dame. Last night they had dinner sent in from a Chinese restaurant. Marge Champion asked Mary if she wasn't excited about Mr. Chipps being made into a musical and Mary was rude. She said she thought she'd wait until they did Mrs. Minniver before she got worked up.

Actually it's going very well although I have no way of judging these things; but Lancaster and Perry are very friendly. We saw some rushes last night and Lancaster manages to look both commanding and destroyed, young and old and when he throws up his face to breathe in the crawl he looks crucified. The colors are very bright. Since I won't play the drunk they've asked me to play the man who appears ballocky but I figure that if I look great in the movies ballocky I'll never get over it and

72. A French nightclub singer who appeared frequently on the Jack Paar "Tonight Show" in the late 1950s, wife of Ted Mills, an Astoria colleague.

if I don't look great in the movies ballocky I'll never get over it and so I've asked them to try and work out something else.

　Best,

　　John

Dear John,

　I expect you must be wondering about me and Burt and this is in haste since I must go down to Westport and see my rushes. Frank called on Thursday and said they had a great spot for me, a triple shot and could I make a ten o'clock call so I got down to the location at ten where they buttoned me into a bush jacket and put some stuff on my face. Well the scene is a cocktail party and the tables are all covered with gin and whisky bottles but these turned out to be dummys. This made me nervous so I said to Eleanor that if I didn't get a real drink pretty soon I would start vibrating and oscillating so then a prop man brought me a scotch. Weak. This was about 11 A.M. I had another at 11:30 and hung around until one when we had the lunch. Shrimp salad. Columbia sets a nice table. Anyhow I didn't get my call until three. Eleanor had told the prop man to keep my glass filled and so I was feeling pretty good. I didn't have a standin so I had to do all the rehearsing including the camera. It was a very complicated shot in which they sort of waltz the camera around, followed by grips with cables. I got very sweaty. Finally I got to rehearse with the stand-ins. What I was supposed to do was to shake hands with Lancaster and say "You've got a great tan there Neddy." Things like that. I was supposed to improvise. So I said to Frank that if a man and woman came to a cocktail party I'd speak to the woman first and Frank said that was allright. So finally Lancaster and this terrific 18 year old dish named Janet Landgard came on. She has natural honey-colored hair and enormous pale blue eyes and slightly crooked teeth and beautiful helpless-looking legs. So we rehearsed about a dozen times and then we got ready for the first take but when this dish came on instead of shaking hands with her I gave her a big buss. So then when the take was over Lancaster began to shout: "That son of a bitch is padding his part" and I said I was supposed to improvise and Frank said it was all right. I asked the girl if she minded being kissed and she said no, she said I had more spark than anybody else on the set. That's what she said. Lancaster heard her. Anyhow on the second take I bussed her but when I reached out to shake Lancaster's hand the bastard was standing with his hands behind his back. So after the take I said that he was supposed to shake hands with me and he said he was just improvising. So on the third take I kissed her but when I made a grab for Lancaster all I got was a good look at the surgical incision in the neighborhood of his kidneys. We made about six takes in all but our friendship is definitely on the rocks.

Hastily,
John

JOHN CHEEVER
Cedar Lane
Ossining, N.Y.

Tuesday
26 July [1966]

Dear John,

Afterwards I drove home because we had asked the Ettlingers for dinner and Genevieve and Teddy had asked themselves and Mary had poached a salmon and then Genevieve called and said to Mary Cheri I am soree mais we cannot come because of le trafic may we come on le dimanche and Mary said no and I got hold of the phone and Genevieve said Cheri, she has le voice of la petit enfant and that was that. So then I decided against going to see the rushes and Frank called and said They're Mahvelous, simply mahvelous but I don't think people will recognize you unless they know you terribly well because the camera seems to have hurtled you and then Mary packed her bags and went up to New Hampshire with Fred and I packed my bags and went to East Hampton with Sharman Douglas and Hope Lang and that man she married and then when I came back a lot of things happened and so I went to a shrink who said that I had developed a tragic veneer of amiability in order to conceal my basic sense of alienation and hostility and I was brooding about this an hour later when the phone rang and it was Esquire saying that they were doing a spread of Janet Landgard and that Janet had asked if dear Mister Shiffers would please write her captions because she didn't want her captions written by anyone but Shiffers and I said that I would write the captions and that's the way things stand.[73]

Hastily,

John

J O H N C H E E V E R
Cedar Lane
Ossining, N.Y.

Saturday
27 August [1966]

Dear John,

This is on Mary's American made electrict typewriter which I haven't mastered yet but I did want to answer Harriet's question without delay. The thing is that Burt and I are closer to Jackie and that set than we are to the Johnsons. We don't dislike the Johnsons but to be perfectly frank with you I haven't seen them since I went there for dinner in May. Burt's best chum is a man named Bill who is married to an Iranian princess. She makes her own perfume. Bill was Vine's doubles partner at Wimbleton. They all flew to Jamaica yesterday. This was embarrassing because the Wrapup Party was last night. I was to have

73. John sent me a message in a letter to his Hollywood agent (July 25): "Tell Weaver that someone at Esquire wrote me to say at the mention of my name 'Janet Landgard was quite visibly moved.' He may have meant that she moved to another table but I think he meant something else."

been a guest of honor but Frank called and said that Burt and Janet and Barbara and so forth weren't coming and that he didn't want to take the responsibility of inviting me to a party of grips. He said he thought I'd be sulky and so I stayed home and got stoned on cheap bourbon. I'm drinking cheap bourbon because I don't get paid for the picture until 120 days after they make a final print. That could be five years from now. Ben says he's sick of hearing about Burt and how I was in the movies and whenever the phone rings he says things like I guess that must be Mary Pickford.

We premiere in Cannes.

Best,

John

Ulysses Kay lived up to his advance billing. By the end of the semester we were hoping he'd apply for cultural asylum.

JOHN CHEEVER
Cedar Lane
Ossining, N.Y.

October 9th [1966]

Dear John,

Ulysses Kay, who is one of the most gifted and pleasant men I know, is teaching this semester in the music department at UCLA and I've written to say that you might get in touch with him. The Music Department phone number is Br 2-8911 and the address is 405 Hilgard Avenue. I hope this isn't meddlesome. I ran into Knox Berger[74] at the Club yesterday and we had a pleasant chat about you and Harriet and your house.

My fell purpose at being at the Club (don't tell anyone) is that my daughter and Robert Cowley appear to have fallen in love. She wants to throw up her job in Colorado and fly east.

74. Knox Burger, then fiction editor of *Collier's,* later a New York literary agent.

I literally sat across the table from him and asked: "What are your intentions toward my daughter?" He was quite lucid up to this point but then he began to stammer. His parents attended our wedding. So it goes.

> Best,
> John

> Cedar Lane
> December 13th [1966]

Dear John,

I used to have two reliable correspondents—you and George Biddle—and now I'm left with George. George is fine but he is inclined to write about the glory and the anguish of the human consciousness. There's been no word from Burt; but Yevtushenko blew in not long ago and Mary and I have spent several brisk evenings with him playing a game called Who Does Zhenya Love Most. Updike cheats. Zhenya lives on a diet of Tums and champagne but he's very energetic.[75]

I've seen Lennie only once since his return. The work goes slowly. We have snow and coasting now and the children all come home this weekend for the holidays. In Fred's class newspaper it said: "Miss Arena's fourth graders are preparing for the holidays in typical Colonial fashion by dipping their six inch wicks into warm wax."

> My love to Harriet,
> John

I had asked John to pass George Antheil's out-of-print autobiography, Bad Boy of Music *(Doubleday, Doran, 1945) on to Malcolm*

75. "John was amused by the buccaneer in Yevtushenko," John Updike recalled in a letter to Scott Donaldson, "and Zhenya (as we called him) was engaged by the debonair, raffish side of John. Both could put away the vodka, and though Zhenya's public performances (and he was never, quite, offstage, even in an intimate gathering) were far from John's muttery, Waspish manner, he admired them . . ."

Cowley at Viking Press in the hope it might be brought out in paper-back. "The prospect for its republication in paper seems rather bleak," Cowley replied.

JOHN CHEEVER
Cedar Lane
Ossining, N.Y.

Thursday
5 January [1967]

Dear John,

I've sent the Antheil letter on to Malcolm. His only, only son (divorced) is going out with my only, only daughter. If they stop listening to Thelonious Monk long enough to get married I'm going to change the name of the house to Clapham Junction. You'll be happy to know that I've never worn a blue blazer and I couldn't have had my horn glasses because I packed them away with the Christmas tree ornaments last year and didn't recover them until this year's Christmas eve. Yevtushenko has gone back to Moscow and when we parted he said: "Something terrible is going on in your country." Whatever could he have meant by this?

Chin chin,
John

"Mary and I find ourselves jockied into the position of Parents of the Bride," John wrote Lucy Moorehead (April 8). "For some reason the roles don't seem to suit us. We stayed up late last night talking about flowers, organ music, wedding dresses, newspaper an-nouncements, etc. We both felt like imposters. I got into my Morning Coat and marched around barefoot but it seems that I'm not allowed to wear this. Mary has settled for a black lace mini-skirt and a hat that looks like a Martian vegetable. Robert and Susie come out today for lunch and I'll make another plea for the Morning Coat. They are to be married in St. Marks in the heart of the New York slums."

JOHN CHEEVER
Cedar Lane
Ossining, New York 10562

Tuesday
[May 2, 1967]

Dear John,

Susie decided on Friday afternoon to marry Robert Cowley at a small ceremony at St. Marks in the Bourie. On Saturday afternoon she decided to invite two hundred and fifty people and have a large reception. Mary wrote an epistle in favor of small marriages which I delivered to Susie yesterday at lunch but she threw it away, marched up to Cartier's and ordered the invitations. I then arranged for a reception at the Century Club but after the steward and I had decided on the wine, the sandwiches and the flowers the chairman of the house committee said there was a by-law forbidding debutante parties and wedding receptions. I then went to St. Marks where there is a small garden or yard which could be used for a reception. Sharman Douglas agreed to get the city caterer to put up a tent and a bar but the minister said that if I didn't have a squad of policemen every bum in lower New York would crawl into the tent, piss in the punch bowl and throw empty Petri wine bottles at my Mother-in-law. I then went to Luchows where they had a room for 140 guests if most of them stood up. I called the Cowleys in Connecticut but Malcolm said this was out of the question because he can't stand up and most of his crowd have bad backs. When I got home Phil Boyer called to say that he had booked the Biddle Room at the Harvard Club. (Cap. 135). I took a bath and a Nembutal and was waked from a drugged sleep by Susie who telephoned to say that she had booked a nice small ballroom at the Plaza. (Cap. 150). The Cowley's haven't been terribly co-operative. Muriel keeps saying: "But his first marriage was so beautiful and we had a lovely reception at the Somerset Club." I've known them for so long that I can't believe knives are being thrown but something seems to go whizzing by my head.

Susie and Rob are very happy and Susie has never looked prettier. He is thoughtful and intelligent but not quite thoughtful and intelligent enough to Elope. I will now telephone Carey's and find how much it will cost to move one hundred and fifty guests from St. Marks to the Harvard Club. "You must be getting a lot of material for stories," said Muriel. That's how much she knows.

Ding dong,
John

JOHN CHEEVER
Cedar Lane
Ossining, New York 10562

Monday
[postmarked 13 May 1967]

Dear John,

I don't seem able to get back to work and so much has happened that I thought I'd keep you posted. I got a letter from the Nobel prize people who want to take a look at me and see if I can walk backwards. This would have disconcerted me except that the letter is addressed to Sir John Cheese, Offining. Then on the twenty-eighth I flew out to Colorado and got mixed up with some girls in the Denver airport. They said they were all tired out because they'd been drinking scotch out of a toilet bowl. "Was I naked?" one of them asked. "You even took off your wig," the other one said. Then she sighed and said: "Remember that night when we had to go to Norway and it snowed?" I then flew on to Colorado Springs where I took part in a literary discussion. After this I was driven up Pikes Peak and when I stepped out of the car, at eleven thousand feet, I fell into a ditch and tore most of the tendons on my left foot. At about the same time Muriel Cowley had a heart attack and Malcolm tore all the ligaments of his right knee.

We spent Friday night in town and were waked on Saturday morning [May 6] by a north wind and a bitter rain. I took a little gin in my orange juice and limped up fourteenth street and bought some umbrellas. There was a lunch for the ushers and then I went over to Waverly Place in a hired limousine to get Susie and Mary. This was about two o'clock. Susie has been living there in a tenement called Sans Souci but there was no name on the mail-box and when I started ringing bells at random women began to scream. I went out onto the sidewalk and yelled Susie, Susie and found she and her mother on the second floor front drinking champagne and looking at themselves in mirrors. We got to the church at twenty past two and Susie really had the wind up. She hadn't been so frightened since I took her into the African Habitat room in the Museum of Natural History eighteen years ago. Anyhow I took her arm and off we went. How radiant she is, people said, and what a wirey old gaffer. After I'd given her away I retired to a front pew and went into a complicated ecclesiastical rigamarole to prove that I am, after all, High Church.

Ben took Mary out and I took Muriel out and the guests—about two hundred—retired to a tent in the church graveyard. It is an old graveyard with flat stones so there was no trouble. We had eighteen waiters and one waitress and wine and hootch and food and tables and flowers etc.[76] After about an hour a bunch of hoody looking winos gathered at the entrance to the tent and I told them to drag-arse which they did. "You could have let them have one glass of wine," said Ben. Everybody acted in character. When the hard drinkers began to settle down for the weekend I asked the waiters to remove the flowers. This nettled Mary's sister who began grabbing center-pieces and

76. "The elder Cowleys played no part in the preparations for an expensive wedding," Malcolm Cowley wrote in *Sewanee Review* after John's death. He sent Mary a draft of the article before publication and she reminded him that "traditionally, at least in my experience, the parents of the groom do not play a great part in wedding preparations." Cowley let the statement stand, along with his comment: "At the reception under an outsize tent in the churchyard, the Cheever connection drank their champagne on one side of the tent, while the smaller Cowley contingent sat grouped on the other. That marked a growing difference in styles of life between the two families."

taking them out to her car. Her husband didn't come to the reception at all. He went to the corner saloon and got stoned at his own expense. Muriel Cowley didn't die as she had expected to and Malcolm got falling-down drunk which couldn't have been good for his ligaments. Susie departed in a flurry of paper rose petals ($10) and we all drove home.

    Best,
      John

News of the removal of the revolving ten-foot chorus girl John had seen from his bedroom window at the Chateau Marmont brought back memories John had recorded in a 1961 short story, "The Angel of the Bridge." The narrator flies into Los Angeles in the late afternoon and describes a sleepless night at his favorite hotel: "Outside my window was a monumental statue of a young woman, advertising a Las Vegas night club. She revolves slowly in a beam of light. At 2 A.M. the light is extinguished, but she goes on restlessly turning all through the night. I have never seen her cease her turning, and I wondered that night, when they greased her axle and washed her shoulders. I felt some affection for her, since neither of us could rest, and I wondered if she had a family—a stage mother, perhaps, and a compromised and broken-spirited father who drove a municipal bus on the West Pico line."

JOHN CHEEVER
Cedar Lane
Ossining, New York 10562

[Fall 1967]

Dear John,

    Every silver linning has a cloud, I guess, and how sorry I am to know she is gone. How vividly I remember those evenings when she revolved and I sat in the window, chain-smoking while her old father—a bus driver on the West Pico line—ate his sandwiches under a palm tree. It was bad enough when you and Harriet left the hill and with her gone I think I never want to return.

    Gin Field called to say that she was giving a small party on the 7th. I am supposed to appear here on the afternoon of the 8th before something called The Spoken Arts Society. It may not be advisable for me to go into New York before I perform my cultural buck-and-wing. These things take the skin off my arse but I'll wait and see how I feel. I am thought by the lecture agencies to be ebullient but my public person consists of a rich blend of Nembutal, gin and Miltown and if I get the mixture wrong I foam at the mouth. We would like very much to get you to Naples in July. All is well here or fairly well. Fred, Mary and I went up to Naples in July and while I interviewed Sophia Loren, Fred went up and down Vesuvio.[77] He loved it. I loved it. When Mrs. Vanderlip died the ownership of the house—Beechwood Hall—was contested by the heirs and the trustees have rented the place—all seventy-five rooms—to Susie and Rob. They walk their dog in the ball-room, drink their gin in the winter garden and seem very happy. Ben was arrested in Nantucket for stealing a sign. He spent seven hours in jail, charged with larceny, but the judge turned out to have read something of mine and they returned him to the custody of his beloved parents. He is home now which pleases me and goes to Antioch in October when I will miss him. You both must be very proud of the Warren book. I found it monumental, comprehensive and intensely interesting and I look forward to telling you how much I liked it when we meet.[78]

As ever,

John

October 18th [1967]

Dear John,

This yellow paper is not a regression; it's just that I'm out of stationary.

I'm very anxious to hear about the Warren dinner and

77. John was interviewing Sophia Loren for the *Saturday Evening Post*.
78. I was planning a trip East in connection with the publication of *Warren*.

what Harriet wore and so forth. I'm also anxious to know what plans Little Brown have for advertising. I had meant to say much more about the book when you were here but my natural ego-centricity seemed exacerbated by pain. The pain mounted as the light failed and I finally called the doctor and demanded the name of a urologist.[79] Specialists in this neighborhood are like tinkers, drifting from Scarsdale to Tarrytown and back again. I finally tracked one down in White Plains—an old man suffering from all the occupational hazzards of a life dedicated to the urinary tracts of strangers. His face was weary and finely linned, his white curly hair (or hair piece) pommaded and when he did what I choose not to describe he was obviously thinking about his retirement to the West coast of Florida. I thought of angels. Lennie and Gin came out on Saturday. Lennie was gentle as ever and Gin seemed much less angular. It rained. They went to England yesterday.

I got yesterday, in the mail-box among the usual, a letter from Sophia. "My dear friend," she wrote, "when I met you I appreciated at once your personality and your intelligence. I do hope we meet again very soon so I will have a chance to reciprocate your friendliness, etc." Glands be damned, I poured a hooker of gin and sat down in the library my head aswim with pictures of me and Sophia at 21, me and Sophia walking in the autumn woods, me and Sophia facing the television cameras at an opening, etc Cha cha.

Best,

John

When Harriett and I made a promotional pitstop in Washington, our congressman, Jim Corman, invited us to a party honoring the Chief

79. John was suffering from prostatitis when I visited him in Ossining a few days before this letter was written. As I was leaving, he gave me a copy of the October 21 issue of *The Saturday Evening Post* with his Sophia Loren interview featured on the cover. ("An eminent writer visits a great beauty and she talks about Streisand, poker, Sinatra, pep pills and Marilyn Monroe.")

Justice. We didn't spill any gravy or knock over any coffee cups and when Harriett inquired about the bandage on Mrs. Warren's left arm, she explained: "I was ironing a shirt for the C.J. and the iron got away from me."

JOHN CHEEVER
Cedar Lane
Ossining, New York 10562

November 11th [1967]

Dear John,

I was very pleased to hear that everything went so well with the Warrens and even if there was a little slip-up here and there I am sure, from your portrait, that the Chief Justice is not the sort of man who would make a scene about spilled gravy or an upset coffee cup. It all sounds fine. I called Lennie's doctor whose secretary made me an appointment for the end of the month. Then I went to dinner at the Century and ran into Doctor Draper who had that ghastly pallor that seems to be one of the occupational afflictions of urology. He was the man, of course, but when I cracked a few jokes about the situation he turned out to have no sense of humor at all. None.

My disease, at the moment, seems more fascinating than it is painful and I think I may get under the wire on medicine. What is most disconcerting is the suspicion that my muse, my unquiet tassel, my divine spark, my childlike sense of wonder my pervasive sweetness of heart may be nothing but a dirty infection. What I want is a large pill—yellow or brown will do—that will stabilize my p——e without any loss of verve. I have always known that part of myself to be foolish but it has never before been vindictive.[80]

80. "The infection seems closely allied to my basic sexual nature," John noted in preparing "some sort of dossier" for Dr. Draper, "and it seems that the blowup could have been caused by alcoholic and other excesses brought on by my anxious and greedy urge to take more than my share of brute pleasure."

But all is well, the weather is splendid, I've put up the storm windows and done a little work. My only brother showed up yesterday. He's had three alcoholic crises and has lost his wife, his children, his worldly goods, his memory, his liver and his teeth, but he seemed in splendid condition. My Father always said that it was an uncommonly hardy family and perhaps he was right.

    Love to Harriet,

    Best,

       John

Wednesday
[January 1968]

Dear John,

    . . . If you've seen Gin and Lennie they may have told you the news but anyhow Ben was arrested in a peace demonstration in Cincinnati and thrown into the work house. The charge was disturbing the peace and the bail was nine hundred. He got the lowest bail. The highest was forty-four hundred. He came home for Christmas with a beard and a short hair-cut. I said nothing about the beard and he shaved it off on his second day here. He remains his manly and gentle-self but he keeps giving me the compassionate looks of a son whose Father has never served time in the Cincinnati workhouse. Mary and I keep telling him what firebrands we were. After all she led the 1936 May Day parade. He's very kind. The trial is in February and he expects thirty days but one of his friends has already gotten fourteen months. The judge spent a year in a German prison camp and wants the defendents to get a taste of what he suffered.

    As a professional biographer what do you think of the Troyat? (I'm enclosing postage.) I'm in the artificial position of regarding Tolstoy with great reverence although I've not read him for twenty years. (Fet's grandson took me through Yashnaya Polyana and we both wept freely.) Troyat offends me when he describes paradoxical behaviour and then calls attention to the paradox. I expect the French to be more luminous and subtle. However I read the book with much pleasure.

My friends the Litvinovs are in trouble and our correspondence is now carried on in lush barometrical similes. "What a wind blew through Moscow last night," writes Tanya and I report deep snow in Cincinnati.[81] So it goes.

Best,

John

I had sent John a copy of my article, "Life Among the Power Children," a light-hearted description of the Executive Seminar Center in Berkeley, where my friends in the Civil Service Commission took delight in exposing midlevel federal bureaucrats to the Flower Children across the street at the University of California.

Friday
[February–March 1968]

Dear John,

It was very good to hear about the jurists, the IRS and I thought your piece spritely and eloquent. I saw Lennie recently who spoke of you and Harriet and the beauties of your house and your cracked crab with tears in his eyes. This was in his office where he has a refrigerator and a bottle of gin. We were joined by a charming young man who lives in Paris and is the mastress of Picasso's old mistress. He was very charming but his charm seemed to me not intrinsic. Then we walked to Lennie's apartment where Gin turned on the fans that stir the mobiles. She was all dolled up and had on a big sparkly ring and looked terribly rich which I guess she is.

Ben got off with a $150 fine, a long lecture and banishment from Cincinnati for life. One of his co-defendents got fifteen months. She is a Quaker and refuses to eat prison food. They

81. When John's publisher, Cass Canfield, went to the USSR in the summer of 1968, he wanted to look up Tanya, but was advised by the American embassy to stay with his bus group and not "take unnecessary chances." He did as he was told.

force-fed her at the end of twenty-eight days. She can't have visitors and won't write on prison stationary. Her poor parents are afraid she will die; and she likely will. Ben, on the other hand seems quite carefree. He has a white MG, a long haired blonde and is sports reporter for the Vandalia Chronicle. We see a good deal of Susie and Rob. They bite one another's ears and call one another on the telephone to say: I love you. I seem to have scored a victory with the New Yorker. I went there with a manuscript and said that the price would be five thousand dollars. Everybody turned white and went to the men's room but then they read the story and said five thousand was what they were going to pay anyhow.

    Best,

    John

Richard Carter, a film publicist and producer, never succeeded in bringing "The Bus to St. James's" to the screen.

JOHN CHEEVER
Cedar Lane
Ossining, New York 10562

April 25th [1968]

Dear John,

    I'm glad to know Carter's your friend and I do hope the picture works out. Henry sold it for peanuts and I'm sore about this. However Spiegel payed off. I deposited fifty thousand in the bank one Thursday.[82] On Friday a teller called and asked if I hadn't made a deposit. He seemed to remember that I had but there wasn't any record. The check it seems got stuck in the maw of the computer in Mt. Kisco and it wasn't until Tuesday that they got the money out of the cog-wheels. I then bought three airplane tickets to Curacao and some tropical toggery

82. Sam Spiegel of Columbia Pictures was making the final payment on the $60,000 purchase price of "The Swimmer."

including a blue jacket with brass buttons. As a direct consequence I was mistaken for a porter in San Juan, Porto Rico. A man tapped me on the shoulder and said: "The two brown bags and the red one. Gate seven." Mary giggled and giggled. We got to Curacao at midnight and were driven to the most remote part of the island. A sign creaked in the wind and in the lobby of the inn there was a radio station where a one-eyed man was broadcasting to Kiev. In the morning when I started off for a walk through the cactus forest I was stopped by the cyclops. "Where do we think we're going?" he asked, turning me around. "Our guests usually stay on the beach and mind their business." He and his wife did a soft-shoe in the bar late each night. I never actually saw the missel base but he was on the radio every night after the soft-shoe. We stayed ten days and got very brown.

I've seen Lennie once and he seems fine. We've had the porch painted, partially. One afternoon the painters settled down to drink beer and listen to the ball-game. When I objected to paying for this they all got into their Impalas and drove off, leaving me with the drop-clothes but I've always wanted some nice drop-clothes. My love to Harriet.

John

JOHN CHEEVER
Cedar Lane
Ossining, New York 10562

May third [1968]

Dear John,

I don't see why you worry so much about life insurance since we both have wives who are independently well-to-do and anyhow we'll all live forever. I remember you used to worry about Serutan. I worry mostly these days about what to do with the empties. The garbage men come twice a week and there is always a can of empties. They have commented on this. My father used to take them into Boston in a suitcase and dump them in a vacant lot but you can't do that anymore. Wouldn't you think they could put the stuff in a disposable bottle. It is a serious problem.

David Susskind, A. E. Hotchner and George Plimpton called last week to ask if I would support Kennedy. We had South African lobster tails for supper and Susie, paying a call (she does her wash here) said: "My parents are racists."

Best,
John

Carter had turned up with cancer.

JOHN CHEEVER
Cedar Lane
Ossining, New York 10562
July 17th [1968]

Dear John,

. . . It is terribly hot here. I'm very sorry to hear about Richard Carter; and I'm going to break with Henry. Donadio has left Russell & Volkening and I've left Harpers.[83] I want to get as much as possible under one roof. The Swimmer is doing very good business but I don't get a percentage. A neighboring blue stocking called me a few nights ago and virtually asked me to refund the price of her ticket. How *could* you have done such a thing, she asked. Ben was home from college for two weeks which he spent in bed with a girl named Nina. He seemed happy. I may be in Rome in the autumn and we could meet there.

As ever,
John

83. "I've changed everything—my doctor, my lawyer, my dentist and my liquor dealer," John wrote his old friend Frances Lindley at Harper & Row and thanked her for her work on *The Wapshot Scandal* ("something I'm not likely to forget"). Candida Donadio negotiated his contract with Knopf for *Bullet Park*.

John, a member of the grants committee of the National Institute of Arts and Letters, was responding to a friendly word I'd put in for Malcolm Braly, whose research for his prison novel, On the Yard *(Little, Brown, 1967), had been done, as the jacket copy indicated, "the hard way."*

JOHN CHEEVER
Cedar Lane
Ossining, New York 10562

[1968]

Dear John,

I should have written sooner but the Braley grant is still pending. I thought it had been cleared. There are two other candidates and a ballot was mailed out today.

Best,

John

JOHN CHEEVER
Cedar Lane
Ossining, New York 10562

Christmas [1968]

Dear John,

The metaphor of the nativity seems to have skipped Ossining this time around; but I remain hopeful. Yesterday the Institute (and this is highly confidential) agreed to give Brayley (the convict) an award. This pleased me. I've written nothing since the novel was completed and have spent a lot of time posing for photographers and mouthing crap about the essentially prophetic nature of literature. The agent continues to speak in half-millions but nothing has been signed. The day after Christmas we—all six of us—go to Curacao where I trust my broody nature will clap hands and sing, etc. My moody but affectionate wishes to you both.

John

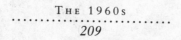

Dear John,

When we meet again, which I hope will be soon, you probably won't recognize me. In December a dentist suggested that I have all my teeth removed. I went to the hospital where there were the usual prattfalls. The anesthiologist was afraid that as an alcoholic I would resist gas and he overdid it. I was out for seven hours and woke in a very dislocated frame of mind. I thought Fred was calling me and kept stepping out into the corridor, ballocky, and saying: Everything's going to be allright, Fred. Then I noticed that my mouth was full of teeth and guessed that the operation had failed. I was about to stage an uproarious scene when I realized that while my mouth was full of teeth they were not my teeth. Now I have a very flashy if portable smile. Cheering a football game on tv my smile flew across the room. In Curacao I had to swim with my mouth shut lest my smile fall to the bottom of the sea. A vehement sneeze can imperil my smile; but I've been told this can be adjusted.

I've written nothing since the book was finished. This has been painful. When the book seemed to be ending I kept striking curious bargains with Time or the Devil. If I could finish the book I didn't care if my life were finished. Someone seems to have taken me seriously and I've never found myself in such a void.[84] This intensifies the booze fight. The spirits in the gin bottle seem to have complete mastery over my comings and goings. I've moved the cocktail hour forward from twelve to eleven and from eleven to ten. I trust this will pass.

As for the book: all movie sales fell through.[85] However it

84. "When the Scandal was done," John wrote Bob Gottlieb, his new editor, "I dreamed that I heard the voice of Hemingway saying 'This is the small agony. The great agony comes later.' I threw away all the shotgun shells and spent a week scything the woods. There's been nothing as bad as this with Bullet Park but I seem to be unable to remember the book."

85. *Bullet Park* was (to use John's word) "poleaxed" on the front page of *The New York Times Book Review*. "I may have made a mistake in using

is Book of The Month alternate for April and Bantam offered seventy-five thousand for paper. Knopf is asking a hundred and fifty. I have given fourteen press interviews including one with a young lady who wanted me to take my pants down. There was a scuffle in the St. Regis in which I had to keep both my smile and my cock from coming undone.[86] Chop chop.

John

J O H N C H E E V E R
Cedar Lane
Ossining, New York 10562

February 20th [1969]

Dear John,

Since I haven't heard from you I'm afraid my letter about teeth depressed you and that was not my intention. In fact the portable smile is quite successful. A beautiful and intelligent young woman whose name is Hope has decided that I am for her. We walk the streets of New York hand in hand, kiss at intersections and feed the lions in the zoo. Her husband does not like me. Her husband does not like me at all. When I come into their suite at the St. Regis he straightens all the picture frames. This makes her irritable. I've never straightened a picture frame in my life, but do you think this is enough to go ahead on?

Burn this.

Yours,

John

---

a suburb as a social metaphor," he wrote Tanya. "One would sooner read about fornicating in mountain passes and storms at sea. The reviews were mostly respectful but strangely diagnostic as if I had been mistaken for a philosopher."

86. "Get the hell out of here," John told her. Fifteen years later, when Jo Brans interviewed him in Dallas, he recalled the incident and said: "She wrote an extremely flattering account."

Cedar Lane
Ossining, New York 10562

April 9th [1969]

Dear John,

I'm delighted to know that you're coming east and I hope to see you here. Three weeks ago I went skiing in my orchard on the year's last snow. A pretty woman came down the driveway to return my copy of Portenoy. "How well you ski" she exclaimed. I then went into a brilliant double Christiania that began with a turn to the left and ended up in the emergency ward of Phelps Hospital. I am now in a cast from my hip to my toes and will be thus until well into May. Mary has been terribly nice and my plans to follow Hope to the coast have somehow gotten vague.

Tell Harriet that I can get Cardinals and Orioles to answer my whistle but I don't think they're as clever as quail.[87] The book comes out in a week or so and I am beginning to feel that it is a new automobile or a line of women's underwear. This is not complaining; but I've never seen such effeciency or heard such sums. Please call as soon as you get to town.

As ever,
John

JOHN CHEEVER
Cedar Lane
Ossining, New York 10562

September 22nd [1969]

Dear John,

It's been so long since I've heard from you that I'm not sure where you are and what you're doing. I trust everything is going

87. In a letter to John I had mentioned the quail that came skittering across our patio when Harriett called to them in what she took to be their native tongue.

well. I seem after six months, to have come through a massive depression. In June Susie and Rob went to Mallorca for the summer and Muzzy and Dazzy followed. Muzzy got sick and Dazzy got drunk. Mary then went onto Madrid and Rome while Fred and I stayed in Deya, baiting Robert Graves and swimming in the pellucid waters there. We returned here on a Tuesday when Ben and his girl [Linda Patricia Boyd] announced that they were to be married on Thursday. She's a wonderful, witty, pretty girl he's known for a long time. Mary wept throughout the service. "The only reason I'm crying," she sobbed, "is because his suit fits him so badly." It did too. It was the kind of suit chimpanzees wear in the circus.[88] Ben's father-in-law is in charge of security for IBM. They don't drink or smoke or read or wear blue shirts or talk much but they're quite nice. Ben is living with them until he returns to college. Ben's mother-in-law sews for him, makes popovers for his breakfast and arranges flowers in his room. He almost never comes to visit his old parents. He has a motorcycle and sometimes he drops in to take me for a spin. I don't like riding on a motorcycle.

Susie and Rob have moved to London for the winter and I expect I'll go and visit them if the reviews are any good. I often think I will come out to the coast to see Hope but I don't know. She's working very hard. I'm still not doing much work—not because I'm depressed but because I don't seem able to hit on a kind of fiction that has enough vitality to compete with first-rate reporting. I think one can but it takes time.[89] I haven't seen Lennie but we did dine with the Ettlingers and they were splendid. My love to you both.

John

88. "You would like Ben," John wrote Tanya. "He is immensely gentle, thoughtful and strong but he's one of those men whose clothing never fits. I've taken him to the most expensive tailors but he still looks like a bear."

89. "If you cannot write a story that is equal to a factual account of battle in the streets or demonstrations, then you can't write a story," John told a *Paris Review* interviewer.

JOHN CHEEVER
Cedar Lane
Ossining, New York 10562

November 20th [1969]

Dear John,

This is simply to report that I saw the Untermeyers at an Institute dinner last week and their vitality, wit, charm, intelligence and warmth would seem monumental if they were not so completely free of pretence. It was a great pleasure. After dinner, which is always heavy, Eudora Welty read a story. Halfway through the story a man at a table in the rear began to snore. It was a very diverse and percussive performance. Eudora continued gallantly in her Mississippi accent. On went the snorer. It was like a dialogue between the flesh and the spirit. Then someone shook the snorer. Being a great snorer myself I had never experienced the consequences of such an interruption. He awoke with a Vesuvian explosion of spluttering, coughing, farting and mumbled oaths. On went Eudora and of course the snorer was back at work a few minutes later. No one dared shake him again and so it went to the end.

Best,

John

I had begun to make carbon copies of my letters to John.

JOHN D. WEAVER
9933 Beverly Grove Drive
Beverly Hills, CA 90210

December 1st [1969]

Dear John:

Yes, Louis is really quite remarkable. He'd just turned 50 when we first met him in Kansas City, where he spent a month as poet in residence and Harriett helped him prune adverbs from one of the books he was working on at the time. Not long after he turned 80 we spent a couple of days with him in Berkeley, and it was wonderful to see the students trailing him across

Sproul Hall Plaza with the same delight. It's the same with Gregory Peck. Last night we went to see him save some astronauts whose retrofire system had malfunctioned. It was touch and go for a while, and the oxygen kept giving out (it used to be the water and Gregory Peck would always give his canteen to the delirious kid whose grandfather owned the mine), and all those lights on the instrument panel were blinking and Gregory Peck was saying things like SRO Negative and I kept waiting for Harriett to lean over and tell me how to fix the damn thing, but she didn't and they had to leave it in orbit, but they got two of the three astronauts back and a Russian cosmonaut helped with the rescue and it was like the U.S. Cavalry coming to the aid of the fort and everybody cheered. The audience was composed of members of the Writers' Guild. God knows what Spiro Agnew would make of it all. On the way home Harriett said she thought one of the astronauts had unwittingly stepped on the orbital guidance system during an extravehicular test program.[90]

Best wishes,

John

90. "A space epic with a horse and buggy script," Pauline Kael wrote of *Marooned*.

The 1970s

❧❦❧

"Tomorrow," John wrote his son Ben, May 9, 1971, "I go to Sing Sing to talk with the warden about giving a course in the short story to convicted drug-pushers, etc. If you don't hear from me you'll know what happened. Clang."

"The prison occupies a good deal of my time," he reported late the following year in a letter to Robert Gottlieb, executive vice president of Alfred A. Knopf. "I had hoped to do something like Camus but the raw material—misery and death—is disconcertingly farcical. Freddy the Killer said: 'I got twenty-five years for icing my old lady by mistake.' He laughs. A comely young man said: 'I chained this dude to the refrigerator and stole his parimutal tickets. He dragged the refrigerator across the kitchen and down the hall to the living room where he telephoned the police. I hid out in a car-wash but they busted me. I'll be eligible for parole in eight years.' One of my students—my favorite— was sprung after fourteen years and in this order got his head cut open, got beaten in an alley, broke his nose and lost all his front teeth at a dance in Peekskill and blew his savings ($200) on a cocain high. They're great company."

John insisted he had not gone to Sing Sing (or, as it is now called, the Ossining Correctional Facility) to gather material for a novel. "One doesn't marry in order to write about women nor have children to write about children nor teach in prison to write about prisoners," he pointed out in a conversation with John Hersey. The prison he called Falconer was his third and last "large metaphor," he explained, following his New England village (St. Botolph's) and his suburban towns (Bullet

Park and Shady Hill). All of them, he added, were "areas of confine-ment."

When he met his first students at Sing Sing, a class of about forty felons, John told them he would be conducting a course in writing, in telling stories, "in making sense of one's life by putting down one's experiences on a piece of paper." Later, when many of them were out on parole, they wrote John to say that by "putting down what they did, who they met, and what they said in the course of a day, they were able to hold onto themselves in a degree that they hadn't enjoyed before."

Meanwhile, John was drinking himself to death. At one point, when he was face-to-face with the Dark Angel, he mistook the hospital's intensive care unit for a tavern and ordered a double martini. In the first three years of this new decade he published only four stories and had not yet tackled another novel. When he was living alone in Boston, a colleague arrived with food Mary had prepared for him in Ossining. John was "sodden drunk," crawling up and down the stairs on all fours, but, John Updike remarked at the time, "even when he was most in a fog, a flash of wit and perception would remind you that it was John Cheever in there."

Before the 1970s ended, he had triumphed over his addiction to alcohol, escaped from his psychic prison and gone back to making sense of his life by putting down his experiences on pieces of paper. With the publication of Falconer *in 1977, he appeared on the cover of* News-week *("A Great American Novel"). The following year he won the Pulitzer Prize for* The Stories of John Cheever *(Knopf). In the Book of the Month Club News,* Clifton Fadiman *anointed John as "our best since Hemingway."*

Our correspondence lagged in the first two years of this new decade when publication of The Brownsville Raid *(Norton, 1970) set me off on a crusade for the exoneration of 167 black infantrymen summarily dismissed without honor by a stroke of Teddy Roosevelt's pen following a midnight shooting spree in Brownsville, Texas, in the summer of*

1906. Two of their five white officers were acquitted in courts-martial that affirmed the black enlisted men's guilt, although no evidence, then or later, was produced on which any one of them could be charged.

In January 1971 I sent a copy of the book to Augustus F. Hawkins, black Congressman from Los Angeles, who introduced legislation calling for the righting of this "grievous wrong." Six months later Secretary of the Army Robert F. Froehlke gave the men honorable discharges, posthumously, except for two survivors.

"That dishonorable discharge kept me from improving my station," eighty-seven-year-old ex-Private Dorsie W. Willis of Co. D, Twenty-fifth Infantry, told a New York Times *reporter. "Only God knows what it did to the others."*

JOHN CHEEVER
Cedar Lane
Ossining, New York 10562

Seventeenth
[June 1970]

Dear John,

It was very good to hear from you and I'm delighted to know that you have a book coming out. I've enjoyed your letters so much over the years that I've missed them but my own letter-writing proclivities seem eclipsed. Who cares that it is raining or not raining or might rain? Whenever I start a story these days I discover that I've written it. I went up to Saratoga last month and walking the three miles down Union Avenue I saw exactly twenty-seven details that I had used in stories—a wooden tower, old parimutuel tickets, a three legged dog, an iron deer, a dying elm, etc. I go on Monday for a change of landscape to Tokio and Seoul but I go with John Updike who is very grabby about the mise-en-scene. He walks a little behind me and hogs all the sensitive observations. Mary and Fred are coming along and I will be a PEN delegate in Korea.

Hope and Alan are getting a divorce but I seem, through some sleight of hand, to have ended up with Alan. Hope has found what she calls an "uncreative" man. Susie and Rob, who are living in London spent a month here and that was pleasant. Ben and his bride are living in New York. The swimming pool situation here is very critical. Most of the pools I use—and their attendants—have grown old. Pools that used to be open in May are not yet painted. I am studying Japanese and can say Good Morning (Ohiyoh) and where is the men's room (Oh-toh-koh noh behn-joh wah doh-koh dehes hah.)

Saranoya,
John

Saturday
[Christmas 1971]

Dear John and Harriet

It was so good to hear from you. I feel that John stopped writing letters once he got into his own swimming pool. George Biddle stopped writing when he hit 87 and while I'm working on a young woman named Beatrice Greene who lives in Bethesda the mail is so discouraging that I've often thought of moving. It snows. It is pleasant. Fred and I have just returned from your sister-in-laws demense.[1] We got into a terrible fight on the banks of the Neva during a blizzard. Night was falling. "If you think," I shouted, "that I am unable to abandon a fourteen year old boy in a blizzard in a strange country you are greatly mistaken." I hoofed off for the Hotel Europe. He followed. I could tell because he kept stepping on my heels. My disposition is no better and no worse than it was on that lovely evening[2] when Harriet pressed my trousers so that I would look neat for Jerry Wald.

Love,
John

In his New York Times *article about the exoneration of the Brownsville soldiers, the day before, Gladwin Hill had described me as "droll."*

1. My older brother and his wife had visited the Soviet Union.
2. It was midday.

Cedar Lane
The day after
[4 October 1972]

Dear John,

I was pleased to read in the paper that you are droll and my sincere congratulations on the force of your work. It must be very gratifying. It's been so long since we've corresponded that I feel awkward, not to say shy. Would you be interested in knowing that Ben is about to be a father, that Susie and Rob are living in San Francisco, and that Fred, at fifteen, is much taller than I? I have grown old, of course. My girth has gone from thirty to thirty-four and I grunt when I lace up my shoes in the morning. My struggle with alcohol has worsened. I go to absurd lengths to get the maid out of the pantry where the bottles are kept. I've done everything but shout "fire."

Fred and I went to Russia in November for the Dostoievsky Jubilee. The Russians said: "We do not think you will like Riga so shall we go to Tibilisi where it is still summer." That's where we went and I never saw a trace of the jubilee. I teach at Sing Sing these days and this is fairly adventurous. There is a collection of stories coming out in February and I hope to write another novel.[3]

I don't see Lennie but I called him and he had no news of you. Please write and tell me how you are and I'll get over my shyness. My love to Harriet.

Yours,

John

My typewriter has broken down and I'm using Fred's which accounts for some of the errors.

3. The short story collection was *The World of Apples* (Knopf).

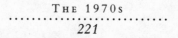

JOHN D. WEAVER
9933 Beverly Grove Drive
Beverly Hills, CA 90210

Nov. 11, 1972

Dear John:

I know the New York Times is supposed to print everything that's fit, but I had no idea it would see fit to describe me as "a droll, youthful man of 60." The story has produced a great many letters, mostly waggish, and none more welcome than yours. I've written you half a hundred letters in the last year or so. I just never got around to committing them to paper and then to the postal service.

We were very pleased to get news of the family, and would love to see Susie and Rob if they ever get down this way. We rarely manage to get up to San Francisco, but would like to have their address in case we do make it someday. It's been God knows how many years since we saw Susie, and it seems hard to believe that Ben is a prospective parent and Fred a teenager . . .

All is well here. Harriett is young and radiant, working on half a dozen different fronts. She has become something of a legendary figure in City Hall. Recently she casually mentioned to a friend in Public Works that the brush at our intersection with Benedict Canyon was so thick it was hard for us to see approaching traffic. A few days later I drove down the hill and spotted four huge pieces of municipal equipment, with a crew of 12, hacking a clear view of the canyon.

As you know, I've always enjoyed research, and lately have been at work on a book about Los Angeles. It grew out of a request I got a year or so ago from the Encyclopaedia Britannica to write the Los Angeles entry for a revised edition. I became fascinated by the pueblo's raunchy past and by how much of the story remains untold. I've been given a parking pass at UCLA, a treasure for which some researchers would happily kill, and I have a place set aside at the historians' luncheon table at the

Huntington Library where I eat with the learned men on nice days.

Thanks to Caskie Stinnett, we have a highly agreeable arrangement with Travel & Leisure. I do a little writing for them, take a writer to lunch now and then (on an expense account) and serve as a consultant on California matters, in exchange for which I get a modest monthly stipend. We'd both forgotten how convenient it is to have a check come in every month. The only trouble is that it reminds us how fast the months are going by. We hardly get to the bank with one check before it's nearly time for another. I guess that's part of getting old, and I really don't mind too much. I'd love to see you and Mary and take a brisk walk on a pleasant day.

Love,

John

Cedar Lane
[early December 1972]

Dear John,

I spent last week in Iowa City where Vance Bourjaily, filling my glass, asked if I could possibly know the Weavers. They love you very much. Mrs. Bourjaily cooked a Giogot en Croute and fell asleep. It snowed and snowed. I walked in the woods with Vance and got hooked on a shaky eight-bar fence. My performance was given in something called The Clapp Memorial. I got hoarse halfway through but I rasped on. Hoarseness is not, thank God, a symptom of Clapp.

It was great to have your news and my love to you both.

Yours,

John

JOHN D. WEAVER
9933 Beverly Grove Drive
Beverly Hills, CA 90210

3 December 1972

Dear John:

We were delighted to get some word of the Bourjailys and we both wish we could have sat in on your Clapp talk. Carl Foreman came to town with Young Winston. Harriett dug out my black tie and we went to the premiere with the Bakers. Herbie had to pass up the reception afterwards to go home to rewrite a sketch for Flip Wilson. The Paxtons have sold the beach house where we used to leave our shoes and socks when we went for walks. Brownsville keeps cropping up in the news and I hope Mrs. Conyers gets a large green check from Washington.[4] I also hope that eventually I'll make back my travel expenses on the book, but I'm not counting on it. We've had a glorious week of summer weather, sunny and in the 80's, but today has turned gray and cool. The Paxtons are coming to dinner, so we'll have a fire and brace ourselves against the winter. Sometimes it can last for three or four weeks.

Harriett joins in love to you both.

John

John was in Phelps Memorial Hospital in Tarrytown, felled by a heart attack brought on by drinking. As he lay in bed hallucinating, he was nominated for elevation to the American Academy of Arts and Letters and critics were praising The World of Apples. *The Sunday Susan brought him a splendid front-page review in* The New York Times Book Review *he thought he was imprisoned in a Soviet labor camp and refused to sign what he took to be a confession.*

4. Mrs. Boyd Conyers of Monroe, Georgia, widow of one of the Brownsville soldiers, later received a tax-free government check for $10,000.

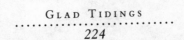

June Fifth [1973]
Cedar Lane

Dear John,

What really happened was that I began to get dizzy at the heads of steep staircases. This involved some psychiatrical research into the erotic significance of staircases in my youth. Then I became short of breath and one day I could hardly breathe at all. I was taken to the hospital where I was diagnosed as having heart failure and a possible attack of DT's. They put me into a webbed straitjacket, plugged me into four wall outlets and put me in a barred bed. My razor was in a table beside the bed and when night fell I got the blade and began to cut the straitjacket. I also cut myself. I got out of the jacket, inched my way down the bed to a hole at the end, landed in a heap on the floor and shouted VICTORY. This brought the cops and I was put into a second straitjacket—leather with brass bindings and four padlocks. I began to howl. First they brought in a black strongman who threatened to break my arm. Then they brought in a sinister Oriental who sharpened a syringe on a stone and knocked me cockahoop. When I came to, about seven hours later, I commenced to die. The family gathered around the bed to hear my last words. These were loud and obscene. The solemnity of the scene was lessened by the fact that Susie giggled. Then my heart took a turn for the better and the doctor says that every day I live my heart will improve.

Having been delivered from the grave has made me very happy. I've not been so happy in years. There is a sinister shrink in the wings who says that my euphoria is regressive, that I am high because I'm forbidden to do what I don't like to do (emptying the garbage) and that if I don't take his advice I'll end up in the stews. I've told him to kiss off. Drink has been no problem. I regard the bottles in the pantry as old and boring backgammon partners. The shrink thinks this is all phoney, but it works. I've not had a drink for a month and don't much want one.[5]

I wonder if you got your copy of Apples. I dictated the list to Susie when I was in an oxygen tent and under the impression I was in Moscow. If you didn't get one drop me a card and I'll see that you do.

Yours,
John

JOHN D. WEAVER
3783 Whitespeak Drive
Sherman Oaks, CA 91403

9th June 1973

Dear John:

We're delighted that you managed to beat off the dark angel, and we know the euphoria that comes with such a victory. We've had a couple of brushes in the last few years that changed our perspective a bit.

We so enjoyed our afternoon with Mary and Fred,[6] and wish you could have been with us. I showed them the Farmers Market, but your fish stall friend wasn't in evidence that day. I also exposed them to Doheny Drive. It is still a reassuring thoroughfare.[7]

We're settling into the new place, and are quite pleased with it. Harriett has been repainting and is now hammering and sawing away at some panelling. The town will soon be awash in editors, writers and booksellers, because of the ABA meeting. We plan to take in two of the parties, one for Mailer and one

5. Two months later he was back in the embrace of his "backgammon partners."

6. They had flown down from San Francisco, where they were visiting Susan.

7. Doheny Drive, the boundary line between Los Angeles and Beverly Hills, was the only north-south street John would take when commuting between the Chateau Marmont and 20th-Century Fox. He said he found it "reassuring."

for Irving Wallace. We weren't invited to the really literary function—the one for Linda Lovelace.

I'm flying back to Washington Tuesday night to testify on behalf of Congressman Hawkins' bill to provide compensation for the Brownsville victims. The hearings are Thursday, but they asked me to come a day in advance to help with the preparations. I'd love to get up to New York, but won't be able to make it, because of commitments here.

I didn't get a copy of Apples, but would love to have one suitably inscribed. Bob Nathan had just finished reading it when we had lunch recently, and was delighted with it.

Harriett joins in love to all.

John

JOHN D. WEAVER
3783 Whitespeak Drive
Sherman Oaks, CA 91403

1 September 1973

Dear John:

Some leaves blew in the pool this morning, so I suppose it's fall, only I can't remember whether we had summer this year. It was spring, I know, when Mary and Fred were here and we had such a lovely day together, and then we were to move. I guess that took care of summer. Anyway, we're comfortably settled and immoderately happy with the new digs.

We've had some good news from Washington. Hubert Humphrey's bill to compensate the victims of the Brownsville dismissal order has passed the Senate and goes to the House next week. The administration has dropped its opposition, so it should pass smoothly. This is the bill I went back east to testify for in House and Senate hearings last June. I'm particularly eager to see a government check go to our friend, Dorsie Willis, the 87-year-old Minneapolis survivor whose wife is packing about 10,000 pounds of Big Mac hamburgers a day to help pay for his arthritis medicine. Dorsie stands to get at least $25,000.

Carl Foreman was here the other day with his English wife

and two English children, Jonathan and Mandy. We had a nice afternoon in the sun. And we had dinner the other night with the Presnells, whom we hadn't seen for quite a spell. The years weigh lightly on Marsha, but Boy Chum is beginning to show a bit of wear. He's had some kind of heart flare-up. Being put in mind of his mortality has mellowed him considerably.

We were delighted to have Apples inscribed, and have placed it on a shelf set aside for the books we treasure most. Harriett joins in love to all.

    John

John had signed on for a semester with the writers' workshop at the University of Iowa. "The Iowa team is terrible but everybody stays for the last down and then you walk home under the elm trees which are numerous," he wrote his Ossining friends, John and Mary Dirks. "Theatre, film, parachuting, rugger, ceramics, weaving, cricket, bookbinding, soccer and LaCrosse are all swinging and the bumper sticker is WELCOME TO IOWA, THE GATEWAY TO NEBRASKA. *There is a ten-foot Paul Bury fountain across the river from my window but it's more of a pool than a fountain. The architecture ranges from the 1840's through brick buildings with Pindar and Aristotle on the cornice to a lot of Abramovitz. The elms and the river help. I missed the rocking chair contest and last night the amateur Topless Go-Go Girls Contest was delayed beyond my bedtime . . . My students are brilliant and diverse and when we bring off a seminar it takes three men to get me off the ceiling. I'd never known that particular high."*

Iowa House
Iowa Memorial Union
Iowa City, Iowa 52240
September 8th [1973]

Dear John,

I'm very glad to hear that the compensation bill is coming through. I guess it's the only case since Dickens where literature has had a discernable and a corrective influence on legislation.

My congratulations. Your letter seemed very contented and this was nice to receive.

They have been abusing raccoons at the Illinois State Fair and I have spent this gloomy, lonely, rainy afternoon in a hotel room clipping newspaper accounts for a friend in Scarborough who has raccoons for pets. I never thought it would come to this. However I'm going to be picked up for dinner by an oriental named Miss Chew and tomorrow is Get Together Day for the English Department Graduate School. There has been some talk about skinny dipping. I'll be here until Christmas teaching Problems of the Modern Novel but if boy-chum asks tell him I'm coaching LaCrosse.

My love to you both,
John

On my way home from a research trip to Wisconsin I touched down in Iowa City, where John had reserved a room for me at Iowa House. I was given this typewritten note when I checked in around 9 P.M.

Friday
room 436
[21 September 1973]

Dear John,

I'll be back by eleven and unless you need sleep and leave a No Disturb note I'll call you. It's very pleasant to know you're here.

John

When John knocked on the door a couple of hours later, he was not drunk, but was obviously back on the sauce. Next morning, walking around the campus on a glorious fall day, John gossiped about academic politics and illicit couplings among faculty and students, including his own arrangement with a coed younger than his daughter. When we got back to Iowa House, he showed me his room, which had little to commend it except a view of the river. He put through a call to Mary, chatted for a few minutes and handed the phone to me. "I'm so glad you're there," Mary said. It was clear to both of us that John was killing himself. When I passed the phone back to him, he ended the conversation with an affectionate exchange, looked at his watch and grinned. "You need a drink." I seldom drink before dusk, but we repaired to a bar, and by late afternoon, when a student arrived to drive us to the airport, I was nursing an untouched Canadian Club and soda and John was stoned. I left Iowa never expecting to see him again.

JOHN D. WEAVER
3783 Whitespeak Drive
Sherman Oaks, CA 91403

27th September 1973

Dear John:

I flew home in a sparsely settled section of the plane and managed to pick up a head cold along the way (there was an unexpected hour's layover in Des Moines), but after a couple of days in bed, I'm up and around again . . .

I was quite taken with my first view of Iowa and I'm delighted you've installed yourself in such a friendly and serene oasis. Enjoy.

Harriett joins in love.

John

PS: And please keep T&L in mind. Caskie would love to have a piece on your pedagogic experiences at Sing Sing or something drawn from the leaves of your Iowa journal.

Iowa House
September 30th [1973]

Dear John,

. . . I am sorry about pushing you into the mud and losing the way.[8] Otherwise your visit was such a pleasure that it is beginning to seem unreal. Nothing has changed, of course. The Iowa River flows under my window and as night falls the light

---

8. I wasn't "pushed." I slipped and almost fell.

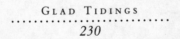

neckers give way to the more serious crowd. Yesterday was a Slavic lunch where it was discovered that all I can say in Russian is Thank you. This was followed by the president's reception for the new faculty. Non alcoholic and I didn't put my pants on until the last minute so they weren't rumpled. This was followed by a cocktail party, given by the Dean of the Liberal Arts College, followed by a dinner given by the head of Oriental Studies. I skipped another party (nude ping-pong) and got to bed early and sober but today there was nothing and I've been miserable. I do wish I were more comprehensive. Tell Harriet that there is an Irish tailor here and that I've ordered a suit and give her my love.

As ever,
John

JOHN D. WEAVER
9933 Beverly Grove Drive
Beverly Hills, CA 90210

12th October 1973

Dear John:

Sometimes I think I'm not cut out for the ceremonial responsibilities of my arrangement with Travel & Leisure. I'm all right as long as I'm picking up the tab for a Big Mac and a Miller's High Life for a broken-down greeting card writer, but when I move up in class I run into trouble. The other night we went to a high-toned affair at the Bel-Air Hotel given by Vicomte Bernard de la Giraudiere, managing director of Laurent-Perrier & Co. I arrived wrinkle-free, and everything went well until we were at table and I found myself sitting across from Governor Reagan's daughter [Maureen Reagan] who seems to regard her father as a bit of a radical. On my left was a very attractive blonde from the Time bureau here, and at one point she complained of a cold draught bearing down on her back. She had just got over a cold and was fearful of catching another one. I got up (only mildly awash in our host's champagne, which Harriett found inferior to our better Napa Valley vintages) and made my way across the room to the PR girl, who pointed to a man standing between tables 17 and 18. She said he would take care of the matter for me, so I walked over to him and explained the problem and he was furious. Turned out he was not the maitre d', but the president of a local wine and food society. He glared at me like he'd spotted an Annie Green Springs stain on my tie. I crawled back to the table and reported the incident to Harriett. She agreed with me that the man *looked* like a maitre d'. Reagan's daughter spent most of her time jumping up from the table and kissing people. She looked like a defrocked Avon lady. Two days later I took Bill Dana to lunch at Scandia. He showed up without a coat and they fitted him out with something oversize in tweed before we reached the maitre d'. Bill explained to me, "This is their way of keeping the riffraff in." Now we're bracing ourselves for a big affair at the Beverly Wilshire on the 29th. It's Harriett's birthday—a big one—and I hope nothing untoward happens.

Best wishes,
John

"It was all very pleasant but I did little work," John wrote Bob Gottlieb on his return from Iowa, and added that he was thinking of giving up his classes at Sing Sing. "They've discontinued the prison newspaper, for which I was an advocate. This was not, as I thought, because of the administration but because my dear friend the printer, was counterfeiting birth certificates and Salvation Army food tickets."

Cedar Lane
Valentine's Day [1974]

Dear John:

I haven't written sooner because there's been so little co-herence in my affairs and because I've done a number of things of which I'm sure Harriet would disapprove. When I came home for Thanksgiving things were all right here. Mary came out to Iowa for a week-end and I arranged a dinner party with the president and the VanAllens and a cocktail party for about sixty. She managed very well and looked lovely; but when I returned for Christmas she hurled at me the fact that I am responsible for all her misery and have ruined her life. A number of other things happened that I do not choose to mention. The Boston University offered me a full professorship for next year and I accepted this. It seemed a decent way of ending things. In the meantime I have been fucking a twenty-two year old graduate student who wakes me in the middle of the night to ask: Are those your own teeth? She's passionate, intelligent and talks a lot about clothes. I returned to Iowa last week. It's a long way to go for that sort of thing but I'll probably do it again. There's been only one mention of marriage. If we marry, she asks, can I have a pitbull?

All of this is bad for my health and I'm drinking. I'll come through. I did a piece for Caskie on Iowa and they paid my plane fare. I'll get back to the novel tomorrow or tomorrow. Last night the oil burner broke down and flooded the basement. This is all bad for my heart but how can I admit that the facts of life are lethal? How I wish I could have written you a serene letter about lasting love, open fires, faithful dogs, etc. Next time.

My love to Harriet if she wants such love.

Yours,

John

JOHN D. WEAVER
3783 Whitespeak Drive
Sherman Oaks, CA 91403

16th February 1974

Dear John:

Harriett and I are sorry. We love you both and we treasure our memories of the thirty years we've watched the kids grow up and seen your work come to enjoy the public esteem that was so long overdue. It worries us to think of your going back on the sauce, because we know—as I'm sure you do as well—that the heart supporting your pervasive sweetness[9] can't tolerate the stuff.

I'm delighted that you're going to do a piece for us on Iowa and will look forward to reading it. Meanwhile, we hope you'll keep the lines of communication open. Where does one write you? And what in God's name is a pitbull? Should I get one for Harriett who joins in love?

John

Cedar Lane
Friday
[postmarked 22 February 1974]

Dear John:

How like you to answer the unanswerable. It was the closest I've come to tears. I think you and Harriet and I share some sense of what love amounts to. I remember standing on the terrace of your old house, by the Cinzano ashtray. The door was open and I heard Harriet flush a toilet and open and close a drawer. The sensation of my aloneness was stupendous. I am, as you both know, quite stupid and callow but I do try to catch myself. It's like chasing someone around a barn.

Caskie took the Iowa piece that you suggested.[10] He also paid my fare so that I could return to Iowa House and discuss pitbulls. A pitbull is (I think) a bow-legged dog with a heavily furrowed brow. They break wind continuously. I was supposed to return next week for a reading, but I shall not. The situation at Mary's school worsens. This will be the second time she's [been] caught in such a catastrophe. She's welcome to come to Boston with me but she does want to teach. Fred returns on Tuesday. He's quite big these days and clumsey but when I hear

9. John's "pervasive sweetness of heart," like his "childlike sense of wonder," had long been one of our running jokes.

10. "An Afternoon Walk in Iowa City, Iowa" appeared in the September 1974 issue of *Travel & Leisure*.

him thump down the stairs at three am on his way to piss (he never closes the door) my coronary pains vanish.

Love,

John

Cedar Lane
Ossining, New York
Ash Wednesday [1974]

Dear John:

That was a gloomey letter I wrote and the mails are not meant to carry such hairy tidings. I think I forgot to say that Fred loves Andover, Andover loves Fred, I love Fred and he returns on the fifth. The headmaster of the school where Mary teaches has been canned and she has some problems about next year. What does a woman of fifty-seven do. Any solution she can arrive at will suit me.

Susie left for California yesterday and I suppose she'll call you if she's in Los Angeles. The fires are blazing, the sun is bright, the cars are running, a man is coming to repair the oil burner, my intellectual, sexual, coronary and digestive tracts all seem to be in order and please forgive my gloom.

Yours,

John

JOHN D. WEAVER
3783 Whitespeak Drive
Sherman Oaks, CA 91403

March 5, 1974

Dear John:

The sun has been shining here, too, I'm happy to report. Dorsie Willis, the last of the Brownsville soldiers, was in town last week with his wife, Olive, who is some thirty years his junior. Every Decoration Day she goes out to a cemetery in Minneapolis and puts flowers on the graves of Dorsie's first two wives, neither of whom she ever met. The Army paid them

$25,000, and it seemed like a lot of money until they called in a plumber and got an estimate on the downstairs bathroom Dorsie would like to put in. On his 88th birthday (it was also their thirtieth wedding anniversary) we drove them down to City Hall, where Mayor Bradley was waiting with a birthday cake and the key to the city. A few days later I arranged a VIP tour of Universal Studios for them. At one point when I was pushing Dorsie around in a wheelchair, we stopped at a men's room and as we left I noticed he hadn't gotten his fly zipped all the way up, so I told him he had to be careful, there were a lot of sex-starved girls running loose on the lot. "John," he said, "if you can't get it up, why take it out?"

If Susie comes through town, we hope she'll give us a ring. It would be so nice to see her and to get fresh intelligence from Ossining. We're both quite distressed about Mary's situation. We can imagine what a splendid teacher she must be, and we hope she manages to hold onto her classroom.

We're expecting a set of Britannica III any day, because it comes with the fee I got for doing the Los Angeles entry. We have no place to put it. Harriett has been calling a contractor about doing some remodeling. She figures that while everything is in such a high state of confusion, it would be a good time to have work done. It's like having your appendix out while you're under an anesthetic for major surgery. She joins in love to all.

John

"I am here as a professor only to make enough bread to keep Mary warm and Fred in Andover," John wrote Elizabeth Collins in a letter from Boston postmarked September 30. "It is not easy for a writer in his sixties to balance the books. Mary and I met in Connecticut last weekend and all was well. I think everything is going to be allright."

JOHN CHEEVER
71 Bay State Road
Boston, Massachusetts 02215

[September–October 1974]

Dear John,

I haven't written sooner because I'm not quite sure where to begin. Firstly I'm delighted about Harriet's health. I've never seen her anything but spritely and generously so. Things here are chaotic. Mary and I are separated perforce although she came down last weekend and brought me some food. Fred, who is at Andover, joined us reluctantly because it was the day of the Exeter game. He loves Andover. I took a professorship here for the money but between the state income tax and the Plymouth Rock laundry I will end up penniless and naked . . . Ben's beautiful wife asked him to wax the kitchen floor once too often. He packed a bag and came home to Mother. He's returned to his wife but things are touch and go. I am frightfully lonely and seem to lack much common sense.

My students are resolved and intelligent but they've stuck me with thirty-two. The administration is in hiding and I've not yet met the head of the English department. There are pleasant walks along the river and I count on these. The campus is scattered all over the city, people take pot and so[me] other things I chose not to mention. I shall go home for Thanksgiving and return refreshed and cheerful.

Yours,

John

My friendship with Ralph G. Martin, biographer of, among others, Jennie Jerome Churchill, the Duchess of Windsor, Cissy Patterson, Golda Meir, and Henry and Clare Boothe Luce, goes back to the fall of 1956 when we worked together at Adlai Stevenson's campaign headquarters in Washington.

JOHN D. WEAVER
3783 Whitespeak Drive
Sherman Oaks, CA 91403

22 September 1974

Dear John:

I put your Boston address in my notebook when I called from the T&L offices, and then managed to lose the notebook on my way to JFK by way of Long Island, where I visited Ralph Martin, who drove me over to Oyster Bay to see Teddy Roosevelt's home. It was littered with the stuffed heads and hides of animals he had done in for pleasure. Ralph and I were overtaken on our tour by a busload of black children, who were bored and restless until they got to the top floor where they went ape over TR's gun collection.

I flew home that evening to a nightmarish situation which has finally begun to brighten. Harriett had discovered a suspicious lump in her groin, on the same side as the melanoma removed from her left leg five years ago. Her cancer surgeon removed it under local anesthetic and it turned out to be another melanoma, so he put her in the hospital for more radical surgery.

He removed the lymph glands two weeks ago. The biopsy showed there had been no spread other than one tumor he had taken out a few days earlier. Then, on a Friday afternoon, the day before she was to leave the hospital, she was given some precautionary tests in the nuclear medicine lab, and the doctor in charge said there appeared to be something in the bowel, so she'd have to come back the following Monday. It was the longest week-end we'd ever gone through, and Monday was interminable. We showed up for tests at 10:30 A.M., and it took only about an hour, but we didn't get results until 4 that afternoon. By then we were well on our way to getting stoned. When the report turned out to be negative, we ordered up a fresh tot of gin for all hands. Harriett is mending nicely, hobbling around on her good leg, and in a couple of months she should be able to run and laugh and play the violin again.

I reread your Iowa piece yesterday, and it brought back

that lovely day we spent together on the campus (as I told Harriett, I'm sure you didn't mean to push me into the mud puddle). Caskie would love to get you back in the magazine, but unfortunately Boston is out, because he already has a piece in galleys. Is there anything else you'd enjoy doing for us? Incidentally, while I was at T&L, the girls showed me a piece Susie had done for the magazine, and they hope to get more work out of her.

Harriett joins in love to all the Cheevers.

John

MRS. JOHN CHEEVER
Cedar Lane
Ossining, New York 10562

September 25 [1974]

Dear John and Harriet,

Lenny Field just called and told me Harriet has had to have an operation. I am so sorry and do hope that pain and trouble was good and worth it and that dear Harriet is resting and mending.

Fred and I often speak of the time we spent with you all in L.A. hardly believing all those wonderful sights and tastes could have been condensed in so little time. He's off to school and loves it.

John's at school in Boston too, teaching at the U. So far it's not as great as Iowa, but his classes please and excite him and he seems to be keeping well, much better than he did at home, with all the care and cares.

I'm trying to keep this place in shape and teaching and making applesauce and jellies and poems.

I expect Susie will be back in S.F. soon, no longer with Robby, sorry to say. Have you seen her on CBS Spectrum? She's improving, I think, beginning to look and talk natural.

Lots and lots of love,

Mary

JOHN D. WEAVER
3783 Whitespeak Drive
Sherman Oaks, CA 91403

1 October 1974

Dear Mary:

It was so nice to hear from you, and I'm delighted to report that Harriett is mending beautifully . . . I hope to be able to persuade her to go to New Orleans with me on the 26th when a national organization of black women, the National Association of Media Women, is to give me an award for the Brownsville caper. We've never been in New Orleans, and it would be fun to celebrate her birthday there on the 29th . . .

Harriett joins in love and thanks for your letter. When we look back on all the years we've spent here, some of our happiest moments, it seems, came when a Cheever passed through town. So come again . . .

Love,
John

Mary's handwritten note on a UNICEF card, "Madonna and Child" *by Fra Filipo Lippi, Christmas 1974.*

This beautiful Madonna looks to me
like Harriet. Don't you agree?
We hope you are both well
and send lots of love,
Mary, John, Fred Cheever

JOHN D. WEAVER
3783 Whitespeak Drive
Sherman Oaks, CA 91403

16th February 1975

Dear John:

Louis and Bryna Untermeyer are in town for a week, and have brought with them a spell of lovely spring weather. We spent yesterday at the beach with them, and had a long, delightful lunch with Erica Jong and her young man, Howard Fast's son, Jonathan . . . Erica is a delight. One of the poems in her next book (she dedicated it to Louis) is called "Cheever's People." She has reread Wapshot Chronicle as often as I have, and was delighted that the house she's rented at Malibu included a copy above the bed (it's a king-size bed, by the way) so she could read it again . . .

It's been a nice week. Harriett joins in love.

John

MRS. JOHN CHEEVER
Cedar Lane
Ossining, New York 10562

April 14 [1975]

Dear John and Harriet:

How are you? Oh, how warm and flowery it must be there now. Here it is very chilling . . .

John left Boston about three weeks ago feeling so shaky that he has consented to go to an A.A. place in New York City. Three weeks confinement with sermons and without any chemical assistance is what it amounts to. He is suffering but resolute. Any kind word from a beloved friend would make a big difference.

Address: Smithers Rehabilitation Center
56 East 93rd Street NYC 10028

Wish we could see you. Hope to hear from you.

Lots of love,

Mary

JOHN D. WEAVER
3783 Whitespeak Drive
Sherman Oaks, CA 91403

19th April 1975

Dear Mary:

We're sorry John is going through such an ordeal, but delighted that he has come face to face with the Creature and we have a strong feeling he'll stare the monster down.

I wrote him this morning and also wrote Lennie Field who has just got back from London and would, I knew, want to know where to reach John.

Please keep us posted . . .

We're in the process of moving again. We've bought another house and sold this one, and we take possession of our new digs May 15th but don't have to surrender this one until July. It's a rather chaotic time just now, but Harriett flourishes on house-fixing-up, and it's turned out to be quite profitable. She did exceedingly well on the sale of this one. She joins in love to all the Cheevers.

John

JOHN D. WEAVER
3783 Whitespeak Drive
Sherman Oaks, CA 91403

19th April 1975

Dear John:

In the early spring Harriett started fluttering around the place with twigs in her mouth and next thing I knew we were in escrow again. She's found a lovely house a mile or two away, with an extra room she can use as an office, and it's on a somewhat quieter street, so I'm in the process of cadging empty boxes from Safeway and going over the books to see which ones I could get along without. We sold our house to a very agreeable young couple with a four-year-old son who should be very happy here for the same reason that I'm not—my workroom faces a cul-de-sac that is a public playground. I think they bus kids in on Saturday . . .

Harriett is selling off some furniture, packing linens and reading the fine print in the escrow papers. Hang in there, she says and joins in love.

John

Smithers Clinic
56 East 93rd Street
April 21st [1975]

Dear John,

This means I've missed two Weaver Houses. I'll never catch up. When I talk with someone like Lennie he will say: "You mean that you never saw the house they moved into after they moved out of the house they moved into after they moved out of Hillside Avenue?" It makes me feel rather left out but in this Alcoholic Rehabilitation Center this is an emotion I should admit to oftener. "But I don't really feel left out," I say. Then they'll ask me why it is that I don't know where my old friends live.

I'm really allright but I can't say so here because only the hopeless lush claims to be allright. I'm to be here for twenty-eight days and I'll make it although the dropout rate is very high. I'm allowed out on Sundays to go to church and on Sunday afternoons I can have visitors. Mary and the children come and I love seeing them. They keep telling me I look much better. I've lost weight but my stomach has not got the word and I'll leave here a skinny man with a great belly and coffee nerves. That's a point of view I'm discouraged from taking because I've ruined my life with false light-heartedness.[11]

Love,

John

On July 4 I sent John a copy of Erica Jong's poem "Cheever's People" and gave him our new Sherman Oaks address.

11. "The counselors at Smithers," Scott Donaldson pointed out after reading *Glad Tidings* in typescript, "did not understand, as these letters make clear, how much that light-heartedness expressed the inner man. As one of his later journal entries put it, 'If I can laugh I can live.' John Weaver was one of the few he could really laugh with."

Cedar Lane
Ossining, New York
July 9th [1975]

Dear John,

Thank you for sending on the poem. I had not read it and it was very kind of Erica Jong. I can't, sincerely, thank you for having written to me between houses. Do you realize that you take up two pages in my address book and that the only house I've ever seen was the one on the hill? When you have settled at Deervale I shall come to the coast. Fred wants to go to Berkeley and I expect we'll come out in the fall for a look, but not if you're moving.

Fred got honors at Andover and is (by my lights) marvelous. Susie is an editor at Newsweek and Ben, very handsome and expensively dressed, is on the staff at Readers Digest.[12] My own affairs seem more antic than most. I could write that I resigned my Boston professorship in March and returned here in time to see the Star Magnolia in bloom. I would sooner write that I was troubled by Ann Sexton's suicide, that I detested Boston, that I called the department head a delinquent asshole and, returning to a bad situation here, had myself confined for a month to a dryout tank on 93rd Street. This was rather like being hung from my thumbs. My room-mates were: 1 con-man, 1 delicatessen clerk (can I help you? he asked in his deepest sleep), 1 ballet dancer (he did not drain the bubble bath) 1 man with an inoperative asshole and 1 pleasant sandhog with whom I played backgammon. I lost twenty-five pounds and a good deal of spiritual dross.[13] Now I work in the mornings, swim with Fred in the afternoons and in the evenings go into damp church basements and say: "My name is Jawn and I am an alcohaulic."[14]

12. As he recalled in his first novel, *The Plagiarist* (Atheneum, 1992).
13. "I came out of this prison 20 pounds lighter and howling with pleasure," John wrote Tanya (June 2). "That was a month ago, and I'm still howling. I howl, write, dance, swim, eat, drink (tea only) and am terribly kind and patient to all dogs and children." He had come to the conclusion that "part of my role is to be buried and arise at fairly frequent intervals."

I weigh myself a lot and count my visible ribs.(8)

Don and I lunched last week. He's writing a play and is happy about this. Lennie writes that he and Gin will go to China in the fall and if it can be managed. Fred and I will see you then.

As ever.

John

JOHN D. WEAVER
3893 Deervale Drive
Sherman Oaks, CA 91403

23d September 1975

Dear John:

We've just gone through a reprise of the ordeal of last September, when, after a trouble-free stretch of five years, Harriett turned up with another melanoma, this one necessitating the removal of the lymph glands on the left side of her groin. Three weeks ago she turned up with a nodule on the scar of last year's operation. The doctor clapped her into a hospital for a series of tests, including a nuclear scan, and late yesterday afternoon we got the good news that none of the tests had come up with anything abnormal. The cancer specialist from UCLA who examined her in the hospital says there is no need for chemotherapy or radiation, so she is back at work on the remodeling of the house. At the moment she is sawing away on some bookshelves.

T&L has undergone an editorial shakeup. Caskie, who reaches the mandatory retirement age of 65 next September, has assumed emeritus status and will be spending most of this year traveling and writing. He and his managing editor, Dave Thomas, have been succeeded by Pamela Fiori and Don Gold,

14. John continued to attend AA meetings regularly for the rest of his life and when he took his turn as a speaker, he often improvised. Temperance could not have had a more persuasive champion than this little chap with the dry nervous laugh and spurious English accent who spun chilling stories of drink, debauchery, degradation, and redemption.

both friends from the old Holiday days and both a delight to work with.

They'd like very much to get you to do something for us, preferably something in the leisure half of our editorial constituency. I suggested skiing, because I thought it might be nice for you and Fred to have a little holiday outing together. In checking our records, I see we've covered skiing in the Tetons, the Rockies (including the Canadian Rockies), New Mexico, Val D'Isere and Heavenly Valley, California. Does that leave any slopes that might interest you?

I had a note the other day from Ken Lamott telling me that Calvin Kentfield had done himself in. Ken gave no details.[15]

The hills are alive with the sound of Harriett's saw. She joins in love to all the Cheevers on this very lovely morning.

John

Cedar Lane
Ossining, New York
October first [1975]

Dear John,

It is not possible, of course, to sympathize with anything so dark, frightening and painful as Harriet's illness must have been; but one can try as I've tried, for most of my life, to pray. My love to Harriet and I can hear the hills ring with her sawing. Twenty-five years ago I wrote: "Which came first? Christ the Saviour or the smell of new wood?"[16] As I remember, when Harriet built book-shelves you sand-papered them and this ought to keep your hands out of mischief. As for prayer I was quoted copiously at Loyola upon the cannonization of Mother Seten. Don't tell Caskie.

15. Ken Lamott, a free-lance writer, lived in the San Francisco area. Calvin Kentfield was the writer with whom John had an affair in Hollywood in the winter of 1959.

16. John's reflection on "the smell of new wood" appeared in *Bullet Park* (1969).

Ben is at Readers Digest. He wears expensive clothes and shoes, eats shell-fish souffles and plays tennis. He doesn't much like me or at least my clothes. It looks now as if Fred and I will be at Stanford in the middle of December. I will perform and Fred will look at the university. I'll write when I know the dates. Fred, by the way, hates skiing. He also cannot ride a bicycle. As soon as I discovered this horrible fact I took him to a psychiatrist. When this failed I was about to push him off a cliff when I remembered that you too didn't ride a bicycle. Such is the chain of being. We've lived happily together ever since.

My love to you both,

John

JOHN D. WEAVER
3893 Deervale Drive
Sherman Oaks, CA 91403

Nov. 8, 1975

Dear John:

The new room has been laid wall to wall with new carpeting and Harriett is busy hanging pictures, rearranging furniture and building some cabinets and bookcases for odd corners. Once it's done, it's going to be the best of the four Harriett Weaver houses. It has something of each of them, and much that is unique to this one. We hope you'll come see it next month when you light out for Berkeley.[17] You and Frederick can have Harriett's workroom. She could use the vacation.

I caught up with Sid Perelman when he breezed through town recently. He was staying at the Marmont, which seems not to have changed a bit since your residency in the Mitzi Gaynor suite . . . It had been years since I'd seen Perelman. I'd forgotten what a joy it is to be with him. In a socialist country he'd be nationalized.

Our new T&L editors, Pamela Fiori and Don Gold, are

17. I had forgotten that Fred wanted to look at Stanford rather than the Berkeley campus of the University of California.

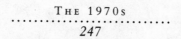

devoting the May issue to the outdoors and would love to have you do the lead piece (about 2,500 words). It occurred to me that perhaps you'd like to work it into your trip west, and show Frederick something of the outdoors. He may not go for ski slopes, but what about some warm, empty stretch of desert in December?

Yesterday I suffered indignities and a degree of pain I hope will never be visited on me again. I got up in the morning pissing claret, which turned to rosé two hours later and finally, around mid-morning, could have passed for a badly made Chablis. Our internist turned me over to a wondrously gentle and compassionate urologist, who said I had a badly infected bladder. He gave me some medicine which seems to be helping, except now I'm pissing orange Koolaid. I remember the pain you were in that rainy day I came to see you years ago, and if I was not sufficiently respectful I apologize. I had no idea what devilment urologists can get into once you're at their mercy.

Harriett joins in love to all the Cheevers . . .

As ever,
John

Cedar Lane
November eleventh [1975]

Dear John,

I want to hear the hammering and the sawing and smell the new wood but this won't be until January. Fred's school and Stanford both close on the 10th of December. Some student organization has offered to "personalize" my stay but they haven't told me what is involved and Snowcroft hasn't settled on a date but I'll write as soon as I know.[18]

You were very helpful the day I had my pisser trouble and it might help you to know that I've stopped looking at what

18. Richard P. Snowcroft was director of the Creative Writing Center.

comes out of there. I turn my head to the left and if I have a stiff neck I shut my eyes. I do hope the bladder condition is cured. I should think that very disconcerting.

As for the Outdoors I am flattered to have been thought of but I may not be the man. I bound outdoors all the time shouting about how glorious it is but then I do the same thing indoors. I don't seem to possess a sage or considered opinion. And I am working on a book that won't be done until spring or summer. I can't say that I'm working on a novel. I say that I'm working on a long piece or revising a collection of stories or writing a biography of Booth Tarkington but I can't tell the truth. I'm sure you'll understand.

Love,

John

JOHN D. WEAVER
3893 Deervale Drive
Sherman Oaks, CA 91403

16th November 1975

Dear John:

Yes, January by all means. The place will be more habitable by then . . .

We're all sorry you can't do the outdoors piece for us, and we hope that once the book is done you'll keep us in mind for something else.

There's a Capra Unit reunion dinner next Saturday. I called Carl Foreman to see if we might go together, and found he'd already arranged to be picked up. By Kitty and Omar Bradley.[19] Sic transit.

As ever,

John

---

19. Carl had done nothing to dampen General Bradley's hope that Sergeant Foreman might make a film based on his life.

JOHN CHEEVER
Cedar Lane
Ossining, New York 10562
January 10th [1976]

Dear John,

This is tardy because I've just bought my ticket and in haste because I'm about to have a tooth extracted. I will arrive in SF on Wednesday afternoon and in LA on Sunday afternoon. I would like to stay with you from Sunday through Wednesday but if this is in any way inconvenient I can stay at the Marmont. I'll be in a dormitory in San Francisco but Stanford hasn't told me which one. I'll call you from there. By Wednesday I mean the 21st, by Sunday the 25th and my departure would be the 28th.

Yours,

John

JOHN D. WEAVER
3893 Deervale Drive
Sherman Oaks, CA 91403
16th January, 1976

Dear John:

We are delighted that you are heading this way (will Fred be with you?) and we'll be awaiting your call from San Francisco to alert us as to your flight to Los Angeles on Sunday the 25th. Hope you can time things to get here by early or mid-afternoon. We thought we might ask Marsha and Boy Chum to come break bread with us that evening. We're having glorious warm, sunny weather. Hope it holds up.

Harriett sends love and has your room in readiness. See you on the 25th.

John

Cedar Lane
January 14th [1976]

Dear John,

This is simply to report that Fred will not be able to come to Sherman Oaks. He remembers you both and is sorry not to see you but Andover has been difficult. They consider California to be some land on the other side of the Charles River. They will not let him out of class until late Thursday afternoon. He arrives in San Francisco on [at] two Friday morning and must return to Andover on Sunday for an early Monday class. All of this in spite of the fact that he has completed all of his college credits and has honors in history, english and russian. We will go to the airport together on Sunday and I'll take the shuttle down to Los Angeles, but I'll call you long before then. Fred and I will be staying in Florence Moore Hall and Richard Snowcroft in the English department will take messages. I've lost his number.

We all seem very excited. Fred called last night and has agreed to go to Brooks and buy a jacket. Susie, who will also be there, seems quite jumpy. I'm worried about wrinkles. Mary gave me a new suitcase for Christmas and if I take it my clothes will be wrinkled and if I don't she will be angry.[20] I am going to take 8 shirts, 5 prs underdrawers, 8 prs socks and a suit I had cut in Iowa. I'll see you very soon.

Yours,
John

John and I had been called on to speak at so many memorial services for departed friends we had begun to compare notes and one sunny winter afternoon we delivered poolside eulogies of one another. I was pleased with his sendoff.

JOHN D. WEAVER
3893 Deervale Drive
Sherman Oaks, CA 91403

2 February 1976

Dear John:

We keep telling ourselves, "This is not a time for sorrow," but we miss you and we hope you'll come back soon. Meanwhile, we have our Breck shampoo (luckily we both have

20. John opted for the suitcase.

Normal Hair), our Cheever azalea (it seems quite at home poolside beside the podocarpus) and the memory of a most delightful reunion.[21] It seemed like only a week or so had passed since the days of the Mitzi Gaynor Suite and North Doheny Drive . . .

I spoke to Caskie's successor, Pamela Fiori, about our talk on Water, and she would love to have your reflections on this recurring theme in your work (baptisms . . . rain . . . the sea . . . Eritren . . . your dowser friend). Such a piece would cause great rejoicing here and in New York. I hope it lies within your paradigm.[22]

Harriett joins in love. It was such a joy to see you big with book.[23]

John

For the first time in our thirty-one-year exchange of letters John spelled Harriett's name correctly, but only for a short while.

Cedar Lane,
Ossining
February 2nd [1976]

Dear John and Harriett,

I'm still struggling with my orientation. I'm not international; I'm not even transcontinental. Lang[24] appeared not to be at the airport when I arrived at midnight. TWA here is cavern-

21. He had overlooked a bottle of shampoo in packing. The azalea was a present for Harriett.

22. On one of our afternoon walks John had brought me up to date on which words were in fashion back East and must be worked into a piece of writing to give it "class." The current favorite, he said, was "paradigm." He used it twice in *Falconer* and *Oh What a Paradise It Seems*.

23. It was also a joy to see John sober, but, as I reported to Louis and Bryna Untermeyer, he was chain-smoking: "At breakfast we'd try not to frown at his cigarette, and then in the evening he'd be equally gracious about our tot of whisky."

24. Donald Lang, one of John's Sing Sing students, had become a family friend following his release in December 1971.

ous with red carpets and white vaults and I wandered through these shouting Lang, Lang, Lang. An old man with a vacum cleaner told me that we were alone. (Lang claims to have been asleep on a sofa in a dark corner.) Then I stood coatless in the cold, waiting for a bus. A friendly cab-driver told me that his mother-in-law had just had a heart attack. On the strength of this I drove with him into New York. This was fifteen dollars. I was about to check in at the Biltmore when the night manager told me that a single room would be forty-eight dollars. It was half-past one when I carried my suitcase back onto the cold and empty street. Had it not been for your fifty dollars I might have spent the night in jail. The Commodore gave me a room for twenty-eight dollars. This room, excepting for a curiously placed mirror, seemed quite homey. I took a local out in the morning, went to AA that evening, lunched at the club on Friday and spent much of Saturday skating with Art Spear. We skated on Sara's pond.[25] Sara was packing to leave for Narobi. Sara is crazy about elephants. She gave us tea. Susie came out yesterday morning and did the Bloody Mary circuit with me. Susie is very chatty. I arranged to go bicycling today but when I woke at five this morning to let the dogs out I found the country buried in snow and howling with a fifty-mile gale.

To try and thank you would be as absurd as trying to calculate how long it had been since we last met. These seem to be non-verbal matters. I do want to be posted on Harriett's condition and the operation. I also worry about the drought and the Times is not reliable. Yesterday they reported the drought, the fire-hazard, the crop failure, the doctor's strike and threw in a possible earthquake. The Times is insecure. Now I will shovel snow which, excepting for cutting my toe-nails at the edge of your pool will be the first practical thing I've done in a week.

Yours,

John

25. Art Spear was a member of John's Friday lunch club and, like Sara Spencer, a friend and neighbor.

Cedar Lane,
Ossining,
February seventh [1976]

Dear John,

The TIMES as you must know, did report the end of the drought but they then predicted a freezing spell. They ended the doctor's strike but they did not mention the man caught in the meat-grinder. As for water I would be delighted to do something for T&L when the book is done but in this connection you should know that a professor named Daniel Subotnick had not read Artemis until he had completed his life's work; a tome called SHIT.[26] He is at the University of Chicago. His tenure is in the department of music. William Morris put the book up for grabs and a reader at Delacorte went to pieces. The reader is named LeSuer. I did not, Harriett, make this up. Anyhow LaSuer wrote: "This dissertation on excrement and defecation examines constipation, diarrhea, colitis, hemorrhoids, toilet tissue, toilet seats and laxatives and is the most beautifully written and exhaustively researched piece of non-fiction to cross my desk in years. This book is unique and liberating!" I guess LaSuer is still on the payroll but Delacorte won't touch the book because of my irreverence in Artemis. So this poor asshole in the music department at Chicago will die if I do not take a public and affirmative position regarding a subject I no longer wish to mention.[27]

26. In his *Playboy* story, "Artemis, The Honest Well Digger," John created J. P. Filler, a college professor who gained wealth and fame by writing a book called *Shit*. "Filler had traveled widely," John wrote. "There were the toilets of New Delhi and the toilets of Cairo and he had either imagined or visited the Pope's chambers in the Vatican and the facilities of the Royal Palace in Tokyo. There were quite a few lyrical descriptions of nature—loose bowels in a lemon grove in Spain, constipation in a mountain pass in Nepal, dysentery on the Greek islands. It was not really a dull book."

27. When Russell B. Adams Jr. wrote John about *The Privy Papers,* his unpublished history of toilet facilities from prehistoric times to the present, he received a prompt reply: "My congratulations and best wishes. You can't

It's cold and brilliant and snow-buried here and I've had a terrible cold ever since I got off the plane. How pleasant it must be to hear the rain.

Yours,

John

JOHN D. WEAVER
3893 Deervale Drive
Sherman Oaks, CA 91403

16th February 1976

Dear John:

. . . I'm sorry that by suggesting a piece on water for T&L I've complicated your already involved relationship with Dr. Subotnick. I reread Artemis last night, and I can see where your handling of SHIT, even though in paperback, could be offensive to a man who has given so much of his life to the crapper. I'll leave you to square things with Dr. S, and will continue to hope that once your book is done, you'll turn your attention to T&L.

Harriett joins in love, and wants you to know that the Cheever azalea, after more than a week of rain and sun, is all abloom, enjoying a premature spring ejaculation.

John

The Walls of Light *was the working title of* Falconer.

Cedar Lane
February 21st [1976]

Dear John,

This is in haste and confusion as I expect everything will be until I finish the Walls of Light. I trust it will be done by June. Your editor wrote me kindly about water and I uncivilly did not reply because the letter didn't seem to demand an answer. The subject seems overwhelming. Reading about the Angor and

---

call it SHIT of course because that's copyrighted by Filler. And anyhow you'd have trouble with the Japanese translation. They have no such word."

Khyber civilizations it seems that the severity and brevity of their monsoons determined their culture. Thus the Angor Wat is a temple to water. Do keep me posted on your health and Harriett's. It is a dark, rainy Sunday here and Mary has crossed the river to see the 12th grade perform Cocteau's Orpheus. She did not tell me she was going until she left because if I can break up Cinderella what wouldn't I do with Orpheus. Harriett won't believe that Roger Wilson has just called and asked if he can come and get some water. Our water is celebrated for its flavor and purity. Tell Harriett that Malraux said: "I do not lie. My lies become truth."[28] It's better in French.

    . . . Eddie Newhouse showed up yesterday. Having polished off Carson McCullers and Joe Liebling he has decided to be of help to my biographer when I die. Anyhow he watched me through lunch where I chatted with a defrocked Justice of the Peace, a German Herptologist and Mrs. Vanderlip's former social secretary. We then went to the bank where I cashed my allowance ($50) and goosed Miss Kennedy. We went from there to the town hall to get tags for my four dogs. There we encountered an ex-mayor who is bananas and was wearing a new Dodgers uniform. He shouted "Walter" and embraced me. Back at the house we found Roger, Art, John and Tom ready for a bicycle trip. I shook hands with Eddie, mounted my 3-speed Oxford and pedalled off into the distance. The only way I can squelch this sort of thing is to outlive Eddie; as I will.

    Yours,
    John

28. One must be wary of John's "quotations." When John Hersey inquired about the source of "Literature is a force of memory that we have not yet understood," a line he had attributed to Cocteau, Cheever said, "Come, John, you know I made that up."

JOHN D. WEAVER
3893 Deervale Drive
Sherman Oaks, CA 91403

March 8th 1976

Dear John:

I'm going to the hospital this afternoon, and tomorrow our internist will take some routine tests, and the urologist will ream out my prostate on Wednesday. Meanwhile, I've cleared my desk, gathered a stack of books and back issues of the New Yorker to read, and after a bowl of chicken soup with Harriett, we'll head for Mt. Sinai by way of the Bank of America. Saturday, to take our minds off medical matters, we went to see One Flew Over the Cuckoo's Nest, and when we came out, I spotted the National Tattler on a newsrack, and there was a big black scarehead: INEPT SURGEONS KILL THOUSANDS. Only the day before I'd gone out to the West Valley to see the councilman who is chairman of the council committee responsible for the public library. He wanted to talk to me about my views on a new central library, but when he heard I was going to be operated on, he lost interest in the library and started talking about my surgery, which was a bit unsettling because when he isn't working in City Hall he's busy running his two undertaking parlors. As I left, he gave me his card. When I got outside I threw it away without looking at it because I didn't want to see which card it was.

Len and Gin Field have been in town, and we've had fun being with them. Len heads back east today, and will probably be ringing you up, conveying our love. Harriett is packing my things. She isn't sure whether she's supposed to sew name tabs on my jockey shorts. I told her I thought that was more for summer camp. But she says it wouldn't hurt, and I guess she's right. She usually is.

As ever,

John

Alexander Graham Bell's friend and coworker, Thomas Watson,
was Federico's maternal great-grandfather.

Cedar Lane
March 11th [1976]

Dear John,

It was truly an epochal day. As you approached the hospital a great snowstorm approached the Northeastern United States. As you approached the operating room my dear son, Federico approached the dais in the great ballroom of the Boston Copley Plaza, prepared to reenact the Discovery of the Telephone. As you were being skewered, Sandra Bell (the grand-daughter of Alexander Graham Bell) said into the first telephone (lifted from the Smithsonian) "Come quickly, Mr. Watson, I need you." "I heard every word you said distinctly," said Federico.[29] At that instant Esther Watson Tipple, in Rome, Georgia, breathed her last. She is the crazy aunt who has been sitting, all these years, on the Watson millions. This part of the world in silent stillness lay of course but the dawn today was brilliant, the snow was beautiful and I am sure you must have experienced some of this radiance. I'm not sure what the tie-in is between your asshole and the 100th anniversary of the invention of the telephone, but I'm working on it.

I went up to Yaddo on the first, slammed out a chapter and came down on the 9th partly to take care of the dogs while Mary went to Boston and partly because I need the company of amiable women I can hunker and friends with whom I can crack jokes. The only woman at Yaddo is a nice waitress but when I came in for breakfast she slipped an end table between us and I heard the choo-choo calling me. That was Tuesday. On Wednesday I drove Mary to a pre-dawn plane for the sport in Boston and she reports that the Bells and the Watsons had a marvelous time. I return to Yaddo on Sunday and plan to

29. The revisionists who crafted Bell's line missed an opportunity to give Watson a classic reply, "Sorry, wrong number."

remain until April first when I hope to have mastered the bulk of the book. I may, of course, be undone by my need for jokes and hunkering. In any case do report when you next splash water on the beautiful, blue-green tiles of your pool.

Love,
John

JOHN D. WEAVER
3893 Deervale Drive
Sherman Oaks, CA 91403

17th March 1976

Dear John:

I'm back home and all is well, but things got off to a shaky start at Mt. Sinai when we were waiting in the Admitting Office to be taken to my room, and a young male attendant came in and clamped a plastic ID bracelet around the left wrist of a middle-aged woman across from us. She took one look at it and shrieked: "But I'm not John Weaver, I'm Mrs. Blumberg." I told her she was about to make medical history, and as they wheeled her away, she said, "Wait till you get my hysterectomy." On the morning of the operation, the nurses forgot to give me a shot to sedate me, so I was wide awake when they wheeled me off to surgery, and while I was lying there waiting for the elevator, I heard the urologist saying, "But Mr. Weaver's chart must be here *somewhere*." There had also been a mixup about my room the first day, and I insisted on being transferred from the one they had assigned me. When I got to the next room and settled down in bed, a nurse came in with a clipboard, beamed at me and said, "You're Mr. Blatnik?" I'm not sure just what operation I got, Mrs. Blumberg's, Mr. Blatnik's or my own, but I feel great, and the surgery was quite painless, with minimal discomfort afterwards. I've come home to a burst of lovely spring weather, and the orange blossoms outside my workroom smell like a Las Vegas wedding chapel. I have to take it easy for another couple of weeks and it will be a while before I'll be able to pose for a Playgirl centerfold. I keep thinking of

Mr. Blumberg, and hear him asking, "Darling, what in God's name did they do to you?" And Mrs. Blatnik may be in for some surprises. *"This* is a tonsillectomy?" How do I address a letter to you at Yaddo? We're delighted that the book marches well and look forward to its completion. Harriett joins in love.

John

Yaddo
Saratoga Springs,
New York 12866
March 25th [1976]

Dear John,

I'm very glad that it's over and thank you for reporting. My interest is not entirely unselfish. It seems to be a journey we must all make and you are the only traveler whose word I trust. Chilly Beckworth, for example, told me he got the giggles during the operation. I didn't believe that.

I came up here on the first and then returned for three days so that Mary and Fred could go to Boston and Celebrate the invention of the telephone. I think I wrote you about this but it doesn't matter since nobody believes it anyhow. Then this morning I decided I'd finished the book. No one else would agree with me but I think the roof-tree is in place and all I have to do is write the three opening chapters, rectify the shadows here and there and arrange tie-ins with the local power, gas & water companies. It looks like no more than a month of very easy running.

This place is quite freaky but good for work although I am the only smoker. Nobody smokes, not even the maids, the garbage man or the fellow who oils the weather-vanes. They would prefer that I left the table when I smoke, they won't ride in my car because it makes their hair and their beards smell bad and they won't come into my room, even when I tempt them with a little hoard of crackers, cheese and cold cuts that I have hidden under the bed. However I'll come down on the second and find some true, blue friends in the smoking car.

Yours,

John

JOHN D. WEAVER
3893 Deervale Drive
Sherman Oaks, CA 91403

17th May 1976

Dear John:

We're enjoying a burst of beautiful spring weather which coincides happily with a respite from doctors' waiting rooms. Harriett's radiologist can find no trace of the nodule that caused us so much worry last fall and my urologist has given me the finger for what I hope will be the last time. He is so pleased with the forcefulness of my stream that he is thinking of applying for federal legislation to have it brought under the Wild Rivers Protection Act of 1974.

We were so pleased to hear that the book is almost finished, and we look forward to reading it. Is there any chance you might be coming out here for a meeting with Paramount?[30] And with the book out of the way, could your thoughts be turned toward T&L? If you shrink from doing a piece on water, what about taking a glance at your journals and doing a Russian reminiscence?

We wish we could share a beaker of orange juice with you on the 27th. We could make it a joint celebration, the start of your 65th year and, on the following day, the start of our, God help us, fortieth year together. In any event, we'll lift a Memorial week-end glass to the three of us and hope we can link forces again soon. Meanwhile the Cheever azalea flourishes poolside and Harriett joins in love to all.

John

30. The studio had taken a $40,000 option on *Falconer*.

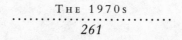

Dear John,

Coming in late yesterday afternoon from a frost-bitten garden party at the Academy where we had lunch with the Untermeyers and chatted muchly about your asshole we returned and found your kind letter here. At times things do seem to tie in. I'm delighted to know that you and Harriet are well and I am touched by your birthday greetings. My love to you on your anniversary. Our's was on the 22nd of March—our thirty-fifth.[31] I was at Yaddo and completely forgot it. However a Star-Magnolia that I had given Mary on our twenty-fifth burst into bloom.

The Untermeyers were exactly what one would expect. Here, of course, there is the invincibility of man. Erica Jong and Jonathan were there. A man, standing with his back to me said, "I am Cinderella. I've sat beside John Cheever for an hour; and tomorrow I must go back to work." You know what I said, of course. I said, "Cut the shit." Also I bumped lightly into a lady who was carrying a martini. "Just because you're John Cheever," she said angrily, "doesn't mean that you can spill gin all over me." She was really ugly.

The book is indeed done and I got through the publisher interview without a fist-fight. They wanted three words changed. Paramount won't get the manuscript until next week. If they do buy it I will come to the coast. I like the book very much but it does seem an ultimate display of my manifest limitations. I do wish it were richer and more various.

On T&L I would like it if you felt like sending me on a trip to anywhere, anywhere in the world. I've thought, for no reason, of Rumania. I think I told you about Lang who, when he was sprung from Sing Sing exclaimed: "I wanna see da Sistine

---

31. He had typed "twenty-fifth," crossed out "twenty" and written "thirty" in the margin.

Chapel." There's a story and I think a good one but he is a dangerous character. Litvinova is now in London and that's a great story but I don't think for T&L.

Love,

John

J O H N   D .   W E A V E R
3893 Deervale Drive
Sherman Oaks, CA 91403

29th May 1976

Dear John:

. . . I wrote at once to Pamela Fiori, suggesting she give you a ring, and I hope something agreeable to you has been worked out.[32] Meanwhile, we are going to be very much at home this summer, so if you head west, we'll be on hand to meet you at LAX.

The Fields have been visiting Italy, and sent us a picture of Bill and the new house he's building. It looks like quite a handsome structure, and we wish we could look in on it. Incidentally Bill has written a very amusing essay for T&L on the quirks and quiddities of the Italian language.

Harriett joins in love. Stay well.

John

32. "John Weaver said, if you could go anywhere in the world on assignment, it would be Rumania," Pamela wrote John. "If you're serious we can have a round-trip ticket in your hands, arrangements made, some advance money within a month and a gypsy as a traveling companion."

"My only knowledge of the country is that my work has been translated into Rumanian," John replied, "that most Rumanians I know claim to be Greek and that my closest Rumanian friend—the poet, Popescue—is such a striking example of egocentricity that I have wanted to check on his origins. His mother, the actress, is the celebrated petite beauty of Bucharesti, that little Paris of the Balkans. However when we went to buy her shoes in London it seems she wears size thirteen." Popescu, John later wrote his son Ben, "lives in Bucharest at 16 Julian Fuck Street."

Cedar Lane

Ossining

June second [1976]

Dear John,

With the privacy of your pool secured I suppose you swim in the "buff" and I hope you fare better than I who was described by my daughter as looking like one of those old men who swim the Hudson on their 80th birthday and who are photographed for the newspaper although the paper never prints their picture. There has been no word from Pamela Fiori.[33] I think now and then of going to Rumania but I think I will remain here until the Paramount goose is cooked . . . We now wait for David Picker.[34] I go to Massachusetts tomorrow to bury my brother and we return there next week to see Fred graduate.

At three thirty, yesterday morning, the phone rang and a man said: "This is CBC. John Updike has just been involved in a fatal automobile accident. Do you care to comment." I began to cry, terribly. "Oh," said the voice, "is it personal?" "He was," I sobbed, "a colleague," and went on crying. I wandered around the house until dawn when I fed the dogs. At nine I called Susie and asked her, through Newsweek, to check with CBC and the Ipswich and Boston police. There was no report of John's death. At ten I called Knopf. John was content in his bed in Boston and they thought me mad. At half-past ten Mary Updike called. She had received the same call, a few minutes before I. Stay tuned.[35]

Yours,

John

33. Her letter was on its way to Cedar Lane.

34. Head of Paramount.

35. In 1949 when Josephine Herbst wrote John about a similar call from her publisher to check Peggy Cowley's report of her death in Paris, he replied: "The way I heard it Katherine Anne [Porter] is the one who's dead. Not in Paris but in Pottsville, Pa., where she was overtaken by fish poisoning on her way east to attend a testimonial dinner given by Somerset Maugham for Glenway Wescott, both of whom have been reported dead. Irwin

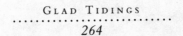

JOHN D. WEAVER
3893 Deervale Drive
Sherman Oaks, CA 91403

6th June 1976

Dear John:

It seems to me that this would be the ideal time for you to pack a bag, slip into something wrinkleproof and fly off to a lovely place you've never seen before or would like to see again. Don't worry about Hollywood. Reading a book—a *whole* book—puts quite a strain on the corporate mind, and it takes time, quite enough to permit you to go away for a while. And if something should break while you're gone, you'd gain considerable stature by having word go out from the Polo Lounge that Paramount had been forced to track you down to some remote European village . . .

Harriett joins in love and we hope a whopping Paramount sale will bring you back our way. I'm nearly out of Breck shampoo.

All the best.

John

A note accompanying a Jill Krementz photograph of John and Louis Untermeyer taken at the Academy luncheon described in John's May 20 letter. It "belonged in Sherman Oaks" because his trousers were neatly pressed and Louis's had a badly wrinkled crotch.

Shaw said that somebody told him that Leonard Ehrlich was dead, but Mary saw Leonard at the dentists a few days later, more dead than alive, to be sure, but who are we to judge? Leonard said that Irwin Shaw was dead. The man in the liquor store said that his wife said that she had heard a radio announcer say that Mayor O'Dwyer was dead and we had a baby sitter some time ago who came in with a long face and said that Frank Sinatra was dead . . ."

Cedar Lane
June 9th [1976]

Dear John,

Jill sent this on and as soon as I took it out of her envelope I knew that it belonged in Sherman Oaks. Thanks to you the man on the left will go to Rumania.

Love,

John

JOHN D. WEAVER
3893 Deervale Drive
Sherman Oaks, CA 91403

12th June 1976

Dear John:

It's a lovely photograph and we're delighted to have it. Harriett was quite pleased with your appearance (Louis could have done with a touch or two of the iron).

We hope you have a grand time in Rumania. Meanwhile, we'll keep a light in the window and fresh flowers in the Cheever room.

Harriett joins in love.

John

The day before John wrote this letter Pamela Fiori sent me a copy of his article on Rumania with the wry comment: "He did a lovely job for a fledgling, don't you think?"

Yaddo
Saratoga Springs N.Y.
September ninth [1976]

Dear John,

I haven't written sooner because I put a deadline on the Romanian piece and wanted to complete it before I did anything else. I mailed it off to Pamela on the day I came here. I do feel that, succeeding Caskie—with whom I had a sort of dog-eat-dog friendship—might be difficult, but while I scarcely know Pamela it seems to me that she enjoys quite enough independence to give me an honest opinion. Should she need encouragement I shall count on you. The fall of these sentences can be accounted for by the fact that this is being written in a castle where the ghost of that socially ambitious and long-winded pig—who sniffed the dust of every second-rate drawing room in London—still prowls.

Everything, alas, seems to stand under the pall of the novel. Paramount did not pick up the option, which is no skin off my ass, but it will influence paperbacks and book clubs. To wait nine months for publication is something George Eliot, for example, would not have tolerated. I have been told that the book is successful and what I want is some tangible and lasting documentation of this. I mean a check. The book clubs decide next week.

Romania was a great help through all this. The government gave me a Mercedez, a chauffeur and an amiable guide who liked to play backgammon and swim. We made a two thousand mile swing around eastern Europe. Carmen Sylva, the Queen of Romania, was the idol of Katrina Trask, the queen of this demesne.[36] I am not in a rut.

I am here for the annual meeting. Mary will drive up on Saturday for the festivities and we return to Ossining on Sunday. Mary's new ten thousand dollar kitchen is completed and I think I have never seen her so happy. Fred leaves in a week for the coast and I don't know when I'll visit him but I think it will be soon.

As ever,
John

36. John liked to tell about Katrina Trask's cables to Queen Victoria signed "To the Queen of England from the Queen of Yaddo." The estate got its name from the attempt of one of her infant children to say "shadow."

JOHN D. WEAVER
3893 Deervale Drive
Sherman Oaks, CA 91403
16th September 1976

Dear John:

Harriett is sewing, pressing and repairing the bags we schlepped to New York for the Fair in '39 (they still have the NRA Blue Eagle). We plan to splash down at JFK in the late afternoon of Monday, October 4, and we'll be in and around the city for a week. I think Pamela is putting us up at the Berkshire, so we'll be close to the T&L offices. I'll give you a ring on Tuesday and I hope it will be possible to get together. We *read* all about Romania (Pamela, as I'm sure you've heard by now, was delighted with it, and once we'd read the Xerox she sent us, we could see why) but we'd like to *hear* about it.

We rejoice in the prospect of having Fred in California. We figure it will bring you out this way from time to time, preferably *not* when we're back east.

Lennie wrote to us confirming Mary's happiness and giving us good medical news of you, which gave us great joy.

Harriett joins in love and we hope the book clubs have chosen well this week.[37]

John

Cedar Lane,
Ossining, New York
September 18th [1976]

Dear John,

I'm delighted to know that you and Harriet are coming East and do call us on Tuesday. I do hope you can get to see the country during the weekend, not so much to see us as to see Mary's new kitchen. The drain under the trap is no longer bandaged like a Russian with a toothache and I think the floor is truly beautiful. I give a reading in Syracuse on Wednesday

37. The Book-of-the-Month Club made *Falconer* a main selection.

night but we return on Thursday. Perhaps Pamela would like to come out and see the new kitchen. Mary has seldom been out of it since it was completed. On Tuesday I go to AA at seven-thirty and return a little after nine so call us before or after then. Until Tuesday,

    Yours,

      John

JOHN D. WEAVER

3893 Deervale Drive

Sherman Oaks, CA 91403

25th September 1976

Dear John:

I'll give you a ring Tuesday (incidentally I don't seem to have your number in my address book, but I assume I can get it from Information, and if not, I'll call Susie at Newsweek), and we'll work out some way to get together. It's a bit complicated, because of your Syracuse commitment, which coincides with the one day and evening we're quite free at the moment.

On Friday we're going up to Connecticut to have lunch with the Untermeyers, and then we're going to Westport to spend the night with Ralph and Marj Martin. Perhaps we could rent a car and drive from Westport to Ossining on Saturday morning, have a look at the kitchen, and then drive on down to LaGuardia, turn the car in and take the shuttle to Washington. Everything's tentative, depending on what further complications may develop when we get back there. But we wanted to see if Saturday mid-morning could be pencilled in.

    Harriett joins in love.

      John

We rented a car in Westport and drove through a cyclone to Cedar Lane. Mary was in her $10,000 kitchen, basting a turkey, and John was reading the bound galleys of Erica Jong's new novel, How to Save Your Own Life, *which he offered to pass on to me.*

Cedar Lane
November 15th [1976]

Dear John,

It is so unlike you not to have written that I can only guess that I offended you when you and Harriet were here for lunch. It may have been that I have not, as I promised, forwarded the Erica Jong book. It was a considered decision of mine not to forward the book and I have experienced nothing that has changed my opinion.

But to go on to matters that might at least interest Harriet the cyclonic wind that blew in Mary's niece just before we sat down to lunch also smashed the glass pane in the door of the upstairs hall. All the doors but this one are paneled. Fifty years ago when a shy child spent the night here the glass door was installed to allay her fears of the dark. It is ugly, rather like the door to a toilet in some institution. At least twelve carpenters have told me that I would find no paneled door of such dimensions in stock. A door would have to be be built by a cabinet maker. No cabinet maker returned my calls. On Saturday, after you left, I knocked the hinge-pins free of fifty years of paint and dragged the door into The Ossining Sash & Door Factory, a temple of wood.

Harriet surely will understand this. Years ago I asked which came first—Christ the carpenter or the holy smell of new wood. This sanctity is exploited by three enormous men named Larsen, the sons of a great patriarch. Their hair, once golden is now white, but their bones are vast and their teeth are like headstones. Their realm is the lumber-yard. Their supplicants are suburban house-owners, dressed in the dernier cri of weekend garb and seeking odd scraps of wood and moulding to build a record cabinet or a cold frame. One stands in line. One does not speak to the Larsens. One waits to be recognized. Compared to The Ossining Sash & Door Factory the ceremonies on the high altar at Trinity are helter-skelter. Against a backdrop of the colors and grains of new wood and in that profound fragrance these three demi-gods sift out the souls of men.

Enter Cheever, dragging his smashed door. I was instantly recognized, led to an inner office (where a secretary was watering a plant) and had my door measured. Then six catalogues were consulted and it was decided that there might be such a door left over from the twenties. Had it been rescued from the flood? Yes. The fire? Yes. It must be in the south, south-east annex and there we went and found the door. Not a word was spoken. Hardware was cut out of the old door and installed in the new. The bill was fifty-four dollars. They carried the door out to the car and when I shook the hand of the senior and thanked him he said—not without pain, not without bitterness—"Well, you see, my son wants to be a writer."

Yours,
John

JOHN D. WEAVER
3893 Deervale Drive
Sherman Oaks, CA 91403

18th November 1976

Dear John:

If put on a witness stand and cross-examined by Raymond Burr I'd have a difficult time accounting for the last month. When we came home, Harriett was down with flu, and by election night, when she was up and around again, still a bit wobbly, a virus of some sort crept up on me during the early returns from Wisconsin. I still feel puny, but take comfort in the memory of Mary moving about in her kitchen while your winter firewood stands so bravely against the winter wind.

We thoroughly enjoyed our Cedar Lane pitstop. The cyclone, the shattered door and the niece gave a dramatic context to a beautiful lunch. It's a lovely house and it has weathered well, as (I like to think) have we all.

As for the Erica Jong novel, I'm sure you have very sound reasons for not forwarding it and I would always be inclined to respect your judgment on such matters.

Harriett is taking me to see the Social Security people to

find out what, if anything, we can expect from them next February when I turn 65. She joins in love and in thanks for providing such a snug retreat. We will be thinking of Mary at work in her kitchen on Thanksgiving Day, while you fetch a holiday log. It's good to know the Cheevers will be warm and well-fed.

Love,
John

Cedar Lane,
Ossining, New York 10562
December 9th 1976

Dear John,

This is a Christmassy note about pant wrinkles but it has gotten to be a serious problem now that I am spending my twilight years journeying from campus to campus, from podium to podium where some people seem to find my wrinkles more compelling than my countenance. How they stare; and when I drape my hands over my crotch this is generally misunderstood. Eight or ten years ago I asked Mary to press my pants. She returned them to me scornfully soaking wet with a wrinkled crotch and no crease at all in the leg. I've tried to press my own pants but I achieve a very limited and fleeting crease and anyhow Mary stands at the kitchen threshold railing at me for posing as a forsaken old creature who claims that he has to press his own pants. She is quite obscene. There used to be an old Polish pants-presser in the village but he died. Now, in order to get the wrinkles out of my crotch I have to have my pants dry-cleaned which takes a week and costs two dollars. Very recently a lady reporter described my face as being linned by some force greater than time. The same seems to go for my crotch. I bought a nice pair of perma-press doubleknits but Susie won't let me wear these, even to clean out the attic. I've thought of kilts of course but all the hair has worn off my legs and there is a ropey, purple vein inside my left knee. I've just displayed my wrinkles at Syracuse, Bennington, Washington, Scarsdale and Cornell and

I'll take them out to Utah after the holidays when I may continue to California for a touch of Harriet's healing iron. Help!

    Yours,

       John

John was to spend a week at the University of Utah before flying to Los Angeles.

3893 Deervale Drive
Sherman Oaks, CA 91403

15th December 1976

Dear John:

    Harriett's steam iron will be at the ready and the car will be gassed and waiting to whisk you here from LAX after your pastoral call on the Mormons. I'll even put ice cubes in the pool for you.[38]

    I had lunch in Westwood with Lennie Field yesterday and then took a stroll through the UCLA Sculpture Garden and stopped by the Research Library long enough for me to Xerox a copy of the Paris Review talk for him.[39]

    Harriett joins in love and we're looking forward to seeing you early in the new year. We just wish the Mormons would get to see your crotch at better advantage.

       John

Cedar Lane,
Ossining, New York 10562
January sixteenth [1977]

Dear John,

    The interviews here for the book start on February third and I won't get down to Los Angeles. I'm grateful for the

---

38. The water was always too warm for him.

39. Annette Grant's interview, "John Cheever: The Art of Fiction," appeared in the fall issue.

attention and I've been through this before but I am uneasy. I will lunch, for example, with the twelve editors of Newsweek and at the end of the lunch they will vote on whether or not to put me on the cover. I don't have any gifts for this sort of thing. The crotch-wrinkle situation is so acute that I cannot discuss it but I will touch loosely on the hanging button problem. The outer coat I wear is Mary's Father's 37-year old Vicuna. When I take the coat off myself I can keep the coat and the linning together but when people insist on helping me out of the coat I am left wearing the linning. This does not embarrass me but it does seem to involve a loss of face. However I noticed last week that one of the buttons hung a good two inches from it's mooring. When I asked Mary—very gently—if she could tell me where I might find a needle and some thread she said no but she could tell me where I might find a tailor. The tailor, of course, tossed the coat into a dry-cleaning vat and the restoration of a single button came to four dollars and fifty cents.

The cold, as you must know, is unusual but my enthusiasm for this sort of thing has diminished. I went skating on Saturday but when I climbed the hill to get the TIMES this morning I was intensely uncomfortable. I have Bill's translation of the new Calvino novel[40] and Bill can turn Calvino's Italian into English without a loss of grace and without a trace of a Latin root. It is splendid. We will have dinner with the Fields and the Ettlingers in New York tomorrow and Lennie says that he has news of you. I know that covetousness is a cardinal sin but I do today covet your pool.

Brrrrr,
John

---

40. *The Castle of Crossed Destinies.*

J O H N D . W E A V E R
3893 Deervale Drive
Sherman Oaks, CA 91403

25th January 1977

Dear John:

We're sorry you won't be coming out just now. We'd much rather have you lolling about the pool than facing a befuddlement of Newsweek editors at lunch. The weather here has been marvellous except for a couple of rains we were happy to see. We have a comforting supply of firewood, so when it rains we hole up by the hearth, and if we're in a mood for self-indulgence, we have a fire going in *both* fireplaces. This, to Harriett, is equivalent to using linen napkins when there's no company.

Last week we went to Cedars-Sinai for Harriett's regular 6-month checkup and her radiologist was quite pleased with her condition, although there has been more swelling and discomfort in the treated area than he'd expected. He said there was nothing to be alarmed about, however, and gave us another six months.

Carl and Eve Foreman are having a birthday party for me on the 4th and I wish you could be here to help pave the way into the sunset years. The first short story I sold dealt with a street car conductor who had never thought of himself as having grown old until an elderly colleague died and he was given the old man's "gravy run." Now, forty years later, I may dig out that issue of Esquire and reread the story.[41]

Knopf, I gather, is beginning to mount a publicity campaign for your book. If you'd like, I'm pretty sure I could get the West View page of the Los Angeles Times Book Review for a friendly piece about you. It might help. As Knopf knows, this is the country's second largest book market. You might mention it to your editor and ask to have galleys sent to me. I'll also drop

41. November 1939.

a line to Arnold Ehrlich at Publishers Weekly. He's an old friend from the good years at Holiday.

Harriett joins in love and the reminder that the pool and the bed-couch in her work room are always available, so there's no need to shiver when you could be swimming & sunning.

John

"Cheever called to tell me I could now go to the races in New York for a dollar," I wrote Louis and Bryna Untermeyer. "I also get a cut on bus fares here, but I've never ridden on a bus here, at least not for about thirty years."

JOHN D. WEAVER
3893 Deervale Drive
Sherman Oaks, CA 91403
7th February 1977

Dear John:

I crossed over into the golden years with a great deal of claret and, I think, some degree of grace. Carl and Eve Foreman assembled two dozen assorted friends and when we had the cutting of the cake and the serving of the champagne, Norman Corwin was warm and eloquent, but I've heard him speak twice in the last year at memorial services, which gave me an uncomfortable feeling.

One of the guests was Digby Diehl, the Los Angeles Times book editor, who said he'd be delighted to give me the West View page of his Book Review section for a few friendly remarks about you. He said he'd check the publication date and pick the Sunday that would be most helpful to the book.

Meanwhile, Harriett and I hope you'll come out for a laying-on of hands. Harriett's work room and steam iron are both at your disposal. And the Cheever azalea is coming into bloom. We'd so love to have you, and you ought to thaw out.

Harriett joins in love to all.

John

P.S. Knopf ought to arrange for you to be interviewed by Michael Jackson. He's civilized and articulate, and his radio show reaches people who buy good books. Also the Dinah Shore show would be helpful and, I'd imagine, relatively painless, and the guests are seated, so crotches don't show.

Cedar Lane,
February 11th [1977]

Dear John,

The big news here is that Mary has bought something called Wrinkles-Away! It is a little steam-engine that, when passed lightly over the harrassed area removes both the wrinkles and the press. I did not need it yesterday for The Lunch because I wore the newly dry-cleaned Iowa suit. For The Lunch I went up to something like the 175th floor of The Newsweek Building where a lot of people were drinking hootch in a big white barny place. Then I sat on a plush sofa beside the editor and the people asked questions. Once, right in the middle of a long answer, I forgot what in hell the question had been. After that we went into a big white barny dinning room where a waiter passed lamb chops. I only took one chop because I didn't want them to think I was a rube or hungry or in any way dependent upon them for food. This left me with nothing on my plate but a chop bone for nearly an hour. I fooled with the chop bone and answered more questions. After this we had something pink in a long-stemmed glass and then I went with the editor down to his office and then I talked with some other editors about whether or not Avedon should photograph me. They kept looking at me. Then one of them said that with my face on the cover there would be a drastic drop of news-stand sales but then another man said this was true of all serious writers. After this I went out on a local and called Knopf to tell them the news and the PR man said: "I've been successful." I also told him that you would house me and introduce me to Diehl but they haven't decided whether or not they could afford to send me that far on a Greyhound Bus. You ought to have a book by now and things are quite satisfactory.

It sounds like a splendid birthday party and I wish I'd been there . . . We go to Boston for Liz Updike's wedding tomorrow and then everything will be quiet until Tuesday when I will cut down a tree for a Saturday Review photographer.

Yours,

John

JOHN D. WEAVER
3893 Deervale Drive
Sherman Oaks, CA 91403
22d February 1977

Dear John:

We were delighted to get *Falconer*, with its affectionate inscription and the engaging photograph on the back of the dust jacket. Harriett had some misgivings about the creases on your right leg, but now that she knows the picture was taken before the acquisition of Wrinkles-Away she feels much better about it.

I read the book at once (Harriett has it now). It was a source of joy, like everything else of yours, and it seemed quite special somehow, like a benediction. It sums up so beautifully the fun you've had at the party, even when you've been served beans and rice, and, having preceded you into life's golden years, I share your intense interest in what's going to happen next . . .[42] I talked to Digby Diehl at the party and he would like very much to have me write something about you for the March 13th issue of his Book Review. I don't know

---

42. Ordinarily John didn't press his Anglican faith on agnostic friends but one afternoon on the beach at Malibu he remarked that there has to be *someone* you thanked for the party: "How could you say you were fearless about leaving the party when it's like a party, even in stir—even franks and rice taste good when you're hungry, even an iron bar feels good to touch, it feels good to sleep," John wrote in *Falconer*. "It's like a party even in maximum security and who wants to walk out of a party into something that nobody knows anything at all about?"

what I'm going to say, but, if it's agreeable to you, I'd like to draw lightly on your letters. Needless to say, my use of them would be prudent. And we still hope you'll get out this way, which would enable us to chat about the piece, and I could stand you a handsome lunch on the Times . . .

Harriett joins in love to all and in every good wish for *Falconer* . . .

Cedar Lane,
Ossining, New York 10562
Saturday
[February 26, 1977]

Dear John,

I'm very happy that you liked Falconer and pleased that you wrote to say so. TIME shit on it this week—a month before publication—because Newsweek is running a feature. It was a bad few hours but only a few. The people whose opinion I value seem to like it. There is, of course, the company of sopranos. Phil Roth called, towards midnight to say in his windiest voice: "Thank you for sending me the book and I'll read it when I next take a vacation but the reason I'm calling is to ask for John Updike's new telephone number."

And I'm also delighted that you will do a piece for LA paper and you are, of course, quite welcome to use the letters. The PR woman at Knopf has not called in ten days and I don't know their plans. They will put me up in a New York hotel room for the 9th and 10th. Mary plans to join me and bring the three dogs.

Yours,
John

Cedar Lane,
Sunday
[March 6, 1977]

Dear John,

When Mary came in this morning—distraught—and said: "Your beloved Bucharest is in ruins and all your darling backgammon companions are dying, waiting to be rescued by police dogs, donated by the Swiss government," I said, "Oh Shit. They'll scrub the Newsweek cover." This is really not what happened but there was some nervousness on Madison Avenue yesterday on whether or not the Pope might die and I did *not* pray that they be kept off the front page. I do worry about Pamela.[43]

Knopf hasn't decided whether or not to send me to the coast. I am running in tandem with the Brook Hayward book.[44] Mary could come out with me and then go up to Palo Alto and see Fred. We're all having a marvelous time and shithead—the unwanted retriever—is wanted by every one including the Auchinlosses. He's now known as the Auchinloss dog. I'm now off to the local bookstore to autograph copies. They expect hundreds. Mary plans to appear, towards the end of the afternoon, frightfully drunk, disheveled and with a torn dress that shows one breast. "A Star is born," she is going to scream, "but only I know that the prick has toe-jam." Confusion. TV cameras. And then a haunting reprise of "I Want That Doggie in The Window," which, of course, was playing when we met.

Yours,
John

JOHN D. WEAVER
3893 Deervale Drive
Sherman Oaks, CA 91403

[March 13, 1977]

Dear John:
We've just come back from Palm Springs and San Diego where Harriett was checking out museums for an article New West asked her to do. We got our first glimpse of Newsweek

43. *Travel & Leisure* held off publication of John's article for nearly a year.
44. *Haywire.*

when we had drinks in La Jolla with Major Geisel.[45] His wife wanted to know why only enlisted men seemed to make the cover of news magazines. Ted winced visibly. Later, when we had dinner with Bill Johnson who was a Time-Life bureau manager here, he said Time was going to do a Dr. Seuss cover once but it got knocked out by a natural disaster of some sort.

We were quite impressed by Newsweek's coverage, but not surprised. When the records of the Brownsville soldiers were cleared, the only comprehensive and accurate report was in Newsweek. We thought they did justice to your childlike sense of wonder, your pervasive sweetness of heart and your crotch. We were especially charmed by Susie's interview.[46]

It's strange that Falconer should be in competition with Brooke Hayward's book. She was our neighbor on Hillside when she was married to Dennis Hopper, and for all we know she may still be living in the rambling Spanish pile we used to see from our kitchen. Harriett helped her with some problems she had in City Hall when they first bought the place. Curiously enough, Brooke occupied the same space last week that Digby saved for me in today's Book Review.[47]

Bob Nathan called last night to ask what I thought of "Newsweek's story on the Second Coming," and to express the hope that you'd pay us a pastoral call. It's a hope we share, and it would be especially nice to have Mary here at the same time. I think Mary might like to meet some of the people at the

45. Theodor Geisel (Dr. Seuss) had presided over a group of gifted, irreverent artists and animators at Fort Capra.

46. "The situation made me very nervous," Susie later wrote. "I would either lose my job or my father's friendship, I was sure . . . I interviewed him one rainy winter afternoon, in front of the fire in the downstairs living room of the house in Ossining. The dogs behaved themselves. My mother peeled shrimp in the kitchen for dinner while we talked . . ." John and Susan remained friends and he wrote her a thank-you note: "The lesson let us help one another was not lost on you."

47. My article, "John Cheever: Recollections of a Childlike Imagination," appeared in the Los Angeles Times that Sunday, March 13, 1977.

Huntington and UCLA which we didn't get to cover on her whirlwind visit with Fred.

We've got to run up north on Harriett's museum piece at some point, probably in early April, but we're quite flexible, and it's very beautiful here just now. Do come and enjoy.

Harriett joins in love.

John

p.s. Bill called from New York last night. He's in town briefly for some opera broadcasts and will be back for a more leisurely stay this fall. He sounded quite perky.

JOHN D. WEAVER
3893 Deervale Drive
Sherman Oaks, CA 91403

5th April 1977

Dear John:

Harriett's research on her New West museum piece is coming to a merciful close. My feet hurt and the Indian baskets are beginning to blur a bit with the prehistoric skeletons. We've just gotten home from a swing through the Bay Area, where water rationing has posed the delicate question of whether a guest should flush his host's toilet. There's a lot less bathing in Marin County, we noticed, and a lot more use of ornamental shrubbery as public urinals . . .

We're trying to cut down on our use of water and there's much talk of which wine is best for filling waterbeds, but the pool is still full and we can still flush freely. We hope you'll come before we have to cope with city-metered toilets.

Harriett joins in love.

John

JOHN CHEEVER
Cedar Lane
Ossining, New York 10562

April 8th [1977]

Dear John,

This is in haste and rather harrassed and only to say that Knopf seems unwilling to send me to the coast and that we will be here all of May. His Excellency, Vladimifr Popov (no shit) is due here on Sunday to present me with an invitation from the President of Bulgaria.[48] This will be for the first of June. We would love to see you here any time before this and our well gives two hundred gallons a minute.

Yours,
John

JOHN D. WEAVER
3893 Deervale Drive
Sherman Oaks, CA 91403

18th April 1977

Dear John:

We're sorry you're not going to get out here, but we can't compete with the President of Bulgaria. We can only hope that Madame Popov is able to wield an iron with the necessary skill to keep you presentable on state occasions.

48. "The day after I returned here," John wrote Tanya (February 6), "I was waited on by a delegation of Bulgarians who came down the icy driveway carrying wine, brandy and red roses. They were very like the jolliest of my friends in Moscow. We banged drinking glasses, banged one another on the back and I agreed to co-sponsor a Peace conference in Sofia in June." In a later letter to Tanya (April 4), he responded to criticism from her and from other friends, including the Robert Penn Warrens: "I represent no class, no party, no ethnic group, no minority and no union. I am merely John Cheever and I can say what I please." On May 20, when Mary left for Holland, planning to meet John in Sofia, he again wrote Tanya: "A great many people have joined you in protesting my appearance there and I have replied that I am going there for the fresh bread."

We'd hoped to get back your way in May, but it doesn't look as though we'll make it. We're distressed at the thought that we may end up getting to New York at a time when you're discussing our balance of payments situation with the Bulgarian trade ministry.

Meanwhile we envy you your well. We never thought the day would come when one of our most highly treasured freedoms would be the freedom to flush.

Harriett joins in love and we both rejoice at seeing Falconer No. 1 here and No. 2 back east, where the memory of Love Story seems fresher and more compelling than it is out here.

John

Cedar Lane,
April 22nd [1977]

Dear John,

Do keep me posted on your dates here. The Bulgarian trip—which is now tied in with disarmament talks—could get sticky. Would Harriet, for example, want to fly on a Bulgarian airline? When Ambassador Extraordinary and Plenipotentiary Lubomir Popov came here for tea he unbuttoned his vest and cut a fart.

Yours,
John

Robert Nathan had married the English actress, Anna Lee, who continues to fly the Union Jack on the Fourth of July.

JOHN D. WEAVER
3893 Deervale Drive
Sherman Oaks, CA 91403

8th May 1977

Dear John:

Our affection for Bob Nathan has landed me on the board of his wife's Royal Oak committee to save the white cliffs of

England. I'm not sure just what I'm saving them from, but as the group's token colonial, I was invited to luncheon yesterday at the Rangoon Racquet Club in Beverly Hills. The guests of honor were Viscount Norwich and Lady Norwich, who had just flown in and were afraid the luncheon would make them late for their tour of Universal Studios. Norrie, as I like to think of His Lordship, turned out to be a delightful chap and I hope he has a good urologist because he had to duck out twice to the Gents. Harriett sat across from a quite decent sort who seems to be the son of the Duke of Suffolk or Essex, she wasn't sure which, but he's a friend of David Niven's. I kept having the feeling that at any minute C. Aubrey Smith would come in and warn us that the Riffs were abroad. Tomorrow night we go to a black tie affair for Norrie at the Beverly Wilshire and, on Saturday, a farewell garden party at the consulate. I don't know how all this is helping the white cliffs, but it beats the hell out of being farted at by Bulgarian emissaries.

John

Handwritten note on a postcard from the Netherlands.

Dear John and Harriet,

There is a mysterious lack of interest here in saving the White Cliffs of Dover but I shall carry the message into Bulgaria.

John

JOHN D. WEAVER
3893 Deervale Drive
Sherman Oaks, CA 91403

4th July 1977

Dear John:

We were distressed to hear that there is little interest in the Netherlands in saving the white cliffs of Dover, but we were even more distressed the other night when a Fleet Street friend on the Daily Mail showed up with a lady magistrate from Nottingham (Sherwood Forest, she says, still gives the sheriff a great deal of trouble), and she didn't know the white cliffs were in jeopardy. Did you spot anything in Bulgaria in need of saving?

Harriett is painting the patio furniture and I'm reading a biography of H. G. Wells, who could write indignant letters to publishers that even Bob Nathan would regard as excessive. Bob's letters are so abrasive that young editors at Knopf were forced to read them as part of their orientation to publishing. Many of them, I understand, decided on some other line of work.

Shitty Hall, as our old Japanese gardener used to call it, has put heavy restrictions on our use of water, so toilets go un-flushed except after bowel movements. Everybody's house these days smells like a BMT toilet.

Otherwise all is well.

    John

John's affection for the Bulgarians is reflected in a letter to Pamela Fiori (June 27): "There is a small city in Bulgaria called Plovdiv, built on the ruins of Philip of Macedon's city. This was an agricultural crossroads in the middle nineteenth century and they have restored about eighty houses in the old quarter. I don't like restorations but my notes for Plovdiv are very enthusiastic and I would be happy to write a piece about the city with the hope of getting some tourist dollars into that place. I have the photographs and literature on Plovdiv, but you would want your own photographs. If you are interested I'll send the literature and I would be happy to do the piece for nothing."

"Shall we call you our Eastern European Editor from now on?" Pamela replied. She offered him the assignment, set an October 14 deadline and insisted on paying for the article, but never received it.

Cedar Lane,
July 7th [1977]

Dear John,

I have a friend here who speaks entirely in corrupted nouns: "I've just lucked into a funded construct," he will ex-claim, "and I think I'll never clinker again." It is infectious (isn't it?) and I will nutshell you into a twilight in Sofia.

It was a cocktail party given by the mayor. Gore Vidal and I represented the Stars & Stripes. Bill Saroyan had passed out under a chestnut tree. My old friend Yevtushenko was calling the shots. "Kiss the mayor and meet me in the limousine," he said. At that point Chuckles (Lord Snow) drank his sixth vodka and said he thought he might die. "Lord Byron died in Greece." said Gore. "How clever of you to have settled in Bulgaria." We kissed the mayor and headed for the mountains in the limousine. This was Gore, Zhenya, Mary and me. In the snowy uplands we were met by throngs in peasant costume who danced and sang and set fire to a small lamb. Zhenya was in top form which is rather like watching a man pitch a no-hitter while playing the Rasamouvsky quartette at a moon-landing. Gore who does not eclipse gracefully, was burning. Anyhow we danced with the peasants and ate the lamb and when we left perhaps a hundred people gathered around Zhenya reciting his poetry and asking him to autograph their shirttails. Gore, who had stopped speaking, was writing postcards to Paul Newman. Our chauffeur, it seemed, was drunk and racing down the mountain we nearly went off a cliff. When some helpful peasants had put the car back on the road Gore said: "Had we gone off the cliff *I* would have gotten all the headlines." Zhenya brushed a feather off his knee and said, "only in the west, only in the west."

Yrs,

John

JOHN D. WEAVER
3893 Deervale Drive
Sherman Oaks, CA 91403

21 September 1977

Dear John:

The summer has passed pleasantly and much too quickly. Now, in keeping with the New Year, Harriett has been busy tidying up our accounts, getting in the winter firewood, having the roof worked on, painting the patio furniture and writing for copyright reassignments. All this autumnal activity, with its reminder of your vulnerability to October storms, has got me to wondering where and how you are.

Best wishes,
John

Cedar Lane,
September 26th [1977]

Dear John,

I got your query the day after I had lunched with Lennie and Don and so I can report on the regiment. I had gone into town with my Roman-born son to buy a suit. The only representations I have seen of myself in the last eight months have been photographs in which both my crotch-wrinkles and those on my face have been mercifully air-brushed. It was a frightful shock to see myself in a haberdashers mirror. My son led me out of Brooks to Sardi's. I had bet five dollars that Don would have called to say that he would be late. I lost this. There he was; vast shades tinted the color of a late summer afternoon, hundreds of teeth, a whooping salutation and his most sweet and amiable self. Lennie's sweetness is more constant. Lennie was wearing a hard-finished check with side-vents and when I asked where they bought their clothes they muttered something that sounded like London. Then Don told two very long stories; one (with screams) about the difficulty of passing a kidney stone and the other (close to tears) about the internment of a beloved pet, closing with a lingering shot of a shovelful of dirt covering a chewed-up tennis ball. I winked at Lennie. Then I told the story about Lord Snow, Gore Vidal and Yevtushenko and Don said that it was too bad I couldn't continue to buy my clothes at Robert Hall. At this point I found in my chicken salad the large heel of a head of iceberg lettuce. Don't tell Harriet. Lennie left us at the door—rather as we used to part at the Milk Bar in Astoria—and Don followed me to J. Press, suggesting that I try Bloomingdale's basement. I hastily bought a suit, the nature of which I do not choose to remember and came home alone on the train.

Yours,

John

JOHN D. WEAVER
3893 Deervale Drive
Sherman Oaks, CA 91403

2 October 1977

Dear John:

I wouldn't want this to get out (it might throw a wrench in the SALT talks), but, by a coincidence, the very night we received your communique on the lunch with Lennie and Don, we went to the Foremans' for dinner and, seated across from Lennie Spigelgass, it was distressingly evident that the western remnants of the regiment are no better equipped to face an enemy in anger than the Sardi's contingent. Spigelgass' account of how he plucked you from the cannon's mouth seems to have lost some of its freshness after years of retelling at God knows what or how many campfires.

Harriett has been invited to present a paper at a conference in Reno of California, Nevada and Hawaii foresters and firefighters on the 27th. We're both looking forward to the outing and Harriett is delighted at the prospect of being able to talk for 30 minutes without being interrupted. She joins in love to all.

John

In his New York Times *obituary Alden Whitman quoted a student who had referred to Louis Untermeyer as "an entire semester of required reading." He was ninety-two.*

JOHN D. WEAVER
3893 Deervale Drive
Sherman Oaks, CA 91403

18th December 1977

Dear John:

Bryna called the other day to tell us that Louis had asked to be brought home from the local hospital to die in his own bed eating vanilla ice cream. He will take a big chunk of our lives with him, the entire forty years of our marriage, and on this rainy Sunday morning at the start of Christmas week I am more than ever grateful for the photograph you sent us of the two of you, smiling and crotch-wrinkled on your way to a men's room. I have it on my work-table alongside the best picture ever taken of Harriett. Bob Nathan snapped it one night when we were going out to dinner together. She is wearing a red dress. Her legs are primly crossed and she is clearly pleased to be within reach of food and drink. We hope our paths cross in the New Year. Meanwhile, Harriett joins in love to all the Cheevers.

John

I had expressed my admiration for John's article a year earlier, when I read the galleys.

Cedar Lane,
April 7th [1978]

Dear John,

I have the T&L from Deervale with my piece on Romania and no comment from you and I trust my enthusiasm for that Communist state did not offend you. It is my feeling today that a vast penetration of the Eastern Carpathians by American Tourists with credit cards will help to bind up the wounds of that part of the world. Things have been crossed up here since Mary picked up a virulent parasite in the Leningrad drinking water in January. I got a bad case of Estonian toe-jam in Tallinn but I'm long-suffering and anyhow my mother was a Christian Scientist. Anyhow Mary was sick for two months and I was alternately

Florence Nightingale and a Prick. At one point I took off for two weeks in the Adirondacks, leaving Mary with a high fever, buried in ten feet of snow. The skiing was marvelous. Mary seems to have recovered and I am as cranky as ever.

I lunched with Lennie at Sardi's about a month ago. I was on my way to see the tax accountant but even through this gloom Lennie seemed contented and interested in his projects. I've seen no other army chums. Your brother Bill, I take it, has been at Columbia, but there's been no word of him. There are still patches of snow in the woods here but my friends in the Golden Age Club keep saying that this will be the most thrilling of springs. We were in Moscow for the worst of the storms and the weather in Moscow was so clement that I went around without a hat or a coat. This was forbidden by a major in the KGB and when I asked why he said: "You are a guest of the Soviet Government and if you don't wear a hat and a coat people will think you don't own one."

Yours,

John

JOHN D. WEAVER
3893 Deervale Drive
Sherman Oaks, CA 91403

15th April 1978

Dear John:

Pamela has just left after a 3-day visit to discuss a special Los Angeles section T&L is doing in October. She appreciated your phone call about the Romania piece, which everybody was delighted with. I sent a copy to Mary Wickes, who was very pleased and would like to see you next time you come this way . . .[49]

Lennie is coming out next month with Gin and the grand-children, and we're looking forward to the reunion. He turns 70

49. Mary Wickes had played a leading role in the short-lived run of *Town House*.

in July and the California trip will, we gather, launch a 60-day celebration.

Bill hasn't settled in at Columbia yet. Just dropped by to see what sort of office he'd have when he comes back in late August. We hope to make our way to New York in the early fall while he's in residence.

When does the book of short stories come out? Wish you could be here Monday night. We're invited to a one-year anniversary party given by the editor of WET: The Magazine of Gourmet Bathing ("Dress Eclectic, Think Electric"). Harriett hasn't decided whether she wants to get into wetness, but she is, as you know, a Baptist. She joins in love.

John

Harriett had been appointed to a city-county advisory fire commission.

JOHN D. WEAVER
3893 Deervale Drive
Sherman Oaks, CA 91403
14th May 1978

Dear John:

Yesterday at breakfast the Commissioner referred to the urban-mountain interface, but so far she hasn't asked for my input or rejected any suggestions of mine because they would impact adversely on our domestic tranquility . . .

Lennie is currently in residence on Wilshire Boulevard and I look forward to lunching with him tomorrow. Wish you could sit in with us.

Harriett joins in love to all the Cheevers.

John

Cedar Lane
May 18th [1978]

Dear John,

My sincere congratulations to Harriet. How mysterious are the ways of time! It was my beloved grandmother—the daughter of Sir Percy Devereaux—who emigrated to this country with the hope of becoming a fireman. She will be pleased. Mary is wild. Yesterday was Prize Day at the Academy and at lunch I sat across from Lillian Hellman who, having lost her looks and her vision, has become the dearest of friends. I waved to Lillian, knowing that she might mistake me for Jimmy Savo, but she spoke my name and blew me a kiss. Then I plucked a rose from the center-piece and tossed it in her direction. When it splashed into her sauce she went after it with a knife and fork. The gigolo who was attending her pointed out that it was not a Brussels sprout and Lillian picked up the rose and asked me if she should wear it in her hair. In your teeth, said I and Lillian then dropped the rose into the front of her dress. "Once an alcoholic, always an alcoholic," growled Mary. Returning here at dusk we found that Harriett had been made a Commissioner.

Yours,
John

J O H N   D.   W E A V E R
3893 Deervale Drive
Sherman Oaks, CA 91403

16th October 1978

Dear John:

We've just come back from Harriett's two-day triumph in Marinette, Wisconsin, where she was the toast of a national fire prevention conference at the Holiday Inn. Foresters and park rangers were sipping champagne from her tennis shoes. The salmon were running and the fall leaves were at their most flamboyant. We had a glorious hour's drive in a Hertz Buick from Marinette to the Green Bay airport, and then flew home to find your book of stories waiting for us. It is the only book I can think of that would pry me away from the new Johnson biography Bill gave me when I was in New York.[50] The stories

50. W. Jackson Bate's *Samuel Johnson* (Harcourt Brace Jovanovich). John's book was the collection of short stories that won the Pulitzer Prize for

bring back so many agreeable memories of 59th Street and Sardi's. We're both looking forward to your winter pastoral visit when Fred returns to Stanford. Meanwhile, all is well here. Pamela came out to launch the October issue.[51] We dined well and Harriett bought me a new pair of shoes, the most expensive shoes I've ever had. They cost more than the suit I got married in. Harriett knew at the time she was not getting a dresser. She joins in love and thanks for the STORIES, and we both wish you and Mary could be here on the 29th to help usher Harriett into the world of senior citizens. I may have her tennis shoes bronzed.

Love,
John

Cedar Lane
October 22nd [1978]

Dear John,

It was good to have your note and your piece on Los Angeles. I think it the most temperate, well-informed and just description of that city I have ever read. I suppose it has some-thing to do with being married to a principle in the government. I was disappointed to find on the map neither our tiny figures on the beach at Santa Monica nor your swimming pool in Sherman Oaks. Here the swimming pools are filled with dead leaves and I spend my spare time hanging storm windows, cutting down small trees, spading up the beets and parsnips. Brrrr, but it is cold in the evenings . . . !

Our son Benjamin is running in the New York Marathon, Susie writes from France that she has just completed a novel[52]

---

fiction. It also won the National Book Critics Circle Award, for which John Irving's novel, *The World According to Garp,* was a serious contender. "I'd have voted for him myself," Irving later wrote Benjamin Cheever.

51. Featuring Los Angeles.

52. It was Susan's first novel, *Looking for Work* (Simon & Schuster). "We are all very proud of you," John wrote her on this same fall day.

and dear Federico just telephoned from Stanford to say that he needs three thousand dollars. Agnes DeMille, Dick Cavett and I are working up a soft-shoe routine for the National Arts Club next Thursday . . .

> Yours,
> John

JOHN D. WEAVER
3893 Deervale Drive
Sherman Oaks, CA 91403

25th November 1978

Dear John:

. . . Last night we came home late from a gathering of old newspaper friends and found a window broken in the room we added to the house. Someone had climbed over a bookcase (plays, mostly) and ransacked the place. It was the first time we'd been burglarized since some goniff broke into our apartment in Kansas City and stole Harriett's Phi Beta Kappa key, which has been replaced by the president of William and Mary. Last night's thief seems not to have hit a free lance writer before, and he must have been keenly disappointed. He found a few bucks in Harriett's purse and rummaged through her jewelry, but found nothing he wanted. A young man named Steve has joined us from a 24-hour window-replacement establishment in Van Nuys and has treated us to forty-five minutes of material on burglaries, including an account of an attractive young divorcee whose intruder stole nothing but her underwear. Every damned stitch of it. Then our Mexican gardener got in *his* story. He'd been at a customer's house, going about his usual chores, when some coyote arrived and said he was from the phone company.

"Scything, I think, is the best thing to do when you complete a work of fiction but I don't suppose you could do that in Fayence without causing some talk. I seed lawns, hang storm windows and fell trees. I also pray—no less—for contrition and humility and when I achieve these—always in excess—I go back to scything."

He was wearing a phone company uniform and wore a leather holster for the tools of his calling. While he fiddled with a phone wire—Juan learned later—two accomplices broke in the other side of the house and stole the color TV and $10,000 in jewelry. I think I've just about got time for a swim before I get the postman's burglar stories. Harriett joins in love to all the Cheevers and, among the other blessings for which we give thanks this fine fall day, is the knowledge that we don't have to tell the president of William & Mary that a failed PhD. has struck us again. And no apparent violence was done to our underwear.

John

John had begun to date his letters.

Cedar Lane,
November 28th, 1978

Dear John,

You seem to have taken your burglary with unprecedented equanimity; but then you and Harriett have reserves that are not possessed by the rest of us. In this neighborhood it takes three or four years to rehabilitate the victims. A stunning divorcee here lost her table silver and her grandmother's beads and got to be such a bore that she was not even invited to fund-raising cocktail parties. She sold her house at an inflationary price, lost her money in Hong Kong real estate and was last heard of doing something I don't choose to mention in a 45th street massage parlor. Thanksgiving reminds me of a dinner you and Harriett gave me in a basement where Harriet shook something in a paper bag. This year I went in town with Ben and my grandson to see the Macy Parade with it's rich, Weaver associations. Santa has gotten mixed up with a swan. Our beginnings never know our ends.

Yours,
John

I had sent John a check and asked him to autograph a copy of Stories *for my sister and her husband, Jane and Jack Poulton.*

JOHN CHEEVER
Cedar Lane
Ossining, New York 10562

December 15th, 1978

Dear John,

The book went out of Knopf to the Poultons yesterday and I am returning your check. Inflation doesn't seem to have reached the west coast with quite the severity we have experienced in the east. To negotiate a check of less than five hundred dollars in Westchester is self-destructive. Twenty-five thousand is the nut; but when Susie telephoned from Chateauneuf de Grasse to say she had sold her novel for twenty thousand we were rather embarrassed. Unless things improve she will have to return home in the spring.[53]

Fred returns home tomorrow at dawn, a little snow is falling and we have a nice woodpile. Mary—and Hope—join me in sending you their best wishes for a Merry Christmas.

Yours,
John

JOHN D. WEAVER
3893 Deervale Drive
Sherman Oaks, CA 91403

31 December 1978

Dear John:

We worked as usual throughout the holiday, but the week was exceedingly pleasant, and we look forward to drinking in the new year with old friends. We spent Christmas Eve with Carl and Estelle Reiner, helping them celebrate their 35th anni-

---

53. Susan had collected her savings and back vacation pay, sold her car, sublet her apartment, and fled to France to write *Looking for Work*.

versary. Carl got a 3-day pass in '43. That was the December I was brought back to New York by Major Spiegelgass and first met you and Lennie and Don and Ted. It was at a Christmas party, I think, that I ran into someone who told me about the West 11th St. apartment I nailed down against the day Harriett would come east. I bought her a signed Benton lithograph that hangs in the hall, just outside my workroom door, and I never thought I'd be acquainted with someone who had gotten an advance of $20,000 on a novel, especially a little girl not yet 2 . . .

My sister was so pleased with STORIES that she called from North Carolina the day it arrived. I was no less pleased to see that the Encino book store's stash was a third printing. We hope you'll put some of the royalties into a trip west to Los Angeles via Stanford. We would so enjoy seeing you, and your Breck shampoo is still in the medicine cabinet, down only half an inch or so. Meanwhile, Harriett joins in thanks for sending Jane and Jack the book and in every good wish for the new year.

As always,
John

JOHN CHEEVER
Cedar Lane
Ossining, New York 10562
February 25th, 1979

Dear John,

This stationary was given me by a kind neighbor on my 66th birthday and I must use it up before May 27th so that I can ask for something lighter only in blue. You might think I could afford my own stationary but the situation here is very cloudy. When I told Mary that I would, before taxes, bank half a million dollars she said that we must sit down at the kitchen table and discuss to whom we would give the money. We have never sat at the kitchen table, she hasn't spoken to me for weeks. "I have finally bought myself a mink coat," she says sadly.[54] I bought the coat, of course, but why should this make me sore? I offered to buy Hope a mink coat but she wanted to go down-town and bargain with some furrier in a basement. She then took off for the coast in order to re-shoot a Dove Soap commercial. In the first version she omitted all the lines that mentioned soap. She's no better about money. She was very excited to find a little dress at Bendel's for what she thought was one hundred dollars. It was, of course, one thousand . . . I will now spend the rest of this day carting horse manure from the stables of Judge Brieant down to my vegetable garden. No shit.

    Yours,

      John

    The Stories of John Cheever *won the Pulitzer prize for fiction on the same day that Benjamin Hale Cheever ran the Boston marathon.*

JOHN D. WEAVER
3893 Deervale Drive
Sherman Oaks, CA 91403

18 April 1979

Dear John:

    We were delighted with the news and called you the moment we heard it, but were told you'd gone to Boston for the marathon. By rights, of course, this should be your second, following the one you earned with Wapshot Chronicle. It is most appropriate, though, that when it finally came it was for the stories, which we continue to reread with such admiration, pleasure and affection.

    54. "If I were the kind of writer I am reputed to be," John wrote Susie, "I would write a story about a suburban matron who wakes up in the morning and taps the barometer. Then she checks the weather reports on TV, radio and in The Times. The weather news sometimes exalts her, sometimes leaves her in despair. She is waiting for that disturbance that springs up out of the northeast and is known as 'The Mink Coat Wind.'"

Harriett, fresh from her triumphs in Tucson, where she was the hit of the foresters' fire management conference, joins in congratulations to all.[55]

John

JOHN CHEEVER
Cedar Lane
Ossining, New York 10562

April 21st, 1979

Dear John,

I think you should know that when we lunched with Joe Pulitzer in Cambridge last year he drew Susie aside and asked: "Is your husband as nervous about being Jewish as he was when he wrote that novel about his father being a Centaur?"

We lunched with Bill last week. I offered to do my impersonation of Eleanora Duse but he seemed disinterested.[56]

Yours,

John

I had run across a copy of Memorabilia of George B. Cheever, DD (1890) *in a secondhand bookstore and sent John a photocopy of the Reverend Doctor H. M. Booth's funeral address. "He had no zeal in the pursuit of dead lions," said Dr. Cheever's eulogist. "The present aroused him."*

JOHN D. WEAVER
3893 Deervale Drive
Sherman Oaks, CA 91403

8th May 1979

Dear John:

As a fellow eulogist, I thought you might be interested in the splendid sendoff the Reverend Dr. Booth gave the Rever-

55. I chose not to cloud this congratulatory letter with the news that when I met her at the airport I was shocked to see her in a wheelchair.

56. With the help of a Guggenheim grant, Bill was working on his biography, *Duse* (Harcourt Brace Jovanovich, 1984).

end Dr. Cheever who, we were pleased to note, had a child's simplicity, wrote better verse than Longfellow, showed no zeal for pursuing dead lions and smote both the slaveholder and the distiller. On May 28th I intend to present Mrs. Weaver a poem to make up for the forty that have gone unwritten since our first anniversary in '38. She joins in love to all the Cheevers.

John

JOHN CHEEVER
Cedar Lane
Ossining, New York 10562

May 14th 1979

Dear John,

Thank you for Dr. Booth's remarks on George Cheever. Since he came from the north shore I guess we were connected but excepting my Uncle Hamlet, none of our family ever went west of Worcester. I didn't get to Englewood myself until I was nearly sixty and left directly after lunch.

We continue, of course, to move in the other direction and on the first of June Ben, his wife and I will leave for Bulgaria. I have had to book tickets, clear visas, and entertain Bulgarians and I seem to be neither here nor there. A dear old lady wrote from Three Mile Island to say that she refused to be evacuated unless she could take with her the Collected Stories.

Yours,

John

Michael Seiler, in a Los Angeles Times *feature article on Ossining—"Prison Town Still Tries to Escape Past"—quoted John as saying it was "a marvelous place to live." He praised the friendliness of his neighbors and their respect for his privacy. "When I go into the village to get a Sunday paper, I know everybody and everybody knows me as the old man who rides the bicycle out on Cedar Lane."*

JOHN D. WEAVER
3893 Deervale Drive
Sherman Oaks, CA 91403
25th August 1979

Dear John:

It was good to have you pop out of the Times at the breakfast table last Thursday. It was the day before Harriett's periodic examination by her radiologist, and I remembered how you'd gone with us to the old Cedars-Sinai for her last look at the lamp. I tend to grow a bit testy just before these checkups, making lists of people who, in my view, might be more justly visited with her pain and anxiety. Happily, the doctor found nothing troublesome and told her to come back in six months rather than four. I will then have entered my sixty-ninth year.

From time to time I take writers to lunch for T&L, usually young writers, representing every creed, color and sex. The other day it was a redhead fashion writer of a certain age who had once worked for Newsweek. She said she was looking forward to reading the Cheever novel this fall. I said "I didn't know John had a new book coming out." There was an awkward pause and I realized she was referring to Susie.

Nice note from Lennie the other day. He seems to be enjoying a prolonged stay in Eaton Place.

Harriett is being interviewed at some length by Richard Reeves for a New Yorker article on the tenuous relationship between Angelinos and their physical environment.[57]

She joins in love to all.

John

---

57. It appeared in the November 5 issue.

JOHN CHEEVER
Cedar Lane
Ossining, New York 10562

August 31st, 1979

Dear John,

Susie was delighted to hear about the fashion writer and we're working on a sort of literary dynasty, not so much to celebrate the Cheevers as to crush the Updikes, Therouxs and Sitwells.[58] We're all ready to publish and I gave my grandson a tape-recorder for his sixth birthday. Fred is working on an historical novel, Mary's poetry is being published in Amsterdam, Ben has completed a book on Marathons, Susie's novel was sold to Warners and Ben's wife won first prize with her apple-pie in Bristol, N.H. and is working on a book about baking. I've stopped smoking and I tell interviewers that my cock dropped off during the Good Friday Vigil.

Yours,

John

58. "He developed a running literary scorecard: Dumas (2), Bellow (1), Theroux (2), Updike (3)—both John Updike's mother and son are published fiction writers—and exulted in our new parity," Susie recalled in *Home Before Dark,* and went on to add: "We joked about what it must have been like at the Dumas dinner table or whether Updike had any cousins in the wings who might upset our score."

The 1980s

❧

"I think that he, with my mother, regarded death as no mystery at all,"
John wrote in his journal when his brother Fred died in the spring of
1976. "Life had been mysterious and thrilling I often hear them say
but death was of no consequence. Some clinician would say that while
I part so easily from my brother I will for the rest of my life, seek in other
men the love he gave me."

Six months later, on the way to Los Angeles for what proved to
be his last visit, he spent a week at the University of Utah. "Lonely
and with my loneliness exacerbated by travel, motel rooms, bad food,
public readings and the superficiality of standing in reception lines," he
recorded in his journal, he fell in love with a personable, talented young
postgraduate student he sometimes referred to as Rip. He persuaded Rip
to give up work on his Ph.D. (it would be of no help to him as a writer
and might be harmful) and come to New York, where he became John's
confidant, literary assistant, and lover. When cancer spread from John's
kidney to his lungs and hip, Rip drove him into Manhattan for cobalt
treatments three times a week and later, as the end drew nearer, to a
Mount Kisco hospital for daily treatments.

"He was pleasant and funny," Susan recalls.

She casually dismissed her "flickering of wondering about the
sexual nature of his friendship with my father." When she found out
from the journals some months after John's death, what surprised her
"was that I hadn't already known." Her brother Ben's discovery came
about gradually and was confirmed by a blunt, explicit phone call twelve
days before his father died.

"I'd suspected as much," Ben told him.

Despite the mistresses and the men in his father's life, his parents "continued to be important to each other," Ben says, and when an interviewer made a passing reference to his "miserable childhood," he was incensed. "Do you have any idea," he asked, "what it was like to have breakfast every morning with John Cheever?" Humor lay always close to the surface of domestic friction. "Bless this table with peace," John would say when parents or children were quarreling at the start of a meal, and if the dogs were underfoot scrounging for scraps, he would add, "both top and bottom." A family friend was witness to a scene in which John walked past Mary with an exaggerated smile. "Wipe that artificial smile off your face," she said, and he replied: "The only thing artificial about this smile is the teeth."

In one of his last interviews, when asked to describe his life with Mary, John said, "She has displayed an extraordinary amount of patience." He paused and added: "Women are an inspiration. It's because of them that we put on clean shirts and wash our socks. Because of women we want to excel. Because of a woman, Christopher Columbus discovered America."

"Queen Isabella," Mary murmured.

"I was thinking," John said, "of Mrs. Columbus."

One evening, after an exhausting day in New York promoting Oh What a Paradise It Seems (Knopf, 1982) he opened his journal and wrote: "I find myself greatly fatigued. I am pleased to make coffee in the kitchen and chat with the old dog. I am Bette Davis and the old dog is Geraldine Fitzgerald in the last scene of Dark Victory. 'Now we have to live again,' says the old dog. And I say, 'If I can laugh I can live.'"

Cedar Lane
Ossining, New York 10562

April 5th, 1980

Dear John,

. . . This is really to ask for an explanation of the new address I see in TRAVEL[1] Should I imagine you and Harriet in a partial construction, hammering and planeing. Do please inform me. Things are quite fluid here and easily imagined. Mary's poetry will be published in the fall by Stein & Day.[2] Hope is at the Beverly Wiltshire having her hair streaked but she goes to Las Vegas on Tuesday to play Omar Sharif's mother. The children are splendid. This is a Saturday morning and I will now clean the chrysanthemum beds, prune the bush roses and plant peas.

Yours,

John

JOHN CHEEVER
Cedar Lane
Ossining, New York 10562

May 9th, 1980

Dear John,

I think it would help your friends if you sent photographs of your new house when it is completed. As a very old man, nearing the end of my journey it is my pleasure, when darkness falls from the wings of night, to recall those domiciles where my oldest friends enjoy repose. This has produced some shocking discoveries such as whips, thumb-screws, needles and other erotic facilities that I do not chose to mention. The wave motif of your last swimming pool has meant beauty and reason to me

1. The *Travel & Leisure* masthead now carried our new Encino address.
2. *The Need for Chocolate & Other Poems,* dedicated to "Fred, Ben, Susan and John."

for many years now and I would like to know what replaces
this . . .
   Yours,
      John

J O H N D. W E A V E R
16314 Meadow Ridge Road
Encino, CA 91436
11th May 1980

Dear John:
   We'd still be living on Deervale Drive if Harriett hadn't
prevailed on me to break the Sabbath, which has never been a
big deal with me because I was brought up to believe that once
you'd made your way to Mass at an acceptable point in the
service, the day was yours, but Harriett was suckled by Baptists
who wouldn't let her roller-skate on Sunday and should have
known better. Anyway, she got me to run the vacuum cleaner
on this particular Sunday, and if the house hadn't been clean, she
would never have let the real estate broker show it to the couple
who turned up at an open house he was showing on our street.
I think we may have been punished sufficiently by a series of
storms that broke on the day our escrow closed and we were
fording a sizeable stream in a 1950s Chevrolet pickup we borrowed from John Paxton.
   Harriett has built three new bookcases and is presently
sawing and hammering away at the bedroom closet, carving a
niche for the TV. She has installed me at a comfortable desk in
a pleasant room looking out on what I hope will soon be the
pool. It will also have a spa, which we didn't have before and
Harriett can put to good use. I've come to feel very much at
home here, but now that she's got everything in place, Harriett
is about to tear the house apart so she can then reassemble it to
her liking. She joins in love to all and we look forward to

reading Mary's poems. When can we expect Federico's collection of essays?

    Best wishes,
    John

John refers to the September 4 birthday of El Pueblo de la Reina de Los Angeles *which, revised census figures indicated, had replaced Chicago as the country's second largest city.*

JOHN CHEEVER
Cedar Lane
Ossining, New York 10562

September 8th [1980]

Dear John,

    I do hope this reaches you in time for your birthday celebration and I was happy to see you on the front page of the TIMES as #2 but I cannot write you until I have your new address. I have the Deervale number, of course, but it is perhaps the vividness of my memories of Sherman Oaks that make it impossible for me to write you until I have some idea of where you are sitting, the view from your window and perhaps the depth of your pool. I lunched with Don a few days ago and would be very happy to report on this and on other matters that might interest you but I can't do anything until I have an address.

    Yours,
    John

JOHN D. WEAVER
16314 Meadow Ridge Road
Encino, CA 91436

14th September 1980

Dear John:

    This was the summer we put in a pool, an ordeal we went through five years ago on Deervale and swore we'd never endure again. It still isn't quite finished (some people from Anaheim are supposed to come here to install a solar cover), but I've been swimming in it every day. It's about the same as the Deervale pool, except that it has a spa. I turn it on around 5 o'clock every day and while it's heating I take my final plunge for the day, then steam for 20 to 30 minutes in a swirl of white water, with five jets streaming from the sides and bubbles coming up from punctured pipes in the floor.

Our contractor turned out to be a born-again Christian who let Harriett do all the work of supervising the various crews (each outfit did its work in such a way as to make it difficult, if not impossible, for the next bunch to function), and then he'd turn up around 6 o'clock, cadge a couple of Scotches and subject us to an hour or so of evangelical ramblings. At one point when work had been held up for several days because a leak had developed somewhere in the underground plumbing, he threw up his arms and shouted, "Sweet Jesus, help me find that leak." Moments later one of the workmen pointed to a spot behind the skimmer and said, "Aqui, aqui." And sure enough there was the leak.

Harriett's game leg is badly swollen (edema resulting from surgery and radiation) and it gives her great pain at times, but she has managed to take the new place firmly in hand and is whipping it into shape (our firewood is neatly stacked against the coming winter and yesterday we got new screens). It will take another six months or so for her to stamp it as a Harriett Weaver dwelling. Meanwhile, we were pleased to learn that New York has a spare $11,000,000 to spend on refurbishing Fort Spigelgass.[3] Do you suppose they will revitalize Borden's?

Love to all the Cheevers.

John

3. "Mayor Edward Koch announced last week an $11-million project to expand the Astoria motion picture studios in Queens into one of the most modern production facilities on the East Coast," the *Los Angeles Times* had reported two days earlier.

I had sent John Los Angeles: The Enormous Village *(Capra Press, 1980). He was at work on* Oh What a Paradise It Seems *(Knopf, 1982).*

JOHN CHEEVER
Cedar Lane
Ossining, New York 10562

September 26th, 1980

Dear John,

Thanks you very much for the Enormous Village. I am in the throes of that tedious lunacy that sometimes produces a book and I can read nothing with discernment or intelligence, but the photographs in your book are marvelous and what I've glimpsed of the text is graceful, witty and exhaustively researched as is everything you do. My congratulations and best wishes. I am also very happy to have your current address and to be able to think of you sitting in a pool as darkness falls from the wings of night. By "Spa" I suppose you mean what is known as a Jacuzzi in Westchester. We, of course, have nothing of the sort ourselves but on these muggy evenings Mother sometimes cools me off with a garden hose . . .

Yours,

John

JOHN D. WEAVER
16314 Meadow Ridge Road
Encino, CA 91436

17th November 1980

Dear John:

Some fleet-footed speculator who got in ahead of adjoining landowners has managed to acquire title to a part of the old John Wexley lot next to our Hillside Avenue house, which we'd always been assured by city officials was "unbuildable." The present owner of our house called to ask us to meet with him and the contractor yesterday morning to provide historical background on the water & power company's easement along a common border. It was the first time we'd set foot in the house since we left (circa 1960). The view was as magnificent as ever (City Hall, however, is no longer the tallest building on the horizon), but the rooms seem to have shrunk. Harriett was surprised to find that the counter tops in the kitchen are still covered with the black linoleum she'd intended to replace fifteen years ago. The shutters she'd hung there were still in place and her brickwork has held up nicely, except for the intrusion of roots from trees we'd planted, including a giant avocado that sprang from a seed I'd stuck in the ground one evening in honor of a remarkable tossed salad.

We're celebrating the end of a 10-year struggle to get Brownsville on television. Carl Foreman has just come to terms with CBS for a 4-hour special. The network is taking an option on the book and hiring me to do a treatment tailored for Gregory Peck (no, he's not going to do it in blackface—the tack I've always wanted to take is the Zola approach, telling the story from the standpoint of Senator Foraker).[4] I was taken out to Peck's home two weeks ago to tell him the story, and he seemed quite pleased with it. I was pleased to spot your collection of short stories in his bookcase, along with a shelf of books on and by Adlai Stevenson. The "front money" will give us a new car and, even more important, another year or two of the Writers' Guild medical insurance.

Do you remember that play of ours that Lennie produced for ANTA right after the war? When we were casting it, a pretty young woman in a sable coat applied for the role of the impoverished heroine. I wish we hadn't turned her down. One or both of us might be getting cabinet appointments when her husband is sworn in next January. Harriett would be a hell of a Supreme Court justice.

Love to all the Cheevers.

John

4. The book, subtitled "The Story of 'America's Black Dreyfus Affair,'" remained under option for most of the next ten years but still has not made its way to the screen.

"Some might be intrigued by the spectacle of Cheever sloshing around in cash he has no particular use for," Mary wrote Lib Collins. "He gets into the welfare check line at the Ossining downtown bank to buy Treasury Bonds (on the advice of a neighbor). He bought Fred a $200 bicycle and when it was stolen, replaced it with a Bavarian Motor Works car, the most expensive anyone in this family has ever had."

JOHN CHEEVER
Cedar Lane
Ossining, New York 10562
November 22nd, 1980

Dear John,

I'm delighted to know that Brownsville will be on TV and I wonder what sort of car you're going to buy. In the last year I've bought three Rabbits, one BMW, one Dodge and one Japanese make, the name of which escapes me. I also bought Susie a house in Vermont. I drive a Rabbit and continue to live here. I feel very well although in the 7th inning of the Fourth game of the World Series I foamed at the mouth, fell to the floor and lost consciousness for several hours and my memory for even longer. This was called a Grand Mal Seizure. There has been no explanation for this but Medicare has sent me a check for $170.[5]

Mary's book will be published on the fourth of December and Susie's second novel comes out in the spring.[6] Ben condescends to lunch with me from time to time.

Yours,
John

5. The seizure occurred at Yaddo during a night game he was watching with friends. "M[ary] is loving and patient," he recorded in his journal, "and I cannot readily recall a time when she has so unselfishly given herself to me."

6. *A Handsome Man* (Simon & Schuster).

JOHN D. WEAVER
16314 Meadow Ridge Road
Encino, CA 91436

5th December 1980

Dear John:

We were taken aback to hear of your seventh-inning seizure and are grateful to Lennie for a reassuring note reporting on
a phone conversation in which you'd said a local shaman had
given you some sort of medication to ward off a recurrence.
Lennie said he and Don were going to lunch with you next
week, and I wish I could be there . . .

Harriett has just finished painting the inside of the house (I
got the job of removing the old shelf paper from the closets). She
joins in love to all. Take care.

     John

MR. JOHN CHEEVER
Cedar Lane
Ossining, New York 10562

September 2rd 1981

Dear John,

I dreamed last night that I saw you both at some crowded
gathering like the Simon Garfinkel reunion in Central Park. I
was hurt to see that you had come east without calling and when
I said as much you said that you had come east to go trout fishing
with Frank Stanton and that you were pressed for time. You
both looked very well and I thought you'd like to know.[7]

    John

7. John makes light of our presumed slight, but he once recorded in
his journal: "Yesterday I discovered that an old friend had returned to town
without calling me. There is probably some personal slur involved here but
it is this complexity that I cannot comprehend. I wish, of course, to be loved
and admired but I also wish for constancy in behaviour and this is perhaps the
most perplexing wish I have. But the significant thing here is the dispropor-
tionateness of the anguish I feel when I find that an old friend has failed to
call me. Then I am cross with my beloved children. My house and my body

JOHN D. WEAVER
16314 Meadow Ridge Road
Encino, CA 91436

28th September 1981

Dear John:

If we'd gone east to get in some trout-fishing with Frank Stanton, we would certainly have called and made our way to the Cheever kitchen with the pick of our catch, but a dream is about the only way we could manage a trip east just now. As a result of the radiation therapy, the bones in Harriett's hip have deteriorated to such an extent that she moves about on a cane with some difficulty and, at times, with considerable pain. There has been no recurrence of the cancer, however, and she still manages to keep City Hall in line. She's been getting some long-overdue recognition for her work in reducing the risk of fire in the Santa Monica Mountains.[8]

Meanwhile, she has become quite adept with the cane and I marvel at the uses to which she puts it. A deft thrust straightens a picture on the wall, retrieves a letter that's fallen behind a bookcase, knocks dead needles off the pine trees. She also uses it in arguments to make up for the shortcomings of the language. She hasn't caused bodily harm with it yet, but I foresee the day when it will have to be registered with the state as a potentially lethal weapon . . .

All our love to you both.

John

---

seem insubstantial. I suppose this is what is meant by a traumatic area. Like those deposits of water and oil that, lying underground, linked to one another like subterranean lakes, if one of them is tapped the fluid in all of them is drained and troubled so this surface injury of no consequence or depth finds a devious way to trouble my whole spirit."

8. Mayor Tom Bradley and the City Council had given her handsome scrolls.

MR. JOHN CHEEVER
Cedar Lane
Ossining, New York 10562

October second, 1981

Dear John,

Harriet's competence as a fire-fighter comes as no surprise to one who can remember her dropping chicken into a paper bag filled with flour in a basement apartment in the village. I believe she cooked the chicken on a curling iron.[9] Her competence will never surprise me. However, I did forget to say that our son Fred will be married on Valentine's Day in a place called Riverside and that you, of course, will be invited. Most of us are planning to wear brown tuxedos. You can rent them from any dry-cleaner.

Yours,

John

JOHN D. WEAVER
16314 Meadow Ridge Road
Encino, CA 91436

20th October 1981

Dear John:

Riverside is where the Nixons got married (Mission Inn, June 21, 1940). Harriett and I had lunch at the Inn a few years ago, but we didn't stay the night, and we were already married, so we didn't have to go through *that* again. At the moment we have no idea what we can plan on for February, but if all is well, we'd love to drive you and Mary down to the wedding and, if there's time, I'd like to take a look at the Indian pictographs outside of town. Meanwhile, Harriett's latest X-rays indicate another hip fracture, which isn't healing, so she's going in for a bone scan at the earliest opportunity, and then will begin preparations for hip surgery. We hope that by February she will be

9. In our one-room wartime apartment Harriett cooked on a two-burner hotplate in a former coat closet with no running water.

able to run and laugh and play the violin again, in which case we would like not only to drive you down to Riverside but also over to the Huntington Library for lunch with the Librarian. The cuisine is about on a par with Borden's, but the company is pleasant and the gardens inviting.

We saw you on a PBS interview the other night. Your jacket looked well-pressed, but you were sitting down the whole time, so we couldn't assess the state of your pants. Harriett says, "Maybe that's why they didn't let him stand up." In any event, it was good to see and hear you, and to get a glimpse of Quincy in living color. The room was filled with your PSOH.[10]

Harriett joins in love to all the Cheevers.

John

[Cedar Lane]
October 24th, 1981

Dear John,

I'm so glad Harriet asked about my pants. They match the jacket and are part of a 3-part suit Susie made me buy at Barney's three years ago. I've only worn it twice so the pants are nicely pressed. However I did have pants trouble on TV only last week when Dick Cavett asked me to do a tandem show with John Updike.[11] When it was time to dress for the show Mary was at her Yoga class and I didn't know what to wear. I put on some real nice shoes but the only pants I could find were very worn

---

10. Pervasive sweetness of heart.

11. "By the time I met him he was a well-established writer, much beset by admirers and would-be claimants on his time, and could be impatient and even rude in a way that surprised me at the time but I have less trouble understanding now," John Updike wrote Scott Donaldson (June 25, 1984), and went on to express gratitude to John for having come "all the way to Ipswich to my daughter's wedding" in 1977 and, four years later, "when he was clearly dying, he came into New York to appear on the Dick Cavett show with me, in order to say a kind word for my book at the time, *Rabbit Is Rich.*"

and the only tweed jacket I have had already appeared in a Cavett show. I dressed this up with a necktie Esse Lee knitted for me when she last crossed from Liverpool.[12] Dick asked about this tie and I told him that dull talk shows had done more for the cravat than Beau Brummel and that when you couldn't tolerate the interlocutor you could always count the stripes on his tie and wonder if it lived in a drawer or on a rack. He snapped at me and said that we would dispense with makeup. Cavett was already made up and Updike was painted like a piece of marzipan . . . When the count-down came for my appearance I went into the toilet and got my fly-zipper caught on my shirt tail. It would not come undone. So then I went into the Green Room with my fly open and asked everybody what I should do. They all looked away. So then I went back to the toilet and took off my pants and ripped my shirt-tail out of its trap and closed my fly. They plan to air the show in November and if you see it this will explain why my hair is mussed, why my face is so red and why I keep looking down at my fly.

    Yours,

      John

    Pamela Fiori called to tell me she had run across a line in the New York Times *about John undergoing some tests at Sloan-Kettering.*

12. The widow of the journalist who wrote the *Time* cover story on John.

29th December 1981

Ms. Pamela Fiori,
Editor-in-chief,
Travel & Leisure,
1120 Avenue of the Americas
New York, NY 10036

Dear Pamela:

I called John this morning. It's bone cancer, left leg and hip. He said he'd had a kidney removed last July for what appeared to be a localized malignancy. Then he recently went to a doctor for what was at first thought to be a pulled tendon. "John," he said of this new development, "it is in no way illuminating." Then he laughed and described the waiting around for radiation therapy as "a kind of laundromat. We sit there in our hospital gowns, not like people who have no washing machines, but like people whose machines haven't been repaired yet." He said he was going back to the hospital today and had been told he would get a clearer picture from the doctors of just what they have in store for him. He said Mary had been "an angel" and that he was determined to come out here in mid-February for Fred's wedding. I look forward with a tightly-knit stomach to seeing him . . .

Harriett joins in love and in every good wish for the new year. We've both had about enough of this one.

John

JOHN D. WEAVER
16314 Meadow Ridge Road
Encino, CA 91436

30th December 1981

Dear John:

It's extraordinary that the two people I cherish most in this world should both be having trouble with the left leg and hip. It can't be "something that's going around," not over a distance of 3,000 miles. I hope that in the new year I'll see both of you entered in the Boston Marathon. Meanwhile, we know what you mean about that surgical-gown laundromat scene. Harriett has been going through it for some weeks now, with a view to finding out whether she can become a candidate for hip-replacement surgery. She goes into the hospital Monday (January 4th) for an arteriogram, and if she gets a passing grade on the blood supply to the left hip, she'll have the operation Thursday.

I keep thinking about our slatternly friend at the Farmers Market fish stall who was to spend Thanksgiving alone in her kitchen with leftovers. If I run into her during the next few days, I'll damn well let her know how we're spending *our* holidays on our respective coasts. If we can stay awake till midnight tomorrow, we'll lift a glass with hope-filled wishes for the coming year. We look forward to seeing you and Mary in February, and I want to be sure she gets to see the Huntington Library, Art Gallery and Gardens. Please give her our love. We long to embrace you both.

John

JOHN D. WEAVER
16314 Meadow Ridge Road
Encino, CA 91436

2 January 1982

Dear John:

I'm on my way to the hospital with Harriett, carrying a flight bag with her nightdress, slippers, comb and brush and traveling iron (in case her surgical gown gets a wrinkle) . . . We'll watch the Shady Hill show at Cedars-Sinai and will check in

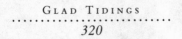

with you and Mary later in the week.[13] Until then, Harriett joins in love to you both . . .

John

John couldn't make it to the wedding.

JOHN D. WEAVER
16314 Meadow Ridge Road
Encino, CA 91436

16th February 1982

Dear John:

We were pleased to hear from Mary that the wedding had gone so beautifully. If Harriett's condition had permitted, I would have driven down to Riverside to represent the regiment, but she had a bit of a setback over the week-end and I wanted to be with her. Sunday evening, for the first time in a week, she was hungry. What started her eating was a nutritionist's suggestion that she order from the kosher menu. Kosher food, we find, is prepared on the premises. The stuff they feed the goyim is catered by an outfit that manages to make French toast out of shirt backings. Yesterday her internist said she could have a tot of whisky before supper, so we clinked Styrofoam cups about 5:30 and drank to her homecoming, which I hope will be soon, but she still has a long, difficult road ahead. She joins in love to you both. You are much in our thoughts.

John

When I drove Harriett home on March 6, we were accompanied by a registered nurse who told us that for some years her father had been taking care of her bedridden mother. "You will destroy each other," she predicted. She was mistaken.

13. PBS kicked off its ambitious series, "American Playhouse," with John's script, *"The Shady Hill Kidnapping,"* on January 12. "A sardonic spoof of middle-class mores," *TV Guide* reported.

JOHN D. WEAVER
16314 Meadow Ridge Road
Encino, CA 91436

10 March 1982

Dear John:

After forty-five years I still don't understand her. In the hospital she took the doctors and nurses aback by saying, "I've got to shit," but now that she's home she tells me she is going to have a "bowel movement." She's entering a new phase, the long, difficult road of physical therapy, but, thank goodness, she's operating from her home base. Over the week-end (she came home Saturday) she read a newspaper for the first time in two months, and yesterday she started going over her tax records. Lennie sent us the New York Times review of PARADISE, and I can think of nothing that would more agreeably lead her back to the pleasures of book-reading. Could we impose on you for a copy, suitably inscribed? We were delighted to hear from Pamela Fiori that she'd run into you at Four Seasons and that there was a possibility you might come this way. We would love to see you. Meanwhile, Harriett joins in love to you both.

John

MR. JOHN CHEEVER
Cedar Lane
Ossining, New York 10562

March 15th [1982]

Dear John:

The Knopf list that I signed seems to have been incomplete. They have no more copies and leaving for the hospital tomorrow I send you my last. I'm going back for Platinum which is working.

yrs,

John

JOHN D. WEAVER
16314 Meadow Ridge Road
Encino, CA 91436

20th March 1982

Dear John:

The book brought a joyful spring afternoon to Golden Pond West, but, unfortunately, it was mauled in the mails, so I'm sending you a fresh copy, along with stamps and a self-addressed label for the book's return once you've signed it. Harriett is gaining ground slowly and painfully, and may be the first hip replacement patient to come home with a glass tube in her throat.[14] We hope we can have the damned thing removed within the next ten days or so. Meanwhile, she joins in love and in thanks for PARADISE. It was liking having you poolside for a sunny, postprandial drowse.

Love to all the Cheevers.

John

MR. JOHN CHEEVER
Cedar Lane
Ossining, New York 10562

March 29th, [1982]

Dear John,

The copy that was mutilated was the last Knopf had. I am afraid of the books going out of print and they are afraid my red corpuscles might run low. How many copies have Tinker and Brigham I ask and they ask my blood count after the last platinum infusion. So it goes.

Yours,

John

14. She had undergone a tracheostomy when her vocal chords became paralyzed. The glass tube was not removed until six months later. Within forty-eight hours it had to be replaced in preparation for additional surgery on her left leg.

JOHN D. WEAVER
16314 Meadow Ridge Road
Encino, CA 91436

22 April 1982

Dear John:

Harriett is reading A Flag for Sunrise. A Santa Ana is blowing in from the desert, raising the pool temperature four degrees. CBS has renewed the option on Brownsville and a television writer is to be put to work on the project this week . . .

We both wish we could be with you on your 70th. Meanwhile, we rejoice in the knowledge that some beneficent use has been found for platinum.

Harriett joins in love to all the Cheevers.

John

John hobbled into Carnegie Hall on April 27 to receive the National Award for Literature and a check for $15,000. "He walked painfully slowly with a cane and the help of his wife, Mary, and his voice was weak," Digby Diehl reported in the Los Angeles Herald Examiner. *"But in a room full of the elite of the literary world, Cheever stood tall as a giant, the subject of genuine and moving adoration."*

MR. JOHN CHEEVER
Cedar Lane
Ossining, New York 10562

April 28th, 1982

Dear John,

. . . The prize-awarding yesterday was rather tiring and I find today that I can barely climb a flight of stairs but I'm off platinum—thank God—and onto some putsresence from the Adriatic that was developed as an insecticide. It costs two hundred and fifty dollars a lump but it makes me feel much better.

Yours,

John

Around four o'clock on the afternoon of Friday, June 18, John died upstairs in the master bedroom at Cedar Lane. "The undertaker," Ben remembers, "handled the body the way one would handle a five-foot-six-inch sack of potatoes." Susan recalls that "they had trouble getting the stretcher around the turn in the stairs—it's an old house—and they lifted it over the banister." They are both writers. They notice that sort of thing.

JOHN D. WEAVER
16314 Meadow Ridge Road
Encino, CA 91436

19th June 1982

Dear Mary:

We were pleased to hear that John was home with you and the children. Time blurs a bit these days and I sometimes wonder how Susie managed to crawl out of that playpen and write two novels. Last January, just before Harriett went into the hospital, we got a warm, nostalgic letter from Don, recalling our days at Astoria and remarking on the closeness of the links formed at those Borden's lunches . . .

From the outset, the day I first read a dozen or so of John's army scripts, I realized that he was by far the best writer of our group and, as I later came to believe, of our generation. I'm glad he lived to enjoy the recognition that finally came his way. People who read the interviews and saw him on television discovered that radiant good humor that enriched and enlivened our gatherings at Borden's nearly forty years ago.

Harriett joins in love and in sympathy for a loss we share so keenly with you and the children. John was such a bright, shining part of our lives.

Love,

John

CHRONOLOGY

1912

John William Cheever is born May 27 in Quincy, Massachusetts, the younger son of Frederick Lincoln Cheever (1863–1946) and Mary Deveraux Liley Cheever (1873–1956).

1924–26

At Thayerlands Junior School in South Braintree, Massachusetts, Cheever's spelling is "unusual," but he wins short story contest sponsored by the *Boston Herald-Traveler*.

1926–28

Attends Thayer Academy across the street from what is now Thayer Middle School.

1928–29

Attends Quincy High School.

1929–30

Cheever returns to Thayer Academy and records his departure in "Expelled," which Malcolm Cowley buys for *The New Republic* and which appears on October 1, 1930.

1931

Cheever goes on a walking tour of Germany with his brother, Fred.

1932

Mortgage on the family home is foreclosed.

1934

Cheever spends his first summer at Yaddo.

1937

With a $400 advance from Simon & Schuster, Cheever goes to Yaddo to work on a novel, *The Holly Tree,* which is later rejected and destroyed.

1938

Hired by the Federal Writers Project (May), Cheever works in Washington, D.C., and lives in a boarding house at 2308 Twentieth Street NW.

1939

Cheever does the final editing on *The WPA Guide to New York City* (reprinted in 1982) and resigns from FWP (May 25). Meets twenty-one-year-old Mary Winternitz in an elevator at 545 Fifth Avenue on his way to see her employer and his agent, Maxim Lieber (November).

1940

Cheever occupies Muriel Rukeyser's apartment on Bank Street in the late spring and early summer.

1941

Marries Mary Winternitz, daughter of Dr. Milton Winternitz, dean of Yale Medical School (March 22). They move into a two-room apartment at 19th East Eighth Street.

1942

Cheever enters the Army (May 7) and, after training at Camp Croft in Spartanburg, South Carolina, is sent to Camp Gordon near Augusta, Georgia, where he is a private first-class with E Company, Twenty-second Infantry.

1943

Random House publishes Cheever's first collection of short stories, *The Way Some People Live*. Cheever is transferred to the Signal Corps Photographic Center, 35-11 Thirty-fifth Avenue, Long Island City, New York. Susan Cheever is born on July 31.

1944

Cheevers enter into communal living arrangement with two other young couples in a town house on Ninety-second Street.

1945

Cheever passes through Hollywood on his way to and from the Philippines. Father dies. Moves into apartment at 400 East Fifty-ninth Street. Discharged from the Army in November.

1946

Goes to Treetops on June 18, and returns to New York on July 15. Drinks champagne at the Plaza with Don Ettlinger and Katrina Wallingford, who are about to leave for Europe on their honeymoon. Attends Ted Mills–Joan Patterson marriage in Andover, New Hampshire, on July 14.

1948

"Town House," a play based on Cheever's *New Yorker* stories and directed by George S. Kaufman, is produced at the National Theatre and closes on September 30, after twelve performances. Benjamin Hale Cheever is born on Mary's birthday, May 4.

1951

Cheever receives a Guggenheim grant and wins the O. Henry Award with "The Pot of Gold." Moves to Scarborough (May 28), occupying a cottage on the Frank A. Vanderlip estate. Random House rejects first *Wapshot* novel on basis of a 100-page draft.

1952

Cheever works on a TV adaptation, *"Life with Father and Mother."* Fred and Iris Cheever move to Briarcliff Manor with their four children.

1953

In February the collection *The Enormous Radio and Other Stories* (Funk & Wagnalls) is published.

1954

Cheever begins a two-year teaching stint at Barnard in New York City.

1954

Cheever is hospitalized with pneumonia. Confirmed at All Saints Episcopal Church. Hemorrhoidectomy (Thanksgiving).

1956

Wins O. Henry Award for "The Country Husband" in January. Mother dies on February 22. Finishes *The Wapshot Chronicle* in June. M-G-M buys film rights to "The Housebreaker of Shady Hill" (April 14). Mary is pregnant when the family leaves for Italy in October.

1957

Cheever is elected to the National Institute of Arts and Letters in January. Federico is born in Rome on March 9 and *The Wapshot Chronicle* is published the same month. Returns to Scarborough.

1958

Cheever wins the National Book Award for *The Wapshot Chronicle* in March. Joins The Century Club. Publishes *The Housebreaker of Shady Hill and Other Stories* in September.

1959

Mary's father dies on October 3.

1960

Receives second Guggenheim grant. Goes to Hollywood to adapt a D. H. Lawrence novel, *The Lost Girl,* for Jerry Wald at 20th-Century Fox. Buys an eighteenth-century house on Cedar Lane in Ossining, New York, for $37,500.

1961

Moves to Cedar Lane in February. Publishes his fourth collection, *Some People, Places, and Things That Will Not Appear in My Next Novel.*

1962

Mary takes a teaching job at Briarcliff College.

1964

Publishes *The Wapshot Scandal* in January. Cheever appears on the cover of *Time,* March 27. In Hollywood for the sale of the film rights to the two *Wapshot* novels (April 3), Cheever meets Hope Lange. Publishes his fifth collection of short stories, *The Brigadier and the Golf Widow,* in September. Makes the first of three trips to U.S.S.R. in October. Frank Perry buys film rights to "The Swimmer." Perry's wife, Eleanor, writes the screenplay.

1965

Cheever takes Mary to Chicago, talks about "the beauties of literature" (May 4). He is awarded the Howells Medal for *The Wapshot Scandal* on May 19. Susan graduates from Brown-Pembroke on June 7. Cheever attends a party at the White House on June 8.

1966

Cheever has a cameo appearance in *The Swimmer,* which is filmed in the Westport, Connecticut, area. He is treated by Drs. Ray Mutter and David Hays for his addiction to alcohol that summer.

1967

Susan Cheever marries Robert Cowley on May 6. Cheever spends two weeks in Naples in July to interview Sophia Loren for *The Saturday Evening Post;* the interview appears in the October 21 issue. Suffers a prostatitis attack (October–November). Benjamin Cheever is arrested in Cincinnati for participating in a demonstration against the Vietnam War in December. He gets off with a $150 fine, but learns what it is to be "roughed up by the Man."

1968

Cheever finishes his third novel, *Bullet Park,* and vacations in Ireland with Mary and Federico that summer. Candida Donadio, Cheever's new agent, negotiates a lucrative contract with Alfred A. Knopf for *Bullet Park.* Cheever has all of his teeth removed in December: "cheering a football game on tv my smile flew across the room."

1969

Knopf publishes *Bullet Park* in April. At Ben's wedding in September, Mary weeps at sight of his ill-fitting suit. Cheever has eleven psychiatric sessions with Dr. J. William Silverberg, May through November.

1970

Alan Pakula and Hope Lange divorce, and Cheever says he seems "to have ended up with Alan" (June 7). Leaves with Mary and Fred for International PEN Congress in Seoul (June 22).

1971

Cheever begins teaching at Sing Sing (now called the Ossining Correctional Facility). Goes to U.S.S.R. with Federico for the Dostoevsky Jubilee in November.

1972

Early in this year Cheever writes in his journal: "In the throes of a grueling booze fight." Turns sixty.

1973

Cheever is elected to the American Academy of Arts and Letters. Knopf publishes his sixth collection, *The World of Apples*. Suffers a heart attack (pulmonary edema). Teaches a semester at the University of Iowa Writers' Workshop. Drinking again.

1974

Cheever accepts an invitation to teach writing at Boston University, and lives in a furnished room off Kenmore Square at 71 Bay State Road.

1975

Cheever is in such bad shape by the end of March that he can no longer teach. John Updike takes over some of his classes. Cheever checks into the Smithers Institute at 56 East Ninety-third Street for a twenty-eight-day dry-out program. Mary drives him home on May 7. His drinking days are finally over.

1976

Cheever's seventy-one-year-old brother, Fred, dies on May 31.

1977

Cheever's fourth novel, *Falconer*, featured on the cover of the March 14 issue of *Newsweek*, is a Book-of-the-Month Club selection.

1978

The Stories of John Cheever wins the Pulitzer Prize and the National Book Critics Circle Award. Cheever receives an Honorary Doctorate of Letters from Harvard in June. Quits smoking and meets the young man with whom he has an affair that lasts until the end of his life.

1979

Travels to Chicago to speak at a ceremony sponsored by the Newberry Library celebrating the acquisition of Malcolm Cowley's papers (October 9). Receives the Edward MacDowell Medal for "outstanding contribution to the arts."

1980

The Public Broadcasting System presents television adaptations of three Cheever stories: "The Sorrows of Gin," "Oh Youth and Beauty," and "The Five-Forty-Eight."

1981

Cheever completes an original script, *"The Shady Hill Kidnapping,"* for public television. Admitted to Phelps Memorial Hospital for a recurrent urinary tract problem. X-rays reveal a cancerous right kidney with, in Mary's words, "a tumor sprouting from it like budding leaves on a wet bean."

1982

PBS introduces its new "American Playhouse" series with *"The Shady Hill Kidnapping"* on January 12. Knopf publishes *Oh What a Paradise It Seems.* Awarded the National Medal for Literature at Carnegie Hall on April 27. Dies at his home in Ossining on June 18, and is buried in the Cheever family plot in Norwell, Massachusetts.

WRITINGS

BOOKS

The Way Some People Live. New York: Random House, 1943.

The Enormous Radio and Other Stories. New York: Funk & Wagnalls, 1953.

The Wapshot Chronicle. New York: Harper & Bros., 1957.

The Housebreaker of Shady Hill and Other Stories. New York: Harper & Bros., 1958.

Some People, Places, and Things That Will Not Appear in My Next Novel. New York: Harper & Bros., 1961.

The Wapshot Scandal. New York: Harper & Row, 1964.

The Brigadier and the Golf Widow. New York: Harper & Row, 1964.

Bullet Park. New York: Alfred A. Knopf, 1969.

The World of Apples. New York: Alfred A. Knopf, 1973.

Falconer. New York: Alfred A. Knopf, 1977.

The Stories of John Cheever. New York: Alfred A. Knopf, 1978.

Oh What a Paradise It Seems. New York: Alfred A. Knopf, 1982.

STORIES

Abbreviations

WSP—*The Way Some People Live*, 30
ER—*The Enormous Radio*, 14
HB—*The Housebreaker of Shady Hill*, 8
SPP—*Some People, Places, and Things That Will Not Appear in My Next Novel*, 9
BGW—*The Brigadier and the Golf Widow*, 16

WA—*The World of Apples*, 10
★—included in *The Stories of John Cheever*, 61

1930
"Expelled." *The New Republic*, October 1.

1931
"Fall River." *The Left: A Quarterly Review of Radical and Experimental Art*, Autumn.
"Late Gathering." *Pagany*, October–December.

1932
"Bock Beer and Bermuda Onions." *Hound & Horn*, April–June.

1935
"Brooklyn Rooming House." *The New Yorker*, May 25.
"Buffalo." *The New Yorker*, June 22.
"The Autobiography of a Drummer." *The New Republic*, October 23.
"Of Love: A Testimony." *Story*, December. *(WSP)*

1936
"In Passing." *Atlantic*, March.
"Bayonne." *Parade*, Spring.
"Play a March." *The New Yorker*, June 20.
"The Princess." *The New Republic*, October 28.
"A Picture for the Home." *The New Yorker*, November 28.

1937
"Behold a Cloud in the West." In *New Letters in America*, edited by Horace Gregory and Eleanor Clark (Norton)
"The Brothers." *Yale Review*, June. *(WSP)*
"Summer Remembered." *Story*, July. *(WSP)*
"The Teaser." *The New Republic*, September 8.
"Homage to Shakespeare." *Story*, November.
"In the Beginning." *The New Yorker*, November 6.

1938
"His Young Wife." *Collier's*, January 1.
"Frère Jacques." *Atlantic*, March.
"Saratoga." *Collier's*, August 13.

1939

"Treat." *The New Yorker*, January 21.

"The Happiest Days." *The New Yorker*, November 4.

1940

"It's Hot in Egypt." *The New Yorker*, January 6.

"North of Portland." *The New Yorker*, February 24. *(WSP)*

"Survivor." *The New Yorker*, March 9. *(WSP)*

"Washington Boarding House." *The New Yorker*, March 23. *(WSP)*

"Riding Stable." *The New Yorker*, April 27. *(WSP)*

"The Edge of the World." *Harper's Bazaar*, June. *(WSP)*

"Happy Birthday, Enid." *The New Yorker*, July 13. *(WSP)*

"Tomorrow Is a Beautiful Day." *The New Yorker*, August 3. *(WSP)*

"The Man She Loved." *Collier's*, August 24.

"Summer Theatre." *The New Yorker*, August 24. *(WSP)*

"I'm Going to Asia." *Harper's Bazaar*, September. *(WSP)*

"The New World." *The New Yorker*, November 9. *(WSP)*

"Forever Hold Your Peace." *The New Yorker*, November 23. *(WSP)*

"A Present for Louisa." *Mademoiselle*, December.

"When Grandmother Goes." *The New Yorker*, December 14. *(WSP)*

1941

"Cat." *Harper's Bazaar*, January. *(WSP)*

"A Bird in Hand." *Mademoiselle*, February.

"Hello, Dear." *The New Yorker*, February 15. *(WSP)*

"The Law of the Jungle." *The New Yorker*, March 22. *(WSP)*

"A Border Incident." *Harper's Bazaar*, July. *(WSP)*

"There They Go." *The New Yorker*, July 19. *(WSP)*

"Run, Sheep, Run." *The New Yorker*, August 2. *(WSP)*

"Publick House." *The New Yorker*, August 16. *(WSP)*

"These Tragic Years." *The New Yorker*, September 27. *(WSP)*

"From This Day Forward." *Mademoiselle*, October.

"In the Eyes of God." *The New Yorker*, October 11. *(WSP)*

1942

"The Pleasures of Solitude." *The New Yorker*, January 24. *(WSP)*

"The Pursuit of Happiness." *Mademoiselle*, February.

"A Place of Great Historical Interest." *The New Yorker*, February 21.

"The Peril in the Streets." *The New Yorker*, March 21. *(WSP)*

"The Shape of a Night." *The New Yorker*, April 18.

"Goodbye, Broadway—Hello, Hello." *The New Yorker*, June 6. *(WSP)*

"Family Dinner." *Collier's*, July 25.

"Problem No. 4." *The New Yorker*, October 17. *(WSP)*

"The Man Who Was Very Homesick for New York." *The New Yorker*, November 21. *(WSP)*

"The Sorcer's Balm." *(WSP)*

1943

"Sergeant Limeburner." *The New Yorker*, March 13.

"They Shall Inherit the Earth." *The New Yorker*, April 10.

"A Tale of Old Pennsylvania." *The New Yorker*, May 29.

"The Invisible Ship." *The New Yorker*, August 7.

"My Friends and Neighbors All, Farewell." *The New Yorker*, October 2.

"Dear Lord, We Thank Thee for Thy Bounty." *The New Yorker*, November 27.

1944

"Somebody Has to Die." *The New Yorker*, June 24.

"A Walk in the Park." *Good Housekeeping*, October.

"The Single Purpose of Leon Burrows." *The New Yorker*, October 7.

"The Mouth of the Turtle." *The New Yorker*, November 11.

1945

"Town House (I)." *The New Yorker*, April 21.

"Manila." *The New Yorker*, July 28.

"Town House (II)." *The New Yorker*, August 11.

"A Trip to the Moon." *Good Housekeeping*, October.

"Town House (III)." *The New Yorker*, November 10.

1946

"Town House (IV)." *The New Yorker*, January 5.

"Town House (V)." *The New Yorker*, March 16.

"Town House (VI)." *The New Yorker*, May 4.

"The Sutton Place Story." *The New Yorker*, June 29. (*ER*, ★)

"Love in the Islands." *The New Yorker*, December 7.

1947

"The Beautiful Mountains." *The New Yorker*, February 8.

"The Enormous Radio." *The New Yorker*, May 17. (*ER*, ★)

"The Common Day." *The New Yorker*, August 2. (★)

"Roseheath." *The New Yorker*, August 16.

"Torch Song." *The New Yorker*, October 4. (*ER*, ★)

1948

"O City of Broken Dreams." *The New Yorker*, January 24. (*ER*, ★)

"Keep the Ball Rolling." *The New Yorker*, May 29.

"The Summer Farmer." *The New Yorker*, August 7. (*ER*, ★)

1949

"The Hartleys." *The New Yorker*, January 22. (*ER*, ★)

"The Temptations of Emma Boynton." *The New Yorker*, November 26.

"Vega." *Harper's*, December.

"The Opportunity." *Cosmopolitan*, December.

"Christmas Is a Sad Season for the Poor." *The New Yorker*, December 24. (*ER*, ★)

1950

"The Season of Divorce." *The New Yorker*, March 4. (*ER*, ★)

"The Pot of God." *The New Yorker*, October 14. (*ER*, ★)

"The Reasonable Music." *Harper's*, November.

"The People You Meet." *The New Yorker*, December 2.

1951

"Clancy in the Tower of Babel." *The New Yorker*, March 24. (*ER*, ★)

"Goodbye, My Brother." *The New Yorker*, August 25. (*ER*, ★)

1952

"The Superintendent." *The New Yorker*, March 29. (*ER*, ★)

"The Chaste Clarissa." *The New Yorker*, June 14. (*BGW*, ★)

"The Cure." *The New Yorker*, July 5. (*ER*, ★)
"The Children." *The New Yorker*, September 6. (*ER*, ★)

1953

"O Youth and Beauty!" *The New Yorker*, August 22. (*HB*, ★)
"The National Pastime." *The New Yorker*, September 26.
"The Sorrows of Gin." *The New Yorker*, December 12. (*HB*, ★)

1954

"The Five-Forty-Eight." *The New Yorker*, April 10. (*HB*, ★)
"The True Confessions of Henry Pell." *Harper's*, June.
"Independence Day at St. Botolph's." *The New Yorker*, July 3.
(Excerpt from *The Wapshot Chronicle*)
"The Day the Pig Fell Into the Well." *The New Yorker*, October
23. (★)
"The Country Husband." *The New Yorker*, November 20. (*HB*, ★)

1955

"Just Tell Me Who It Was." *The New Yorker*," April 16. (*HB*, ★)
"Just One More Time." *The New Yorker*, October 8. (*BGW*)
"The Journal of a Writer with a Hole in One Sock." *Reporter*,
December 29.

1956

"The Bus to St. James's." *The New Yorker*, January 14. (★)
"The Journal of an Old Gent." *The New Yorker*, February 18.
"How Dr. Wareham Kept His Servants." *Reporter*, April 5.
"The Housebreaker of Shady Hill." *The New Yorker*, April 14.
(*HB*, ★)
"Miss Wapshot." *The New Yorker*, September 22. (Excerpt from
The Wapshot Chronicle)
"The Clear Haven." *The New Yorker*, December 1. (★)

1957

"The Trouble of Marcie Flint." *The New Yorker*, November 9.
(*HB*, ★)

1958

"The Worm in the Apple." In *The Housebreaker of Shady Hill*.
"The Bella Lingua." *The New Yorker*, March 1. (*BGW*, ★)

"Paola." *The New Yorker*, July 26.

"The Wrysons." *The New Yorker*, September 15. (*SPP*, ★)

"The Duchess." *The New Yorker*, December 13. (*SPP*, ★)

1959

"The Scarlet Moving Van." *The New Yorker*, March 21. (*SPP*, ★)

"The Events of That Easter." *The New Yorker*, May 16. (Excerpt from *The Wapshot Scandal*)

"Brimmer." *Esquire*, August. (*SPP*, ★)

"The Golden Age." *The New Yorker*, September 26. (*SPP*, ★)

"The Lowboy." *The New Yorker*, October 10. (*SPP*, ★)

"The Music Teacher." *The New Yorker*, November 21. (*BGW*, ★)

"A Woman Without a Country." *The New Yorker*, December 12. (*BGW*, ★)

1960

"Boy in Rome." *Esquire*, February. (★)

"Clementina." *The New Yorker*, May 7. (*BGW*, ★)

"Some People, Places, and Things That Will Not Appear in My Next Novel." *The New Yorker*, November 12. (*SPP*, ★) (Reprinted as "A Miscellany of Characters That Will Not Appear")

1961

"The Chimera." *The New Yorker*, July 1. (*WA*, ★)

"The Seaside Houses." *The New Yorker*, July 29. (*BGW*, ★)

"The Angel of the Bridge." *The New Yorker*, October 21. (*BGW*, ★)

"The Brigadier and the Golf Widow." *The New Yorker*, November 11. (*BGW*, ★)

"The Traveller." *The New Yorker*, December 9. (Excerpt from *The Wapshot Scandal*)

"Christmas Eve in St. Botolph's." *The New Yorker*, December 23. (Excerpt from *The Wapshot Scandal*)

1962

"A Vision of the World." *The New Yorker*, September 29. (*BGW*, ★)

"Reunion." *The New Yorker*, October 27. (*BGW*, ★)

"The Embarkment for Cythera." *The New Yorker*, November 3.

"Metamorphoses." *The New Yorker*, March 2. (*BGW*, ★)

"The International Wilderness." *The New Yorker*, April 6. (Excerpt from *The Wapshot Scandal*)

"Mene, Mene, Tekel, Upharsin." *The New Yorker*, April 27. (*WA*, ★)

"The Wapshot Scandal." *Esquire*, July. (Excerpt from the novel)

"An Educated American Woman." *The New Yorker*, November 2. (*BGW*, ★)

1964

"The Habit." *The New Yorker*, March 7.

"Montraldo." *The New Yorker*, June 6. (*WA*, ★)

"Marito in Citta." *The New Yorker*, July 4. (*BGW*, ★)

"The Swimmer." *The New Yorker*, July 18. (*BGW*, ★)

"The Ocean." *The New Yorker*, August 1. (*BGW*, ★)

1966

"The Geometry of Love." *Saturday Evening Post*, January 1. (*WA*, ★)

"The World of Apples." *Esquire*, December. (*WA*, ★)

1967

"Another Story." *The New Yorker*, February 25.

"Bullet Park." *The New Yorker*, November 25. (Excerpt from the novel)

1968

"The Yellow Room." *Playboy*, January. (Excerpt from *Bullet Park*)

"Playing Fields." *Playboy*, July. (Excerpt from *Bullet Park*)

"Percy." *Esquire*, September 21. (*WA*, ★)

1970

"The Fourth Alarm." *Esquire*, April. (*WA*, ★)

1972

"Artemis, the Honest Well-Digger." *Playboy*, January. (*WA*, ★)

"The Jewels of the Cabots." *Playboy*, May. (*WA*, ★)

1973

"Triad." *Playboy*, January. (*WA*, ★) (Reprinted as "Three Stories")

1974

"The Leaves, the Lion-fish and the Bear." *Esquire*, November. (Excerpt from *Falconer*)

1975

"The Folding-chair Set." *The New Yorker*, October 13. (Excerpt from *Falconer*)

1976

"Falconer." *Playboy,* January. (Excerpt from the novel)

"President of the Argentine." *Atlantic,* April.

1977

"Falconer." *Ladies Home Journal,* July. (Excerpt from the novel)

1980

"The Night Mummy Got the Wrong Mink Coat." *The New Yorker,* April 21.

1981

"The Island." *The New Yorker,* April 27.

1982

"Expelled." *The New Republic,* July. (Reprinted from October 1, 1930, issue)

ARTICLES

"Happy Days," review of *The Gospel According to St. Luke's,* by Philip Stevenson. *The New Republic,* May 6, 1931.

"While the Fields Burn," review of *Now in November,* by Josephine Johnson. *The New Republic,* September 26, 1935.

"Way Down East," review of *Silas Crocket,* by Mary Ellen Chase. *The New Republic,* December 11, 1935.

"The Genteel Engineer," review of *Pity The Tyrant,* by Hans Otto Storm. *The New Republic,* December 8, 1937.

"Cape Codders," review of *Cranberry Red,* by E. Garside. *The New Republic,* February 8, 1939.

"New Hampshire Holiday." *Holiday,* September 1950.

"Where New York Children Play." *Holiday,* August 1951.

"Moving Out." *Esquire,* July 1960.

"Sophia, Sophia, Sophia." *Saturday Evening Post,* October 21, 1967.

"Recent Trends in Writing and Publishing." *Intellect,* July 1976.

"Fiction," review of *The Ewings,* by John O'Hara. *Esquire,* May 1972.

"An Afternoon Walk in Iowa City, Iowa." *Travel & Leisure,* September 1974.

"Romania." *Travel & Leisure,* March 1978.

"Fiction Is Our Most Intimate Means of Communication." *U.S. News,* May 21, 1979.

"My Friend, Malcolm Cowley." *New York Times Book Review,* August 28, 1983.

ACKNOWLEDGMENTS

From time to time over the nearly forty years I exchanged letters with John Cheever, I used to trot out one or two of his reports from suburbia to read to friends on evenings when wine and talk had blended well. Three years after his death in 1982 I began depositing the letters in the memory bank of my first Macintosh (a 512 that has evolved into a IIsi) with a view to publishing them when I felt the time was right. I wanted to wait until his children had had their say.

Susan had just brought out her moving memoir, *Home Before Dark,* and would in time get around to a sequel, *Treetops* (Bantam, 1991). Ben followed up *The Letters of John Cheever* with an amusing novel, *The Plagiarist* (Atheneum, 1992), in which Icarus Prentice, described on the dust jacket as "an aging, acerbic, alcoholic and much-acclaimed American writer," talks like the old friend who used to come to our breakfast table in the Hollywood Hills, speaking in sentences as gracefully turned as those he wrote for *The New Yorker*.

In 1990, when Chica and I settled in North Carolina, Ben got me started on the annotation of his father's letters by giving me access to a whiskey carton filled with file folders containing the raw material he had drawn on for his volume of letters. He also told me a scholarly friend of his had once mentioned a delightful cache of uncatalogued Cheever letters in the George Biddle Collection at the Library of Congress. My friends, Ann and Jack Womeldorf, who have worked at the library for years, dug out the letters, which included John's reports on his friendship with Duck Biddle. Ann and Jack also produced the tape of a reading John had given at the library and described in one of his letters.

I am grateful to Yale's Beineke Library for permission to use material in John's correspondence with Josephine Herbst, and to the Sterling Library for access to the papers of Dr. Milton C. Winternitz, John's father-in-law, who, on June 9, 1951, reported to the family that in his grandson's new home in Scarborough Benjamin Hale Cheever was now permitted to roam around without a leash.

I am indebted to Scott Donaldson, professor of English at the ancient College of William and Mary, for permitting me to browse through the correspondence, clippings, notes, and drafts of his biography, *John Cheever* (Random House, 1984). The material has been deposited with the Swem Library, where Margaret Cook, the library's curator of manuscripts and rare books, made me feel at home and guided me around the spacious campus that has replaced the meadow I remember as an undergraduate (class of 1932). I was especially pleased to come across the letters Donaldson exchanged with John Updike and his former wife, Mary (now Mrs. Robert Weatherall). I am grateful to them for giving me permission to quote remarks that complement John's glad tidings from the Soviet Union in the fall of 1964.

I am also grateful to Digby Diehl for his eloquent account of John's last public appearance, and to Elizabeth Johnson for her recollections of the part she played as one of the judges who gave him the National Book Award for *The Wapshot Chronicle*. Two of my dearest friends, Caskie Stinnett, a college classmate, and Pamela Fiori, Stinnett's successor as editor of *Travel & Leisure,* were helpful in running down information on John's articles for that magazine and for its predecessor, *Holiday*.

John did not hold academics in high regard, but he got on well with Frederick Bracher, a professor of English at Pomona

College in Southern California. I am indebted to him for giving me permission to quote John's letter of November 2, 1962, which introduces our correspondence of the 1960s in *Glad Tidings,* and to Nicole Bouché of the Bancroft Library, University of California at Berkeley, for providing photocopies of this remarkable series of letters.

When I started work on *Glad Tidings* in California, I turned, as I had done for thirty years, to the libraries of the University of California at Los Angeles. For their help in gathering background information and pinning down dates, I am indebted to David Zeidberg, Anne Caiger, and Simon Elliott. John's original letters, along with those of his family and mutual friends and associates, are part of the files I've given Special Collections, University Research Library. This material is catalogued at UCLA as Collection 1206. Harriett's files on her twenty-four-year involvement with fire, flood, and landslide management in the Santa Monica Mountains is Collection 1447.

Since my defection to Durham, I have found the library of the University of North Carolina at Chapel Hill (the country's oldest state university) equally hospitable and equally short of parking spaces.

From the outset, *Glad Tidings* has been a joint venture with the Cheever family. Ben not only got me started but also kept me going, and if Chica could work things out with Mary and Janet, he would be our adopted son. Susan, the family researcher, was helpful in tracking down useful sources. I owe a special debt to Mary, who read an early draft and, reverting to her bachelor days as a New York editor, suggested changes that improved the arrangement of my notes.

When Master Sergeant Don Ettlinger and Private First-class Leonard Field read a later version of the book, they caught several errors that were promptly corrected. For the three of us, reading *Glad Tidings* was like a spring morning at Borden's—sharing coffee, bagels, lox, and cream cheese with John while he held us spellbound with his stories, parts of which would later turn up in *The New Yorker*.

And, finally, as the dedication indicates, this is Chica's book. Without her love and laughter it would never have come to life. Nor would I.

INDEX